SOUTH AFRICAN STUDIES
No. 3

General Editors:
ANTHONY ATMORE
School of Oriental and African Studies

SHULA MARKS
Institute of Commonwealth Studies

STANLEY TRAPIDO
University of Durham

MY LIFE AND
THE ICU

CLEMENTS KADALIE

MY LIFE AND THE ICU

The Autobiography of
a Black Trade Unionist in South Africa

CLEMENTS KADALIE

Founder of the Industrial and Commercial Workers' Union of Africa

Edited, with an Introduction by
Stanley Trapido

NEW YORK
THE HUMANITIES PRESS

First published in 1970 by
FRANK CASS AND COMPANY LIMITED
67 Great Russell Street, London, WC1

First published
in the United States of America 1970
by Humanities Press Inc.
303 Park Avenue South
New York 10, N.Y.

ISBN 391 00045 4

Printed in Great Britain

CONTENTS

PREFACE

CLEMENTS KADALIE completed the first draft of his auto-biography in 1946 and attempted, without success, to find a publisher. In 1949 he approached the late Edward Roux who had recently published his pioneer and invaluable *Time Longer Than Rope: A History of the Struggle of the Blackman for Freedom in South Africa*. Kadalie asked Roux to assist him in revising the MS to make it more readily acceptable to a publisher. Roux and Kadalie spent two weeks together and certain elaborations and omissions were made but by the time Kadalie died in November 1951 a publisher had not been found. After Kadalie's death the second draft of his MS was sent to Roux in 1954 and he was asked to find a publisher and if necessary to re-edit it before doing so. To begin with Roux appears to have made only minor excisions and, although a new copy was typed of what was now the third draft, the second draft survived with the sections to be deleted ruled out in pencil. A copy of the third draft was given to Professor Gwendolen Carter, now head of the Program of African Studies at North Western University, in 1954. Roux appears to have had second thoughts and decided to summarize some of the many memoranda, resolutions and proceedings of conferences that Kadalie had included in the belief that it would improve the literary value of the autobiography and make it more acceptable to a publisher. Draft two, with its pencil cuts, appears to have been used again, and Roux introduced summaries of the lengthy documents which Kadalie had included although he meticulously indicated where he had cut the original MS. In spite of Roux's efforts and those of Professor George Shepperson, Professor of Commonwealth and American History at the University of Edinburgh, and George Padmore, the god-father cum-chronicler of Pan-Africanism, a publisher could not be found.

In 1963 Professor Carter suggested that I might interview A. W. G. Champion who had been Kadalie's lieutenant and had played so important a part in African trade union and nationalist activities between 1925 and 1950. For five months Champion came once a week to record his reminiscences, and began providing me with documents and pamphlets to illustrate events in his career. Champion produced a Kadalie MS, together with a collection of newspaper cuttings which Kadalie had accumulated between 1925 and 1946. The MS contained the sections that Roux had crossed out in pencil but did not include the later deletions. Champion and Kadalie had at the height of their political activities turned from being allies to being foes and in his autobiography Kadalie was critical of his one-time colleague. Nevertheless, Champion had been given the MS by Mrs. Kadalie who had asked him to find a publisher, and he in his turn asked me to do so. The draft given to me by Champion was re-typed, and passages pencilled out were restored. Eventually the present publishers learnt of the MS and after seeing it at once agreed to publish.

While writing the introduction to Kadalie's *Life* I became aware of the draft in Professor Carter's possession and she kindly let me see it. I have thought it appropriate to restore the lengthy quotations which Roux removed, because they add to the book's value as a primary source. One of the most important aspects of *My Life and the ICU* is Kadalie's ability to communicate his egoistic vitality. Edward Roux may have attempted to give the book a more polished literary form but anyone who has read any of Kadalie's correspondence will immediately recognize his style. Comparing the two versions of the MS available it is possible to detect an occasional change in the word order of a sentence, or more rarely, several sentences have been shuffled but not re-written. Occasionally Roux tried to impose a sense of modesty upon Kadalie but this was a hopeless task and where possible I have reverted to the words Kadalie originally used.

In preparing an introduction to *My Life and the ICU* I have drawn on Chapters XV and XIV of *Time Longer Than Rope* and two excellent and thorough re-evaluations of the ICU by Dr. Sheridan Johns of Brandeis University, 'The Birth of Non-White Trade Unionism in South Africa' in *Race* October 1967 and 'Trade Union, Pressure Group or Mass Movement' which is to appear in *The Tradition of Protest in Black Africa*, edited by Ali Mazrui and Robert Rotberg. In addition to the transcript of the Champion interview, Dr. W. J. Argyle of Queen Mary College, who was a colleague of mine at the University of Natal and who continued to interview Champion after I left South Africa, has let me see an extract of an autobiographical sketch by Selby Msimang and a transcript of an interview with Msimang. Champion, archivist as well as political activist, continued to provide pamphlets for his interviewer and Dr. Argyle has let me see copies of these. The Kingston-upon-Hull public library provided me with a microfilm of Kadalie's letters to Creech-Jones in the Winifred Holtby papers and I am grateful to Ian Taylor, a former research assistant in the University of Durham, for typing these letters for me. Finally I wish to thank Mrs. Anne Argyle who typed the Kadalie MS and the Champion and Msimang transcripts. I have retained the original foreword written in 1950.

STANLEY TRAPIDO

December 1968

INTRODUCTION

CLEMENTS KADALIE was the National Secretary from 1921 to 1929 of the first African mass movement in South Africa, the Industrial and Commercial Workers' Union of Africa which became known as the ICU. A highly critical commentator, Edward Roux, has described Kadalie in *Time Longer than Rope* as a man 'full of restless energy, a born orator, a capable organizer'. Kadalie, Roux claimed, had shown great ability in his 'meteoric' rise. 'Intelligent, versatile, passionate, he possessed those qualities of personality which drew others to him and made him a natural leader of his fellows.' He created an organization which began with twenty-four members and before it burnt itself out within the decade it laid claim to a hundred thousand members. Inexperience, the lack of success, which bred factions among the leaders and disillusion among its followers, together with the hostility of White society and the State, led to its collapse. But in the light of recent experience in Africa, it is apparent that Kadalie had the misfortune to have been born in the wrong place at the wrong time. A leader in tropical Africa who built an organization like the ICU after 1950 would have led his followers to an independence which a colonial power would readily have conceded. Kadalie's task was more difficult and more complex. Kadalie rated his own contribution to the political and social life of South Africa very highly. Partly this was vanity. But it should be remembered that he began writing his autobiography before the impact of the ICU upon later organizations was felt and before Roux's book had appeared, and Kadalie sought acknowledgement of his achievements in a country which denied him the recognition he deserved.

Clements Kadalie was born in what is now Malawi, in the last decade of the nineteenth century, and christened at Easter 1896. He received secondary education at a Scottish mission school, and after a brief career as a school teacher began a journey in

1916 to South Africa in search of other employment. Then, as now, this was not an atypical journey, but, unlike the vast majority of his countrymen, Kadalie did not become a miner on the Witwatersrand. Instead, he continued southward to Cape Town to what was, in comparison with other parts of South Africa, a less harsh environment. To some extent this was the result of the Cape's qualified franchise which had survived the unification of South Africa and permitted non-White men to be enrolled as voters. The existence of this franchise gave Kadalie an early opportunity to establish his organizing ability. As a result of a chance encounter he met A. F. Batty, who was about to contest the Cape Town Harbour constituency in a by-election as a Labour Party candidate. Batty enrolled Kadalie as one of his electoral agents and, although he failed by a small margin to win the election, he continued to interest himself in Kadalie.

Batty suggested that Kadalie should form a trade union in the Cape Town docks for non-White workers. Possibly, as Kadalie surmised, the prospect of a General Election, which was then in the offing influenced Batty in making this proposal, for such an organization would provide him with a ready-made network when electioneering began. The union, which was called the Industrial and Commercial Union, enrolled twenty-nine members at its first meeting and Kadalie was elected secretary. Shortly after its formation, the ICU was involved in a dispute that led to a strike. Rapid inflation had followed the end of the European war in 1918 and it was widely believed that the export of South African food products was helping to raise local prices. The White Railway Workers' Union approached the ICU and asked for assistance in preventing the export of food. The ICU agreed to help, but added its own demand for an increase in wages for its members. On December 17, 1919, Kadalie brought the African and Coloured dock-workers out on strike, and this, it was claimed, ended the export of food. Having succeeded in gaining their objective, the Railwaymen refused to support the ICU because, they alleged, it had gone beyond its original agreement, and after three weeks the strike collapsed.

The creation of the ICU in Cape Town coincided with attempts by Africans in other urban centres in South Africa to improve wages and working conditions and to gain civil liberties.

In Johannesburg in 1918 African municipal sewerage disposal workers came out on strike but the strikers were arrested under a Master and Servants Act. In 1919 there was a campaign of civil disobedience directed at the pass laws which limited the movement of Africans in all provinces except the Cape, and which were resented not only as a technique of control but also because they were seen as a social stigma. In 1920 a strike of 40,000 African migrant mineworkers on the Witwatersrand whose wages had declined in real as well as absolute terms since the turn of the century, and who were forced to live in isolated all-male barracks, was crushed by the authorities with great severity. In 1919 Selby Msimang, a Bloemfontein lawyer's clerk, who had been involved in the formation of the South African Native National Congress in 1912 (it was to change its name to the African National Congress in 1924) and who was still closely involved in its activities, attempted to organize local Africans to achieve an increase in wages. Msimang was arrested in March 1919 under the Riotous Assemblies Act and this led to a demonstration, widely reported, which added to his prestige. Msimang was acquitted, and he was invited to address a meeting of the Cape Town ICU in August 1919. Elsewhere, in Port Elizabeth and East London, Africans were forming general workers unions and Msimang and Kadalie at their meeting in August agreed to attempt the co-ordination of local African Workers' associations. Msimang made these proposals known to the annual meeting of the South African Native National Congress in Queenstown in 1920.

The Congress was unsympathetic, for it was committed to a programme of moderate reform which suited its members, drawn from the new African middle class. Their attitudes to political participation and methods of change had been acquired from missionaries, educationists and paternalistic administrators. These attitudes were reinforced by the existence of limited African participation in the Cape where most of the Congress leaders had originated or had been educated. Although the 1919 anti-pass campaign in the Transvaal had been led by the Congress, the organization was not given to mass activities and preferred those methods of participation more in keeping with its own beliefs, deputations, petitions and law suits. It is not too much to claim that the courts provided one of the most important political arenas for Africans in the first sixty years of this century.

The South African Native National Congress's impressions of trade unionism had come from the practices of White workers in South Africa and these were seen not only as being antipathetic to the values and institutions which African leaders supported, but also as being directed against their interests. In the twenty years after the end of the South African War in 1902, White trade unions, particularly those on the gold mines, challenged both their employers and the State, in attempts to secure the position of highly-paid White workers at the expense of low-paid African workers. In a series of strikes, often accompanied by violence, where the union leadership lost control, White workers fought, not only for increased wages, but for the exclusive reservation, in the mining industry, of trades and crafts and even some unskilled occupations for themselves.

Although the South African Native National Congress would not accept Msimang's suggestion that his activities be encompassed by its organization, his announcement of the proposed co-ordinating conference at the 1920 meeting gained the attention of Samuel Masabalala who was leader of the Port Elizabeth African workers' association. The co-ordinating conference was held in Bloemfontein in July 1920 and it was agreed to call the organization which was formed the Industrial and Commercial Workers' Union of Africa. Msimang was elected president, and Kadalie, who had expected to be elected secretary, found that office given to a Christian minister, the secretary of the Congress in Kimberley. Msimang probably wished to have Kadalie elected for this post but the conference had far more representatives from Bloemfontein and nearby Kimberley than from the distant Cape Town which, probably because of the cost, had only sent five delegates. Kadalie and his delegation withdrew from the conference, apparently taking with them the only draft of the new organization's constitution.

In Cape Town Kadalie continued to build his own organization and in August 1920 he prepared to bring the dock-workers out on strike in an attempt to secure the increase in wages that they had previously failed to obtain. On this occasion the threat of a strike led all employers except the State-owned Railways and Harbours to agree to an increase in wages.

In Port Elizabeth, in October 1920, Samuel Masabalala, one of the delegates at the Bloemfontein conference, who had affiliated his organization to the Industrial and Commercial Workers' Union of Africa had come out on strike for a general increase in wages. The Reverend W. B. Rubusana, who had a long career in African electoral politics and had represented the Tembuland constituency in the Cape Provincial Council between 1909 and 1913, was asked by the municipal authorities to act as an intermediary between themselves and the strikers. In attempting to approach Masabalala, Rubusana was assaulted by the former's followers. Rubusana accused Masabalala of being responsible for the assault and the latter was arrested as a result. This led to a demonstration outside the police station, and white vigilantes, followed by the police, opened fire on the crowd, killing twenty people. As a result of Masabalala's arrest, an official of the Industrial and Commercial Workers' Union of Africa sent Msimang a message requesting him to come to Port Elizabeth and give the organization his assistance. After his arrival Msimang successfully urged the ending of the strike and arranged for the funeral of the dead to prevent its being turned into a demonstration which might have provoked further violence. He also attempted to pave the way for negotiations between local employers and Masabalala whose release he had managed to secure after persuading Rubusana to withdraw the assault charge. Masabalala considered that Msimang had weakened the bargaining position of his branch and he was apparently supported in this view by Kadalie who sent him messages of support. Masabalala now drew closer to Kadalie and when the first anniversary of the Port Elizabeth deaths was commemorated Kadalie was not only one of the main speakers, but he claims to have taken charge of the organization of the demonstration which took place. The result of the Kadalie-Masabalala alliance was that Msimang was ousted from the leadership at a conference shortly after the Port Elizabeth demonstration. Kadalie became National Secretary, Masabalala Organizer in Chief, and a Cape Town nominee replaced Msimang as President. Msimang appears to have withdrawn from the organization and the Bloemfontein and Orange

Free State branches became dormant. From 1922 to 1924 Kadalie consolidated his position in the Cape Province and branches were directly affiliated to a unified organization which officially retained the title Msimang had given it, but continued thereafter to be known as the ICU.

The ICU, whether under Msimang or under Kadalie, was anxious to avoid involving itself in activities which might be described as political. Its definition of political would seem to have included any activity which questioned the structure of existing society, but excluded participation in elections. The ICU sought to present itself as a conventional trade union to the White population and the White trade union movement in particular. In addition it did not wish to challenge the authority of the older South African Native National Congress. Kadalie played a prominent part in the 1924 General Election but he did so in a way which must have been widely accepted as legitimate. He persuaded the ANC meeting in Bloemfontein in 1924 to urge its Cape members to vote for the Nationalist-Labour alliance against the South African Party led by General Smuts. The South African Party had antagonized the white working class by its handling of the 1922 strike on the coal and gold mines, and the ICU had supported the government's action in suppressing an ultimately violent strike which aimed at securing the position of White workers at the expense of non-White workers. But Africans could also point to the excessive use of force against members of an African religious sect, the Israelites, who refused to give up land at Bulhoek in the Cape Province on which they were squatting. Over a hundred people were killed in the forced eviction of the Israelites, and the ICU accused the government of unnecessary violence. Immediately after the Bulhoek deaths, Kadalie asked for a commission of enquiry. A Labour party member of the Opposition, Arthur Barlow, who held one of the Bloemfontein seats, made a similar request, but the government did not respond. Kadalie, in attempting to raise funds for the survivors of Bulhoek, organized a concert to which the leader of the Opposition, General Hertzog, was invited. Hertzog did not attend but expressed his sympathy for the bereaved and sent a token donation to Kadalie's fund. If Kadalie's willingness to associate himself with the Nationalist and Labour Parties against the South African Party was a bizarre misreading of the situation, it was one he shared with others on the left. In the last resort conviction that the South African Party was the voice of the mining financiers was sufficient to unite these disparate groups. Each held the South African Party responsible for the major problems which beset South Africa, although each defined the problems very differently. Immediately after Kadalie had won the ANC's support for the Nationalist-Labour alliance Arthur Barlow arranged a meeting between Kadalie and General Hertzog in Bloemfontein, where Hertzog agreed to pay for a special election edition of the ICU paper, *The Workers' Herald.* Both the meeting and the provision of funds for the paper may have been out of keeping with political conventions in the northern provinces, but this kind of collaboration had long been the rule rather than the exception in the Cape. Leaders of the Afrikaner Bond and their English-speaking liberal sympathizers who together formed the Cape's South African Party had after 1898 gone out of their way to court African political leaders. The most prominent of these, John Tengo Jabavu, had been asked by an Eastern Cape branch of the Afrikaner Bond to stand for Parliament in 1904. Jabavu's paper *Imvo Zabantusundu* had been given financial assistance at elections by members of the South African Party and *Imvo*'s rival, *Izwi La Bantu,* had had its election issues distributed free by the Cape Progressive Party which drew most of its financial support from mining interests. Hertzog provided Kadalie with travelling expenses to enable him to attend the convention of the Cape Native Voters Association, where Kadalie again narrowly succeeded in getting a vote in favour of supporting the Nationalist-Labour alliance.

With the ICU established in the Cape, Kadalie set out, after the General Election, on an organizing tour which was to extend the Union to other parts of South Africa. After some difficulty he established a branch in Durban in September 1924. Thereafter, he regulated the activities of the young men in Johannesburg who had formed a branch of the ICU just before his arrival. At the same time he noted the disapproval of his activities with White liberals in an organization called the Joint Council of European and Bantu where he thought he detected the influence of the Chamber of Mines. Kadalie then moved to the Orange Free State where he resurrected the ICU and, after taking in a small and distant village of the north-west Cape, he returned to Cape Town. Initially his attempt to extend the ICU did not incur Government hostility. Although Natal members of Parliament urged the Nationalist Minister of Justice, Tielman Roos, to restrict Kadalie's activities, Roos did not respond. This seemed to Kadalie to be a vindication of the support he had given the Nationalist-Labour alliance. But as Government policy unfolded, Kadalie's opinion changed. African men were excluded from the Industrial Conciliation Act and a Minimum Wage Act was introduced which only included Africans where its effects would be to drive them out of employment if they could not be paid less than White workers. Farming, mining and domestic service, where legislation for a minimum wage could benefit African workers, were excluded from the Act. As a result, Kadalie became unambiguously hostile to White society, attacking all its major institutions, the Chamber of Mines, the Christian Churches and Parliament. At the same time the ICU began to consider an assault on the pass laws and its National Council attempted to persuade an unresponsive ANC to initiate a pass-burning campaign.

The ICU appeared to be transforming itself from an organization attempting to win wage increases and minor patronage from electoral participation to a movement which was set on challenging the structure of society. But although Kadalie's speeches, and even more so those speeches of some of his new recruits, were a response to and an evocation of the mood which the Government's legislation and its proposals on African land ownership and the abolition of the franchise rights in the Cape had created, the ICU's structure did not enable it to mobilize the widespread support which it was given. Nevertheless, White society took fright. The National Secretary of the ICU became a figure of national importance and in the middle of 1925 the Prime Minister is reported to have said of him in the House of Assembly, 'Kadalie had been a very active agitator, and one of no mean culture, with the result that through his action, and the actions of one or two others, there had been a scare for the last six or seven months throughout the Union'.

The ICU caused particular dismay among Whites in the rural

areas of the Orange Free State and Natal where African agricultural labourers and squatters were willing recruits to an organization that promised them land. If the sole criterion for judging an organization's strength was its opponents' perception of it, then the ICU was a very powerful body. Its membership increased rapidly from 30,000 in 1924 to 39,000 in 1926 and 100,000 in 1927. In 1927 branches were established in Southern Rhodesia. Midway through 1925 Kadalie began to consider it necessary to move the ICU's headquarters from Cape Town to Johannesburg. Johannesburg, the major industrial centre of the country, also housed what he considered to be the ICU's major enemy, the Chamber of Mines, and potentially its major ally, the White trade unions. Moreover, Johannesburg had a number of enthusiastic young Communists who were giving help to the ICU, and there were trade unionists, both Communist and non-Communist, who were willing to provide the skilled assistance which Kadalie felt was necessary. The decision to move the headquarters from Cape Town to Johannesburg was agreed to by the National Conference, but it was a decision which the Cape Town branch deeply resented and which it attempted, unsuccessfully, to forestall. Moreover, the move to Johannesburg was to lose the ICU some of its most proficient Coloured organizers for whom advisers could be no substitute. This was not immediately noticeable, however, because the ICU was carried on a wave of enthusiasm. Communists urged their members to join the ICU and some of the most able African and Coloured recruits were Communist Party members. But within a short while, Kadalie and his Zulu lieutenant, Allison Wessells George Champion, whose Natal region had the largest number of members and the largest income, became hostile to the Communist James La Guma, General Secretary of the organization, who alleged that constitutional and financial irregularities existed and did not hesitate to indict those he thought responsible, including Kadalie himself. The result was that Kadalie, fearing that the Communists were trying to gain control over the ICU, called a meeting of the National Council in December 1926 and succeeded in ousting the Communists by introducing a regulation that members of the National Council could not be members of the Communist Party. When the Communists refused to resign from their Party, they were expelled from the ICU. Kadalie now denounced the Communists not only because of their ideological position but also because they were members of a largely White organization. In April 1927 Kadalie carried the support of the National Conference and the ban was extended from members of the National Council to members of the entire organization.

Kadalie's depiction of the conflict between the Communist and non-Communist members of the National Council is of rival ideologies; Communist against Garveyist, the latter being members of that Universal Negro Improvement Society, formed by the Jamaican Marcus Garvey. Undoubtedly some of the contestants saw it in those terms, but cutting across this conflict was another, between the militant and non-militant leaders. The Communists, among the former, were equally critical of what they considered, despite Kadalie's inflammatory speeches, to be his fundamentally non-radical approach. When Kadalie was prohibited from entering Natal by a statutary ban Communists urged him to call a strike, but he chose to defy the ban and challenge its validity in court where he was found not guilty.

Even before the expulsion of the Communists, Kadalie had attempted to create an image of the ICU as a conventional trade union organization. In 1926 the ICU had attempted, unsuccessfully, to exchange fraternal delegates with the White Transvaal co-ordinating body, the South African Trade Union Congress. The April 1927 Conference of the ICU suggested boldly that the White unions join with it to create a single confederation. Later in the year Kadalie asserted, after his return from Europe, that he would press for ICU membership of the South African Trade Union Congress and that if he failed to achieve this, it would expose the bad faith of the White South African trade unionists to the international labour movement.

After its rebuff in 1926, the ICU applied for affiliation to the British Trade Union Council and the Independent Labour Party. Both organizations stated that they could not accept overseas affiliates and suggested instead that the ICU apply for membership of the non-Communist International Federation of Trade Unions. In these efforts to gain international recognition, Kadalie was assisted by a group of White liberals associated with the Joint Councils who persuaded Kadalie to overcome his earlier antipathy to them. With its contacts in England, including Arthur Creech-Jones, then Secretary of the Transport and General Workers' Union, the Joint Council group helped Kadalie to seek advice from the British Trade Union movement. In 1927 Kadalie was presented with an opportunity for bringing the conditions of the non-White working class to the attention of the British and European Labour movements. The International Labour Organization was to hold a conference in Geneva and the SATUC and the Cape Federation of Labour Unions, the two White trade union co-ordinating bodies, could not agree on whom to send as the workers' delegate. Kadalie, claiming that the ICU had a larger membership than either White body, asserted the right of his own organization to nominate the workers' delegate. Predictably, the South African Government and the White unions would not accept this claim, but the ICU agreed to send Kadalie to Europe. Kadalie's credentials were not accepted in Geneva, but he was given an opportunity to state the ICU's position. In Geneva Kadalie began, at the suggestion of an ILO official, to redraft the ICU's constitution, and this was continued in Britain with the assistance of Arthur Creech-Jones. Kadalie spoke at a large number of ILP and trade union meetings, describing the general conditions of the non-White workers in South Africa and attempted to arouse British public opinion against the Native Administration Act which was then passing through the South African Parliament.

During his stay in Britain, Kadalie made a conscientious effort to study the methods of organization in British trade unions and came to the conclusion that it would benefit the ICU to have an adviser from Britain to assist in re-organizing it. Kadalie tried to persuade Creech-Jones to take on the task, not only because he would prove a valuable adviser but also because Kadalie hoped that so eminent a British trade unionist would add prestige to the ICU and bring the White unions closer to co-operating with it. Creech-Jones could not come, but agreed, if Kadalie received the support of his National Council, to help find a suitable adviser.

Ultimately Kadalie returned to South Africa, apparently aware that the ICU was running into difficulties in his absence. A. W. G. Champion, the Natal secretary, had been left as acting National

Secretary and he had quarrelled with the staff of the National headquarters, including members of the National Council. In Natal Sam Dunn, who was acting for Champion, was jailed for embezzling ICU funds; in the Western Cape rival factions had fallen out with one another; the Eastern Province, which before 1925 had been a hub of ICU activity, had collapsed, and the leader of the OFS region, Keable 'Mote, was refusing to accept National Council directives. To add to the ICU's difficulties the Government had, earlier in 1927, responded to the ICU by embodying in its Native Administration Act a 'hostility clause' which was directed at the ICU's activities. The 'hostility clause', which carried with it the penalty of a year's imprisonment, was to be invoked against anyone whose utterances or acts were intended to 'promote feelings of hostility' between Africans and Whites. The implicit intention of the Legislature was to restrict criticisms of the colour-bar, although as Kadalie's experience was to show the judiciary read the Act otherwise.

Kadalie arrived back in South Africa in October 1927 armed with a new constitution which, with minor amendments, was accepted by the National Conference, as was his proposal to invite a British adviser. Kadalie began his promised campaign of reform but, before it had made much progress, the ICU experienced another blow to its prestige following a libel suit which Champion had instigated against a Durban member, John Lenono, who had accused him of using ICU funds for his own purposes. The judge who heard the case found that Lenono's accusations were justified, though Champion claimed that irregularities were the result of inefficient accounting rather than deliberate misuse of funds. Moreover, even when he used ICU funds for a private club registered in his name, he later claimed that this was because he was one of the very few Natal Africans who had succeeded in getting a certificate exempting him from Native law, and who could own property in a White area which, in practice, meant the centre of the city. This enabled him to provide a service to the Africans of Durban which had not existed before. Kadalie had an auditor check the Natal region's books and the report supported the judge's findings. The auditor's report was presented to Kadalie immediately before the 1928 National Conference, which sought to have Champion arrested immediately, but

Kadalie interposed and succeeded in reaching a compromise. Champion was suspended while a further investigation took place.

Champion's handling of the Natal funds may have been irregular, but his standing with his members remained high. Champion had taken the Durban municipal borough to court and challenged their right to compel newcomers to Durban to purchase a permit to enter the city and submit themselves to the humiliating process of being dipped in disinfectant. The court held that the municipal authorities were acting beyond the powers given to them, and Champion, a prolific publicist, turned this victory to good account. His suspension was not accepted by his following and the Durban branch seceded from the national organization. This secession was followed by other Natal branches and Champion was invited to become the Secretary of the ICU yase (of) Natal.

The 1928 conference which led to the Natal secession also committed the ICU to an attack on the pass laws and although Kadalie had preferred a more conciliatory approach the delegates forced a radical stance upon him. It was as a result of this conference's decision that Kadalie attacked the pass laws in a speech in Pretoria and was charged under the 'hostility' clause. The magistrate before whom Kadalie appeared rejected the prosecution's charge and the National Secretary of the ICU achieved another notable court victory. Now, however, with the Natal secession, and with other difficulties within the organization, Kadalie found himself in a weak position. He hoped that the adviser from Britain would help him regain his pre-eminence. Creech-Jones, and those who helped him, found it difficult to find a suitably qualified trade unionist who was willing to go to South Africa. Eventually they suggested to Kadalie, who continued to press them to find a candidate, that William Ballinger, a Scotsman who had served in local government and had been secretary of the Motherwell Trades Council, might be considered for the post. Creech-Jones was insistent that the ICU should make the decision and feel free to reject his suggestion, for Ballinger was clearly not the sort of figure that Kadalie had originally envisaged. Nevertheless, Ballinger was accepted by the ICU's National Council. It is probable that Kadalie and the other members of the National Council thought that Ballinger would

c

bring substantial funds with him. This may have helped to stay the revolt in the National Council which seemed imminent when an anti-Kadalie faction within it drew up a manifesto demanding a 'Clean Administration' and had this published in the White press. But when Ballinger came he had little money of his own, and on the contrary, expected to have his expenses paid by the ICU. Ballinger's backers in Britain, when they learned of the position, managed to provide him with a small income and it is possible that his ability to win the National Council to his side against Kadalie was assisted by his having some resources. Initially, however, despite an early misunderstanding, Kadalie was full of praise for Ballinger's attempts to disentangle the chaotic state that he found in the organization. Ballinger urged the National Council to limit its office holders and reduce the size of its branches. Eventually Ballinger became more and more critical of Kadalie, who, feeling himself isolated, and it is suggested, compromised in his private life, asked for a year's leave of absence on January 5, 1929. But on the 29th of the month he announced his resignation from the post of National Secretary of the ICU because, he stated, he could not associate himself with the activities of the new régime. Two weeks later on February 13, Kadalie announced that he was withdrawing his resignation and proposed a new National Council. The names he suggested for his Council were all dissidents but his attempt to reassert himself was met by Ballinger and the existing National Council, and Kadalie found himself out-manœuvred and forced to tender his resignation once more.

Kadalie's resignation was not an abandoning of his attempt to regain power within the organization and on March 13, 1929, he announced the establishment of the Independent ICU with a highly decentralized constitution. The leader in the Orange Free State, Keable 'Mote, who had for a long time been a law unto himself, accepted Kadalie's proposals as did a large number of branches in the Southern Transvaal. Moreover, negotiations with Champion resulted in a satisfactory formula being worked out to have the ICU yase Natal enter into association with the Independent ICU. In practice this agreement was of little significance and even the Orange Free State-Southern Transvaal network which had seemed so promising had come to exist more on paper than in actuality. Kadalie attacked Ballinger on the grounds of his being in league with the Chamber of Mines and appealed for funds to the Comintern organization, the League against Imperialism. The South African Communist Party advised against the League's support of Kadalie, since it considered that the left-wing position that he now adopted was unlikely to remain constant. By the end of 1929 Kadalie was reduced to one stronghold, East London. It was from there that early in 1930 he led the ICU's last major strike. The strike was brought to an end when he and his strike committee were arrested by the use of a subterfuge and Kadalie was found guilty of incitement and fined. He returned to East London to a hero's welcome and from then on made a series of forays attempting either to revive the ICU on a national basis—the Ballinger fragment had also disintegrated—or to take up economic or political interests of African workers. He was associated with the attempt to prevent the final disfranchisement of Cape Africans in 1936 and he continued to take an active interest in the welfare of non-Whites both in the political and trade union spheres.

The ICU had failed to undermine White society. Its critics, particularly Edward Roux, thought that it had missed the opportunity to do so, but this was far too harsh a judgment. The state was easily able to cope with the ICU, and both its allies and its enemies had probably over-rated it. The achievement of Kadalie and the ICU was to change the methods of African political organizations in South Africa and Rhodesia. Unlike the narrowly based ANC, it sought mass support, used demonstrations and rallies, and considered the use of strikes for political and economic ends. These techniques of political action were inherited by the later nationalist movements of South Africa and Rhodesia in the 1950's and early '60's. If these methods failed to win power they did succeed in giving political expression to widespread grievances. These nationalist movements have been suppressed, and it is difficult to assess exactly the historical importance of Kadalie and the ICU. But when the time comes to write the definitive history of South Africa, it is probable that both will occupy important positions in that history.

FOREWORD

to the Original Manuscript

THE Publishers[1] of this book have had their doubts; not about the subject-matter, which is plain South African industrial history, but about the style. They have put their difficulty to me, and I discuss it here and now, giving my conclusion first. *I believe the book should be published.*

The problem may be thus: how far will this book put off incipient liberal opinion? The answer is that the basis of liberalism is understanding. The illiberal will always cavil, for he believes in uneducated non-thinking unegotistical servants. Their time is passing. To the critical liberal let me say that there is only one CLEMENTS KADALIE, there was only one man capable of initiating the ICU and of building as he did. There are about 100,000 reasonable educated Africans (Bantu, natives, aborigines, what you will); they call themselves Africans: a wider term than Zulu, Basuto, Bechuana, Pondo, Hlubi, Baca, Fingo, Tembu, Gcaleka, Tambookie or just Xosa. Of these 25,000 are parliamentary voters of the Cape Province. Only if one assumes that these men constitute a menace instead of a safety valve to 10,000,000 Africans need one deplore the fact. Only if one assumes that a great African leader is a yet greater menace, will a liberal be afraid, will an educated man shudder, will a Christian shirk his duty and close his eyes to 'loving his neighbour'.

Here is the story of a man who frightened South Africa's fanatical liberals from 1919 to 1930. Read what he did and why. He is actually stabilizing as a gyroscope, using an economic gale to reach a higher level and a wider calm for his people. I know or have known every African leader in the Cape Province since 1904. Clements Kadalie was and is a phenomenon. No others are like him. He combines colossal self-assurance with colossal self-sacrifice—an African Xavier. He is utterly devoid of hyprocrisy. He blows the trumpet he knows, his own. He knows his worth and states it unequivocally and vocally, and the proof of his worth is his work.

The beneficiaries are his people, drawing treble and more of what they drew before he came to their help. Kadalie's approach is probably revolting to the subtler European. We prefer our undoubted worth (have we any real doubts, my brothers?) to be a matter of necessary deduction, not of direct claim. And so does the average African big man. The chief has his 'Mbongo'. The president of an African National Congress has his special paper; the head of a teachers' association has his secretary to write the minutes. Clements Kadalie is his own mbongo. But do not for a moment take him as the rule: he is the great exception.

This book is correct. Wherever checking is possible it has been checked. Where it quotes, it is documentary. Where checked, it is accurate. Read it, forgetting any pedantic annoyance from the unusual style. Consider the achievement. On one point only is Kadalie silent. He tells the reader of when he drank too much; he does not tell the reader that many years ago, when his attention was drawn to its effect on his work and his efficiency, he cut it out completely. Try giving up your cigarette, you critic, you self-controlled white man!

If Clements Kadalie is a great egoist, so were Tshaka, and Kruger and Rhodes. So are all of us, mitigated by civilization and manners, sometimes fructified by Christianity. Critics, consider the Law of Christ when you read this book; there was an unpleasant scene with the money-changers in the Temple. Come on, you stone-casters! Clements Kadalie formed in ten years the greatest Trade Union this country has ever known, a trade union of the previously non-privileged, of our own untouchables. He used this intractable material with a master hand, and he used it for its good. His gains for his followers were immense. He doubled, he trebled, he quadrupled rates of pay. He readjusted African labour to the depreciation of the pound sterling that followed the first Great War. He should be read by everyone who has not yet adjusted African rates of pay to the further depreciation of the second Great War. He cannot be devalued even by his egoism. Because he stands alone, the question 'How far will this book put off incipient liberal opinion?' can be answered negatively.

Lastly, there are thousands of Africans, with gentle manners, who use their education, who respond to liberal thought as the natural gentlemen they are: thousands of these are true Christians, the early Christians of the twentieth century. These are the rule. If Kadalie is an exception, it is only that he is fearlessly what he is without veil or compromise. Personally, deliberately, I would trust Kadalie on a point of honour sooner than most men, black or white. If the 'Keep the African down' school, or the 'Keep him an agriculturalist' school, or 'Teach him just to use his hands' school can use this book to deplore the effect of the Law of Christ on the African, a point of style or manners, let them remember that Kadalie's honesty of purpose shines everywhere from behind his frankness of style.

WILL STUART, M.P.
House of Assembly,
Cape Town.
January, 1950

NOTE

1. The Publishers in question have not been identified, but this statement in no way refers to the present Publishers.

CHAPTER I

My Early Life

I WAS born at Chifira Village, near Bandawe Mission Station on the west shores of Lake Nyasa, where the first Scottish missionaries, led by Robert Laws of Livingstonia, began their ministerial work in East Central Africa. The exact date of my birth is not known, but it was recorded in the mission register that I was christened on Easter Day, 1896. My father, Musa Kadalie, was the first son of Chief Chiweyu by his first head wife. Chiweyu was then the paramount chief of the Atonga tribe of the well-known Askari group in East Central Africa. It was customary for an African chief to have as many wives as possible. I was the second son of Musa Kadalie. There were three boys (all of us eventually landed up in South Africa) and two sisters.

My grandfather, my father and mother were very fond of me. It was a crime for anyone to hit or rebuke me, even if I were at fault. I must confess that I was very naughty when a youth, and perhaps my father spoilt me. He did not like to be separated from me. On one occasion he had to leave home and go among the Angoni tribe, descendants of the Zulu, who reside in a distant part of Lake Nyasa. He was engaged there in building the church at the London Mission Station, where Dr. Donald Fraser was stationed. My father made special arrangements so that I could be with him. When at home, my father took special interest to see that I went to school every day. I remember one day when I absented myself from school, he looked all over the big village and found me playing with other boys, including my elder brother, Robert. He took us both home, where he thrashed Robert until he fainted. My father was a determined man. No one was able to stop him, not even his own father, the paramount chief, when he decided on a course of action. My father died in London in 1904.

On his death our mother, who like him was an ardent Christian, took upon herself the responsibility of looking after the five children. Her brother was a school teacher, and was thus interested in my education, which was jointly cared for by my other uncle, also a school teacher, on my father's side. This uncle, Alick Banda, took great interest in my welfare; for it was he who clothed me while I was a student at Livingstonia College. He made it possible for me to enter the Livingstonia Missionary Institute in 1908. During an interval in my school career I acted as private secretary to my grandfather, who once told me the story of his first meeting with 'Mzungu'—a white man, who was no other person than Dr. David Livingstone, although he did not know him by that name at the time. He further told me of seeing a boat which sailed along the shores of Lake Nyasa and which anchored near Bandawe. Dr. David Livingstone sent for my grandfather as he was the leading chief.

I went to Livingstonia College for the first time in December 1906, to attend the continuation classes for a month, but returned home thereafter. It was in the following December 1907 that I joined Livingstonia College as a boarding student, paying 30s. school fees a year. This fee was increased to 50s. yearly. I had reached Standard III before I came to the college. I passed two entry examinations in one single day, finding myself in Standard V. From Standard V all our teachers were Europeans. It meant, therefore, that at Livingstonia I passed through the hands of only Scottish teachers.

My college life was very interesting. I got on famously with nearly all the teachers of both sexes, including the Principal, Dr. Robert Laws. In 1912 I acted as the Principal's private secretary, and at the same time was secretary of the YMCA. Every Sunday morning I had to go to the Principal's house at 7 a.m. to carry Mrs. Laws's books. We walked together to the Sunday School class which she conducted.

In classes I was considered brighter than many of my fellow-students, and in examinations I always managed to come first in a given subject. With the final examinations I topped the list with first-class honours. While at college I went through a theological course, which I think has helped me since to understand the sufferings of my fellow-men. I was offered a bursary from

Motherwell, Scotland. The bursars wrote and suggested to me that I should proceed to Scotland for higher education, but I was too young to appreciate this offer at the time, and did not go.

Having passed my final examinations at the end of 1912, I returned home as a fully qualified teacher. The missionary in charge at Bandawe was confronted with a problem when schools opened in January 1913. I was too young to be entrusted with my own school as head teacher, but I held first-class honours from Livingstonia. With the acquiescence of my uncle, it was decided to send me to a school under an elderly master. My age at this time was about 16 years. Reluctantly I accepted this arrangement, but did not abide by it for long. I was of the royal blood and was brighter than the head teacher, who belonged to an ordinary family. At our school I was more popular than the head teacher, who consequently became jealous of me. It was not very long before I forced the issue. I refused to take orders from the head teacher, whom I looked upon as not my equal educationally, while inherently he belonged to an inferior class. Our dispute was brought to the notice of the missionary in charge at Bandawe, who sent for my uncle. I stood firm, insisting that I would not take any orders from a man who was educationally inferior to me. I won my first strike single-handed and was later given my own two schools in a district where another uncle, Reverend Z. Mwasi, was stationed, with a view that he would have an eye over me. Here I made my name as a head teacher well established. The Reverend Yesaya Z. Mwasi was a brilliant scholar and also a very powerful emotional preacher. He had known me as a boy at the Mission Station at Bandawe, so it was fitting that he should take care of me as I grew up. His influence over me was beneficial. With him I gained much experience as a preacher on the pulpit.

After I had taught in schools for one year in Nyasaland, I left home early in 1915 in quest of a higher civilized life. My cousin, Alexander Muwamba, now Acting Chief Chiweyu, went to join another young uncle, Isaac Clements Katongo, in the Northern Rhodesia's civil administration. I travelled on foot with two men who were both older than myself to a cotton estate in Portuguese East Africa. Here we were all three employed, the two men as

33

carpenters, making farm wagons, while I worked in the office. We stayed only one month at this farm, for I organized my second strike there. The cotton planter, who was an Englishman, was very cruel. He daily sjambokked[1] labourers for petty offences. At times he shot at the native labourers. I informed my friends of the danger in remaining any longer on the estate, as our turn would come to be treated in similar manner to the local labourers. At the end of the month, after we had received our pay, we left the estate at dead of night and trekked to Southern Rhodesia. The two men knew the road, but I was in charge of operations. I persuaded them that in no circumstances should we touch European settlements for fear of being arrested. After one week's trek we reached the Shamva Mines in Southern Rhodesia, where I got employment on the second day after our arrival.

At the Shamva Mines I worked as a clerk at first in the compound office. From there I was transferred to the General Manager's office to perform the same sort of work as in the compound office. It was here that I first experienced the effect of the colour bar. A European female typist (she must have been in her fortieth year) could not tolerate seeing me in the same office at my desk doing the same clerical work as herself. As I had neat and good handwriting, I was given to keep and write some registers and to do some typing. Perhaps it was the first time this European woman had met an African doing this type of skilled work. She definitely hated me, and I was relieved when I was transferred to the hospital, where I again encountered new experiences. In view of my good handwriting I was put in charge of the hospital register of all patients.[2]

After one year's stay at the Shamva Gold Mines, I moved on to Salisbury, the capital of Southern Rhodesia. I did not succeed in finding work to suit me there. One day I was confronted by the chief of the Southern Rhodesia Criminal Investigation Department, who wanted me to take up police work as a detective. He promised me quick promotion, as he reckoned that my intelligence was above that of any African he had so far seen in the Colony. I told him that I had not acquired my education to further police work. He threatened to deport me from the Colony if I refused to accept his offer. As I was unable to obtain employment in Salisbury, I went to Umvuma, near Fort Victoria, where I was taken on in the Compound Manager's office of the Falcon Mines. Here I had another very bitter experience. Wherever I was employed the mine authorities recognized my intelligence to be above the average of my fellow-Africans. Thus I had some advantage over them. The compound manager here was cruel. He was a good native linguist and also spoke Afrikaans. It was the first time that I had heard this language spoken. This man used to get up at about 4 a.m. daily in order to send out various shifts. Every morning he sjambokked the African miners, while his cruel dogs would come to his aid by biting his victims to death at times. The African clerks in the compound office, too, sometimes had a dose of his sjambok. However, he took a special interest in me, for he went out of his way to speak to me in English instead of in the native language which he used to every African.

The Great War of 1914-18 was in full progress during my sojourn in Southern Rhodesia. I decided to enlist in the army. With this object in view, I sent an application to the Nyasaland Government at Zomba for a clerical post in the army. Zomba is the capital of the Nyasaland Government. I received a favourable reply which stated that I should approach the nearest Native Commissioner who, in turn, would arrange for my passage to Zomba, Nyasaland. On receipt of this letter I left this mine, but the Native Commissioner at Umvuma, after perusing my letter from Zomba, told me to enlist in the Southern Rhodesia Native Regiment, which was badly equipped. As we could not agree, I left Umvuma for Bulawayo, with a view in my mind to proceed farther south in order to enlist in the army.

Having taken leave of the mines, perhaps for good, I reached Bulawayo in 1916, where I obtained employment in the Traffic Manager's office of the Rhodesian Railways. As fate would have it, again I became popular with the European staff, including the heads of all departments. Wherever I was employed I was asked where I had obtained my education. After a few months' employment on the Rhodesian Railways, I changed to an insurance office, still in the capacity of a clerk. Here I met an ideal employer who took some personal interest in me. Our clients, of course, were mostly Europeans. In Bulawayo I organized some social activities among the African community, which were characterized as revolutionary by many people. I remember well a great concert which I organized in conjunction with two of my countrymen in the Market Hall, situated in the heart of the town. For selling mineral waters as refreshments without a licence during the concert, summonses were issued against us. But we were acquitted by the court.

In the summer of 1917 my employer left Bulawayo for Muizenberg, Cape Town, on holiday. As our business catered largely for Europeans, my employer asked a young European man, Mr. Knight, to take charge of the office during his absence. Mr. Immelman, my employer, trusted me so much that he left all his keys and the boxes containing his personal clothing, etc., in my charge. The young gentleman who was to be my new boss moved into the building where our offices were established, as flats were provided upstairs. I did not remain long with my new supervisor, for we soon quarrelled on the ground that I refused to do his wife's kitchen work. The young European lady asked me one day to buy milk for her from a dairy. I did so on two occasions. But on the third occasion I refused, saying I was not in her employment. This led to a quarrel between her husband and me. I demanded my wages which were paid to me. In return, I gave Mr. Knight all the keys of my employer. I immediately sent a telegram to Mr. Immelman at Muizenberg, informing him of what had transpired. He wired back to me saying that I should remain in office until his return.

Notwithstanding this telegram, I collected all my belongings and sold two bicycles, one of which had been given me by Mr. Immelman. Early in February of 1918 I boarded a passenger train at Bulawayo for South Africa, with Kimberley as my first destination. I spent hardly a month at Kimberley with my cousin Don Bright Mwasi. At the time the Germans were bombarding Paris with the Big Bertha gun. I reached Cape Town one afternoon. My elder brother Robert Victor Kadalie welcomed me at the station. When we reached his house at the top of Waterkant Street, my brother's wife, a Coloured woman, said to him after she had shaken hands with me, 'Look here, Robert, there is something in this boy and you will see.' Quietly I pondered over her remarks.

The next day I obtained a job as a packer and messenger with Fraser and Company, harness manufacturers in Darling Street, where I did unskilled work. My next employment was at a handy house establishment, and during the armistice of that year I was in the services of Jagger and Company, wholesale merchants. I worked at first as a packer. Later I was engaged delivering parcels and goods by motor van. I remember one Saturday afternoon we were delivering furniture in the garden suburbs of Cape Town, when I informed the Coloured driver to return to the firm, as one o'clock had struck. I told him that since we were not being paid for overtime work, we were to return goods which were not delivered before 1 p.m. He reluctantly complied with my suggestion, and we returned to the firm. When I was asked by the store foreman why we had not completed our delivery, I promptly told him that since we were not paid for overtime work it was impossible for me to work overtime.

I left Jagger and Company to take up another good post arranged for me by Mr. A. F. Batty, who was instrumental in the formation of the ICU at the beginning of 1919. I was employed as a clerk in a co-operative stores in which Mr. Batty had some voice. The majority of the employees here were European girls, and it was not long before they resented taking orders from a black man in the office; for I was responsible for keeping stock of the goods of the co-operative. In a body they demanded of the manager that I be removed from the office. This he did reluctantly. I was transferred to a suburban branch store, back to my old job of delivering parcels.

I record this experience here just to show the reader how deep-rooted is the colour bar in our land. On leaving this co-operative store I got employment with a firm of waterproof manufacturers, again delivering parcels. Here I had an ideal employer, who was considerate towards me, but it turned out in the end to be my last job under a white employer. One beautiful morning I approached my employer to allow me a few hours off to meet a friend of mine at Cape Town Docks who was due from the coast. When I went down to the docks that morning I did not visualize what fate had in store for me.

NOTES TO PAGE 34

1. *Sjambok*, shambok, n., a stiff strip of dried hide used as a whip; to flog with a sjambok. (S. African Dutch from Malay.)
2. I referred to my experiences at this mine hospital when I gave evidence before the Economic and Wage Commission of 1925 when it sat in Johannesburg, as I shall explain elsewhere in this book. C.K.

CHAPTER II

Birth of the ICU

THE ICU was born in this manner.

One Saturday afternoon during the influenza epidemic of 1918 I was in the company of two Nyasaland friends in Cape Town. We were strolling in Darling Street when the *Cape Argus*, the afternoon daily newspaper, was out in the streets for sale. I bought a copy of the paper, and as soon as I perused it, I began to inform my friends that the end of the war was in sight, for Sir Douglas Haig had launched his offensive in Flanders. Suddenly appeared a European constable, who pushed me off the pavement, assaulting me at the same time. I informed my friends of my intention to report the matter at police headquarters. My two friends, who did not possess the meagre education and little courage I had at the time, refused to accompany me there. As I was arguing with my friends a European appeared on the scene. He must have been walking behind the policeman. After asking us a few questions, to which I replied without hesitation, he handed me his business card, informing me I could mention his name to the police, as he had witnessed the unprovoked assault on me. Alone I went to the police station to lay my complaint against the constable. It was unusual at the time for an African to report a European constable in South Africa, as I was told by the sergeant-in-charge. Instead of accepting my complaint, he hurled questions at me. Where had I come from? Where had I obtained my education? I was probably to him unlike the ordinary African usually seen in Cape Town. I pressed my complaint, how-ever, brushing aside these irrelevant questions. Finally I was ordered to call again the following day, which was a Sunday.

On the second call the sergeant-in-charge resumed cross-examining me in regard to where I had come from and obtained my education. At last he made an apology on behalf of the constable, stating he made the assault on me because of his mental weakness arising from overwork with the epidemic cases which were raging in the city. Thereupon I retorted that if I were to assault European citizens and when caught give as my excuse for my action mental suffering on my part, would such an excuse be accepted? My logic apparently appealed to his conscience, for he raised again the question of my education and home. He eventually promised he would thoroughly investigate the matter.

The following day I called on my European sympathizer in Long Street, where he was carrying on a cutlery business. His name was A. F. Batty. When he stood for a parliamentary by-election for the Harbour constituency, he invited me to join his election committee. We fought the election, but Batty was defeated by a small majority. After the election Batty called me to his shop where we discussed the advisability of forming a trade union. He informed me that he was satisfied I could be useful to my people if I could embark on trade union activities instead of politics. I readily agreed to his suggestion, although I anticipated difficulty in getting people together. We planned to invade the Cape Town docks, as the Harbour constituency fell in that area.

Our first meeting was staged in Excelsior Hall, Buitengracht Street, on January 17, 1919. The majority at the meeting were Coloured men engaged at the docks. There were about half a dozen Africans, including myself. Batty, who was a good platform speaker, presided. In his address he stressed the necessity for the non-Europeans to help themselves instead of depending on politicians like himself. He strongly advised the formation of a trade union, although one should not forget the fact that he wanted to solidify the non-European vote in the Harbour constituency for the next election. By a unanimous resolution the meeting decided to form a union with the name 'Industrial and Commercial Union'. On a motion by Batty I was unanimously elected secretary. Twenty-four members were enrolled that first night; they each paid a shilling entrance fee, making twenty-four shillings in all, with which the first banking account of the ICU was opened. At this first meeting it was resolved that weekly meetings of the new union should be held.

Thus the ICU was born immediately after the Great War of 1914-18. The aftermath of war brought about a rise in the cost of living throughout the country, which affected all sections of the population. The rise in the cost of living was largely due to the fact that most essential foodstuffs were exported overseas. The question of the exportation of foodstuffs to Europe became a public matter, and was widely discussed in the daily press here. The Cape Federation of Labour Unions, which also considered this matter, declared that a check on the exportation of foodstuffs to Europe was necessary. At that time it was the policy of official white trade unions to leave the semi- and unskilled labourers unorganized. But it was necessary that the dock labourers should be approached if a check on the exportation of foodstuffs to Europe was to be brought about. Consequently the new union which catered for the docks, that is to say, the ICU, was approached by the Federation. The ICU Executive readily agreed to tackle the job. We decided, however, that if a strike was to be called we should also take advantage of the situation to put in demands for a minimum wage of six shillings per day. The National Union of Railwaymen, consisting exclusively of Europeans, agreed to support our demands. The day for action was fixed for Wednesday, December 17, 1919.

During the first year of the ICU's existence, I was employed in Greenmarket Square, Cape Town, with waterproof manufacturers. On the appointed day I was early at the factory in order to ask for permission to be absent from work for a couple of hours. Leave was granted, and I went straight to the docks at the East Pier where mail steamers were then berthed. Immediately on my arrival at the docks I boarded the *Norman Castle* and got into touch with Joe Paulsen, a Coloured man who was the first chairman of the ICU and who was one of the foremen of the Union Castle Company. I ordered him to 'down tools' as a signal to others. He, however, hesitated, as he was not sure whether the native workers employed by the Railways and Harbours Administration would respond to strike action. Eventually, Paulsen ceased work and was followed by his 'gang'. The *Norman Castle* was immediately deserted by its non-European employees. I managed to borrow a bicycle and cycled throughout the docks calling on workers to down tools and to follow me outside the dock gates.

41

By 11 a.m. the whole vast Cape Town docks was at a standstill, with hundreds of Coloured and African workers streaming out of it. Outside the dock gates I addressed the huge crowd, officially inaugurating what I believe to be the first organized strike of non-European labour in South Africa. I declared that the objects of the strike were, firstly, to stop the exportation of foodstuffs to Europe and, secondly, to demand a minimum wage of 6s. a day.

In conducting a strike I have always maintained that discipline and good behaviour by the workers are essential if public sympathy is to be obtained. The strikers were, therefore, advised not to roam about in the streets. Two strike meetings were to be held daily, one at the Grand Parade at 11 a.m., another at the bottom of Adderley Street (the main thoroughfare of Cape Town) at 6 p.m. The strike committee was formed, composed of non-Europeans and Europeans. The Cape Federation of Labour Unions, which had its offices at the corner of Darling and Plein Streets, with Robert Stuart as its secretary, permitted the ICU to conduct the strike from their offices. To everyone's amazement the strike became very effective as days passed by. Both the *Cape Times* and *Cape Argus* gave prominent accounts of the strike. It will be remembered that the ICU had not completed a full year's existence when the strike took place. Consequently our funds were not sufficient to wage a long struggle. Some European unions donated to our strike fund. From Benoni, Transvaal, we received £50 during the first week, which was telegraphed to us by Walter Madeley, M.P., who afterwards became Minister of Labour, and Bob Waterson, M.P. for Brakpan.[1] We decided to pay out strike pay of ten shillings per week for Coloureds and Natives residing outside the two locations. Most of the natives who were employed by the Railways and Harbours Administration lived in the Ndabeni and Docks Locations. To them food, including meat, was distributed daily.

During the first week of the strike the Government declared the stoppage of exportation of foodstuffs to Europe. We had expected, however, that the National Union of Railways and Harbours, in accordance with the undertaking made before the strike was called, would give moral and financial backing to the strikers. Instead the European railwaymen started scabbing on the strikers. The Railways and Harbours Administration, who were now losing heavily financially, were infuriated by the Natives' effective participation in the strike. The so-called European 'experts' on Native Affairs, officials from the Johannesburg Central Pass Office and from the Transkeian Territory, were rushed to Cape Town to advise the Natives not to be misled by the ICU and the Coloured people. A meeting was arranged in the Docks Location at 5 p.m. I managed to be present, but was afterwards ejected. This meeting was a complete failure. An old Native man told the officials present that if they were the true friends of the Natives they purported to be, there was no need to bring in troops to the City, since the Natives were not rebels. After this man had thus addressed the 'experts' courageously, he shouted to the audience in Xhosa, 'It is too late now. Let us go to Kadalie, our leader, at the bottom of Adderley Street'. In an orderly body they marched through Somerset Road to the bottom of Adderley Street, where I addressed them.

On the morning of that Docks Location meeting I was in my office in the Trades Hall when Dr. Haagger telephoned from Wynberg to Robert Stuart saying that a troop train was leaving there for the city. Stuart got so excited that he came rushing into the adjoining room and told me to close the office. He left the Trades Hall in haste. The troops reached the city and marched through the streets down to the Docks Location. The Natives, having refused to betray their Coloured fellow-strikers, were forcibly ejected from the Docks Location and were sent to Milnerton camp. We made arrangements to buy food, which was daily sent by wagons to feed the strikers. It was during this time I came to know J. G. Gumbs, who afterwards held the position of ICU President for many years until his death in 1929.

The meeting held in the evening at the bottom of Adderley Street on the day the military paraded the streets of Cape Town was remarkable. On the strike committee we had a number of white supporters. As a matter of fact, the chairman of the strike committee was a European, J. H. Dean. This day all Europeans disappeared, as did Bob Stuart, from the streets. The meeting was a very large one. I became the chief speaker. A powerful oration was delivered by me. The *Cape Times* next morning described my speech as 'sensible'. I said that the Government was unreasonable for sending in troops, as the strikers were not rebels. General Hertzog, who was at the time the leader of the Nationalist opposition in Parliament, had just made a violent speech at Smithfield, demanding a republic for South Africa. I suggested that the Government should have directed the military force to Smithfield, where rebellion was openly advocated.

The dock strike lasted for three full weeks. The ICU had been in existence barely a year, consequently its funds were not sufficient to carry on a long struggle. Jointly, with our own funds in the bank and from donations, we actually paid out in strike pay £506. The Railwaymen's Union, after the Government had announced the cessation of food exports to Europe, withdrew its moral support from us. Our funds in the bank were depleted; outside donations practically stopped. We had no alternative but to call the strike off. So, after a historic struggle of three weeks, the strike was officially ended. The stevedoring employers, without any reference to our union, made some scanty increase in the wages of the dock labourers.

Here I may mention in parenthesis that during the whole time of the strike I was on 'French leave' from my employment in the city. On my return to work after the strike I was summarily dismissed. I never dreamt, however, that the dismissal was destined to play an important part, not only in my own life but in the history of African trade unionism. That strike was the beginning of a movement which spread to the four corners of South Africa. Immediately after the dock strike was called off a general meeting of the ICU was summoned in the Excelsior Hall, early in January, 1920. Over 400 members attended the meeting. We took stock of the strike, while at the same time the future had to be planned. A strong executive committee was elected, with myself now as paid secretary at a salary of two pounds per week.

It was not long before it dawned on me that I had a big part to play in the trade union movement. I therefore decided to equip myself intellectually. At college in Nyasaland I had passed the Normal Course, which is today equivalent to matriculation in South Africa. But this did not satisfy me. I had to do justice to my new calling. I therefore decided to forge ahead. With this object in view I enrolled as a student with the Efficiency Institute, especially taking lessons in the art of public speaking, for which one guinea a month was paid as fees. This school had hitherto exclusively enrolled Europeans. I was informed later that many European public men, like J. W. Jagger, who was Minister of Railways and Harbours, were among its students.

In August 1920, at a special meeting of the Executive Committee of the ICU, it was unanimously resolved that another attempt for a minimum wage in the Cape Town Docks should be launched. Letters demanding increased wages for the dock labourers were sent out by the ICU to the various private stevedoring companies and to the Railways and Harbours Administration. As was expected, the Railways and Harbours Administration were not prepared to recognize the ICU. On the other hand, the stevedoring companies, led by the Union Castle Steamship Company, who had learnt a lesson from the dock strike hardly six months before, readily agreed to meet representatives from the Union. A letter was addressed to me as secretary, inviting the ICU to meet the employers' representatives at the offices of the Union Castle Company in Adderley Street. This reply came so suddenly that it was impossible to convene a special meeting of the executive committee of the Union. But I managed, however, to get J. G. Gumbs, who at the time was the Vice-President of the union, and S. M. Bennett Ncwana, who had come to visit the ICU office on that day from Zonnebloem College, where he was a student. This man unofficially joined our delegation. The employers received us very cordially, and their spokesman expressed the hope and desire for an amicable settlement of our claim for increased wages. We were assured by the employers' representatives that an early reply would be sent to us. I was the spokesman of the delegation. Hardly a week passed when letters poured into our office from employers, with the exception of the Railways and Harbours Administration, offering a minimum wage of eight shillings per day for labourers; nine shillings per day for winchmen; twelve shillings and sixpence per day for foremen (generally known in the docks in those days as 'serangs'), with double pay for overtime.

The excitement of the docks victory had hardly subsided when the so-called friends of the Natives began to plan my expulsion from South Africa. At this time relations between my elder brother, Robert Victor Kadalie, and myself were strained. It was alleged at the time that he was approached to supply the authorities with information regarding my birthplace. On the afternoon of November 24, 1920, I was on my way from the bank where ICU funds were deposited when I was accosted by a European gentleman who introduced himself as a CID man. I was placed under arrest and in less than ten minutes was standing before the Chief Immigration Officer of Cape Town. He handed me a Deportation Order which read:

'UNION OF SOUTH AFRICA
The Immigrants Regulation Act, 1913

'To Clements Kadalie, on board or at the Cape. Take notice that permission to remain in the Union (or this Province) is refused to you on the grounds that you are a Prohibited Immigrant as defined in Section 4 (a) of the Immigrants Regulation Act, 1913. You are notified that in terms of Section 2 of the Act you may appeal to the Board of Appeal, and if you desire so to appeal a form of Notice of Appeal will be furnished to you. Such appeal must be noted within 3 days forthwith.

> (Signed) E. BRANDE,
> Principal Immigration Officer,
> The Union of South Africa:
> Department of the Interior.

Cape Town,
24th *November*, 1920.'

I asked for my solicitor to be sent for. A telephone message was put through to him, and he immediately joined us. The immigration officer seemed to be quite a decent fellow and was somewhat sympathetic towards me, but he had to carry out his official duties, however harsh some of these might be. I was set free on my own recognizances, on condition that I reported periodically. I was also informed that I was not to attend any ICU or public meetings while waiting for a coaster steamer which was due in a fortnight's time. My passage was actually already booked and paid for by the Government. To me this was a sad blow, for my work, which was now growing in volume and promise, was to be suspended, perhaps for ever as far as I was concerned. This deportation agony was borne alone. I was a

single man in my early twenties. My own elder brother had for-
saken me, for he was now pleased that my political activities
were over.

If the story of the contemplated deportation could be written
in full, it would rank as one of the most interesting episodes in
the annals of South African history. At the zenith of the ICU's
rise, parliamentarians, as well as the daily press, discussed the
cancellation of the deportation order. In these pages it is impossible and inappropriate to disclose the secret drama that was
responsible for the cancellation of the deportation order.[2] While
the deportation order was hanging like the sword of Damocles
over my head, the General Election of 1921 was pending. My
solicitors, Messrs. Dichmont and Dichmont, who belonged to a
well-known Cape family, and Advocate Will Stuart, who was then
an M.P. for the Tembuland constituency in the Union Parliament
and who belonged to the Schreiner family, put up a magnificent
defence before the Immigration Board. The Minister of the
Interior at the time, the late Sir Patrick Duncan, K.C., who afterwards became the Governor-General, was a Scotsman. It will be
recalled that my education was obtained from the Scottish missionaries of the famous Livingstonia College in British Nyasaland. In
short, the fight for cancellation of the deportation order was
conducted through various channels. The Scottish Church took
some share in it, while, politically, the late Dr. A. Abdurahman,
although we did not see eye to eye in politics, also exerted
pressure on influential members of the Unionist Party. ICU meetings passed resolutions calling on the Government to cancel the
order. Early in January 1921 the order was cancelled and I
became as free a citizen as anyone could wish. Thus political
pressure, plus early association with the Scottish missionaries, were
responsible for bringing me unconditional freedom.

I should like to close this chapter on the birth of the ICU by
quoting a passage from Dr. Donald Fraser's book, *The New
Africa*. He wrote:

'Once when I was on my way home I was accompanied to the
docks at Cape Town by one of the local ministers. As we
walked along he said that he had asked us to meet there an
African lad who was secretary to the Native Industrial Union,
and had just brought off a strike peaceably and successfully. To

47

everyone's amazement he had combined members of tribes that were very suspicious of one another, and had obtained better conditions and pay for the workers. As we rounded the wharf to which the steamer was tied, two handsome young Africans came forward to greet us. One was secretary of the Native Industrial Union, the other had arrived from Europe where he had been serving in Flanders. They were immaculately dressed, and, as they lifted their hats and addressed me, my eyes opened in amazement as I recognized that they were both natives of Nyasaland. While we spoke together my mind flew to the land in Central Africa from which they had come, with its recent emergence from primitive conditions, and tried to pierce the future. One thing was plain, that the old days of exploitation of helpless people by slavers or the ruthless foreigners were gone, and that the present generation is stretching out its hand in new demands undreamed of by their fathers.

'These lads whom I had just met represented the product of education, but not of mission schools alone. In school they had received their literary education, and their emancipation from their old faith. But since they left Nyasaland an intensive education had been given them in Flanders and in Cape Town. The things they had seen, the treatment they had received, and the men and women they had met with, had led them a long way, and has led them further still since that day in Cape Town. The Scottish Missionary who had taught the Trade Union Secretary would possibly have been shocked at the idea of Native workmen combining to make demands. But, this clever lad had gone to another school, and other teachers had been educating him since he was a pupil in a mission school.'

NOTES

1. (p. 42) Madeley's interest in African trade unions is confirmed by the Msimang interview. Msimang claimed that before the 1922 strike there were 'certain Europeans who were running a workers' organization known as the World . . . [probably the Industrial Workers of the World]. It was an organization from England. And the treasurer of that, of the fund that they sent down for this particular work of organizing the African people, was the late Mr. Madeley, of Benoni, the Labour Party man. And he told me they were looking for an African who could organize the workers under that organization'. Msimang acted as a paid organizer in Johannesburg for a month when the strike broke out and he ceased

his activities. When the strike was over he discovered that the fund was exhausted. Msimang transcript, p. 16.

2. (p. 47) Among Kadalie's newspaper cuttings was an extract from a Parliamentary debate reported in *The Star* of Johannesburg on July 20, 1925. 'Mr. Reyburn (Labour, Umbilo) took the opportunity of reading the correspondence recently laid upon the table relating to the deportation order against Clements Kadalie. He read a letter from a Cape Town firm of solicitors to the Minister of the Interior in 1920, after the order had been made, but ordered to be stayed. It read: "Please state whether proceedings against Kadalie withdrawn or only stayed. Meeting of Native Labour Union to be held here tomorrow night to decide whether to support the South African Party." A confirmatory letter followed written on this letter: "Reply to say man will be allowed to remain. Arrange refund of the deposit.—H.V.S." '

CHAPTER III

The Grass Fire

WHILE I was fighting for freedom against the deportation order there appeared an interesting visitor to South Africa. The American Methodist Episcopal Church of Cape Town were privileged in having a new distinguished Negro bishop, the Right Reverend William Vernon, D.D. He arrived soon after I obtained my freedom, but he, too, met difficulties before he could land here. I was approached by some of the leading men of the AME Church for advice. It was impossible for me to give information as I was still confounded with my new freedom and victory. The incident is mentioned here because it brought about intimate friendship with Bishop Vernon during his stay in South Africa. The Bishop took keen and personal interest in me and in the affairs of the ICU. Bishop Vernon wanted to send me to America for further studies, but I was reluctant, as I thought my work would be interrupted if I left the country. Whether I was wise in this decision only future historians may say.

During the great strike of white miners on the Rand in 1922, the ICU staged a public meeting to protest against the shooting of African miners by white miners. Bishop Vernon actually drafted the resolution which was moved by me on the Grand Parade at the time. The *Cape Times* commented on the resolution as a sensible one.

We have seen in the foregoing chapter how the first trade union minimum wage for non-European labour in the long history of South Africa was brought about at Cape Town docks. This was to be the signal for a general awakening throughout the Union. Other centres in the country were bound to follow suit. Port Elizabeth was the next centre to grasp this opportunity. This was in October 1920. Unfortunately, at Port Elizabeth the demand

for a minimum wage was not conducted soberly and constitutionally by the local leaders, led by Samuel Masabalala. The
agreement between employers and non-European labour in Cape
Town was published in the daily press. At Port Elizabeth, Samuel
Masabalala, who had attempted to organize a union, put in
demands for an increase in wages for non-European labourers
there. The agitation for increased wages, which we learnt after
Port Elizabeth had linked up with us in Cape Town, was conducted intemperately by the leaders there. The local authorities
also made a blunder by inviting the late Dr. Rubusana from East
London to Port Elizabeth in order to pacify the workers. They
were told not to listen to Masabalala and his union. Instead of
pacifying the workers, the interference of Rubusana provoked
the workers into strike-fever which, although it never did take
place, brought about the arrest of Masabalala before the strike
was ever called. There was a riot in the Market Square of Port
Elizabeth in which more than twenty people were shot down
by police and European civilians. A Commission of Inquiry into
the riot was appointed by the Government. The ICU passed a
resolution which was forwarded to the Government, demanding
that a non-European be included in the Commission. For the
first time in the history of South Africa, a non-European, Dr. A.
Abdurahman, was appointed on the Commission of Inquiry. Masabalala was criminally arraigned. The ICU in Cape Town engaged
Will Stuart to defend Masabalala in the Supreme Court at
Grahamstown, where he was honourably acquitted.

With the acquittal of Samuel Masabalala the attention of our
Executive Council in Cape Town was focused on the unification
of Port Elizabeth with us. Selby Msimang from Bloemfontein,
however, slipped first into Port Elizabeth, but did not succeed in
putting this centre on a proper trade union footing. The ICU
Executive arranged to invite Masabalala to Cape Town where
he came in the summer of 1922.

In 1921 I went to Port Elizabeth and spent two months there
in order to put the affairs of the Union on a proper trade union
footing. It was decided to commemorate the shooting of 21 men
and women—African and Coloured—who lost their lives in
Market Square of that city in the previous year. The exact day
of the shooting fell on a Monday, and I suggested to the com-

mittee to observe it on that particular day which fell on a Monday. We obtained the permission of the City Council to have a street collection on behalf of the victims of the tragedy. African and Coloured girls raided the streets of Port Elizabeth with collection boxes obtained from the City Hall. We began the parade from the ICU Kopje in Korsten at 8 a.m. and reached the cemetery at 10 a.m. Thousands of workers participated. The Rev. Edwin Binda—a scholarly African minister—officiated at the graveyard near the sea. The Rev. Edwin Binda, who was an emotional preacher either in the English language or in Xhosa, delivered a very powerful political sermon which caused some of the thousands of his hearers to weep, while European spectators took fright and began to withdraw from the scene. In the afternoon, the demonstration moved to the Market Square in the North End of the City, where I was the chief speaker. Just as was the case at the graveyard where Rev. Edwin Binda stirred the demonstrators, I, on my part, must have added burning oil on the audience, which by this time—5 p.m. after the closing of business—had swelled into many thousands. In view of the sad occasion we were commemorating, my speech was another denunciation of the methods employed by the police, assisted by civilians, which culminated in the death of twenty-three innocent men and women of my race.

In sum, the affair passed off quietly, although there was rumour on the next day that I would be charged for the speech I delivered. Since there was no law on the statute books at the time under which I could be indicted, the firm of printers who printed the handbill announcing the event of that day was charged for printing it instead. I was subpœnaed to give evidence on behalf of the Crown to state that I had placed the order with him. A large sum was raised as a result of our street collection, and this was distributed among the victims of the Market Square tragedy. Thus, with blood, the ICU was set on its way to work for the amelioration of African labour in the twenties.

Masabalala was a good platform speaker in the African languages, for he spoke both Xhosa and Sotho fluently. He was also fluent in High Dutch, but was a poor speaker in the English language. For trade union work he was not properly equipped, as he did not avail himself of private study. The riot at Port

Elizabeth, his arrest and acquittal in the Supreme Court at Grahamstown, made him somewhat of a hero. As an administrator of an organization he was wholly unsuited. He was also deficient in many other qualities that make up good leadership. It was not too long before the Executive Committee dispensed with his services as organizer-in-chief of the ICU. During two months that I spent in Port Elizabeth putting the Branch affairs in order, the ICU was forced to lay a criminal charge against the former Branch Secretary, who appeared before the court.

At last I managed to put the Port Elizabeth branch upon a proper trade union footing, inviting James A. La Guma from Luderitz, South-West Africa, to take up the secretaryship there. ICU activities in Port Elizabeth during this period were at a later date eloquently commented upon by the late Sir Thomas Graham, who was then Judge-President of the Cape Eastern Division of the Supreme Court of South Africa, in the following terms:

'In Port Elizabeth the other day he tried a case in which a Native came before him who was then the secretary of an organization representing 14,000 Natives. He was a highly intelligent Native, and gave his evidence with the greatest possible clarity, although he had to go into large numbers of figures and details. He did so without hesitating for a moment. Asked where he came from, the Native said he came from Nyasaland. That was a remarkable thing—a Native coming down from Nyasaland and taking charge of an organization of Coloured and Native people in South Africa. He had been educated in one generation.'

Having completed the re-organization of Port Elizabeth and having installed James La Guma as secretary, my attention was now directed to extend the ICU further afield. My next call was at East London, reached in the summer of 1922 from Port Elizabeth by a mail steamer which berthed in the roadstead, as large vessels could not enter Buffalo Harbour at the time. On my arrival at East London, I was a total stranger, and knew not one person. However, shortly after my arrival I was directed to the Standard Bank, where I met for the first time T. B. Lujiza, who was employed there. Lujiza had, of course, read about the ICU and Kadalie. I found him very friendly. He directed me to a boarding house in the location. In the evening after his work, he joined me. After exchanging greetings, a programme was mapped out for the first week-end at East London. With my own funds we had handbills printed for the first open-air meeting at the dipping tank. This was held on a Sunday, and was well attended. I spoke for nearly two hours with Lujiza as interpreter. After a few questions had been disposed of, a resolution was unanimously adopted accepting the ICU proposal for a branch of the union to be opened at East London. Over 300 people enrolled as members on that Sunday. A second meeting in the afternoon at the football grounds brought a very large crowd. It was decided that the ICU representative should continue to address meetings every afternoon at 5 p.m. until his departure. Before the second day's meeting, while resting in the afternoon at the boarding-house, I was suddenly awakened by the proprietor, who informed me that an African detective, one Tyobeka by name, wanted to see me. After introducing himself as Chief Native Detective, Tyobeka boastfully told me that I was under arrest. A few yards outside the boarding-house was a European detective. They marched me to the charge office, where I stood before a deputy-commissioner of the South African Police. The proprietor of the boarding-house, old Mr. Mkambi, followed me to the charge office. While I was ushered into the Deputy Commissioner's office by the European detective, the native detective, Tyobeka, remained outside. To the astonishment of the European detective, the Deputy Commissioner of Police greeted me cordially, even mentioning my name properly. He told me that he had been informed that the ICU representative was preaching sedition in the location, but he did not believe the story, since he had heard me already addressing meetings at Port Elizabeth, advocating the peaceful organization of the Native and Coloured workers. I put a few questions to the European detective, who by this time looked stupid when he discovered that one could speak so freely before his master, who apparently was not against non-European trade unions. After a few more questions, the commissioner wished me good luck in my effort to organize my fellow-men. Thereupon I withdrew and hastily rushed to the location to conduct the afternoon meeting. During the day Tyobeka had boastfully spread the rumour that he would 'fix that American chap'. Many people at this time took me for an American Negro, since I could not speak any of the South African native languages. At this meeting, after the police incident, I used strong language for the first time at East London. The local police for the first time, it seems, were humiliated by an African.

After a week's stay, East London was definitely linked to the ICU. Over 400 members were enrolled, and a banking account was opened, with Lujiza as branch secretary. Having secured two important centres to the ICU, namely Port Elizabeth and East London, I returned to headquarters at Cape Town, fully satisfied with such splendid achievements in spite of my short-comings with regard to the language question.

The organization of the Cape Province having been completed in the summer of 1923, it was essential to call all the branches together in a conference. This was held at Cape Town from January 17 to 25, 1923. At this time the Union had seventeen branches registered at headquarters. This third conference of the ICU was given prominence in the daily press, for at its opening session some distinguished guests were present. Thomas Boydell, who afterwards became the Minister of Labour in the first Pact government, Robert Stuart, who was secretary of the Cape Federation of Labour Unions, the Rev. Max Yergan, B.A., representing the YMCA of America, were present. But it was the presence of Tom Mann at this conference which brought about more publicity. Tom Mann, an avowed Communist, was visiting South Africa at this time. He was invited to address our conference, not in his capacity as a Communist leader, but as a veteran trade unionist of Great Britain. We had read before of Tom Mann, Ben Tillet and others who were pioneers in organizing the semi-skilled and unskilled labour in the old country. The press, however, exploited his presence at our conference to the full, and later for a long time the ICU was suspected of Communistic tendencies. This suspicion by the public and the powers-that-be was responsible for the appearance of a newspaper known as *African Voice*, run by I. B. Nyembolo and S. M. Bennett Ncwana[1] (both Africans), which violently kept up its vicious attack on the ICU and me. This diabolical misrepresentation of the ICU and its secretary culminated in the scare that appeared in *African Voice* with regard to my first visit to Lovedale Missionary

College at Alice, when I was accompanied by J. A. La Guma. In large type the paper published our visit with this heading: 'Bolsheviks visit Lovedale'.

While at Lovedale I was specially received by the late Dr. James Henderson, the principal. It was a great pleasure for Dr. Henderson to welcome me to Lovedale, for he came from the Livingstonia College, Nyasaland, where I had received my education. Both Lovedale and Livingstonia are the products of the Scottish Missionary enterprise in Africa. During our visit to Alice we were accommodated at the Anglican Hostel by Bishop Smythe.

Having failed to suppress the activities of the ICU and those of its representatives, *African Voice* ceased publication altogether. This was followed by the political demise of both Nyombolo and Bennett Ncwana, while the ICU grew from strength to strength.

At the 1923 conference in Cape Town the ICU declared its policy to the world in the following resolution: 'This organization resolves unreservedly to dissociate itself from any political body whatever, and declares that its objectives are solely to propagate the industrial, economic and social advancement of all the African workers through industrial organization on constitutional lines.'

Besides discussing labour questions, this conference of the ICU also discussed educational matters as affecting both the African and Coloured communities. A deputation from the conference waited upon the Minister of Education, Sir Patrick Duncan. Another interviewed J. W. Jagger, the Minister of Railways and Harbours. In our foreword to the official report of the proceedings of the conference at the time, which was published in a pamphlet, we correctly wrote:

'The conference of January 1923 differed in many respects from its predecessors. Firstly, it was remarkable because of the fact that the delegates were drawn from what is commonly known as the "rank and file", meaning that they were neither members of any distinguished college or university, nor all paid officials of the organization, but men employed for wages by employers. Secondly, one could ascertain its remarkability on the grounds that upon entering the conference rooms, he will find Coloured and Native peoples recognizing themselves as comrades in arms in their deliberations.'

The 1923 conference also considered a report from its Special Committee for launching a printing press and for building a headquarters in Cape Town. In view of the misrepresentation by its enemies, it was found imperative for the organization to publish its own newspaper. The building programme did not materialize, but the newspaper for the union was inaugurated and was christened by me as its editor, *The Workers' Herald*. The paper ran for over five years and was very successful. With the appearance of *The Workers' Herald* I decided to take up journalism seriously. With this end in view I took studies in journalism with the London School of Journalism by correspondence. During the year 1923 our activities were confined to consolidating the Union in the Cape Province.

NOTE TO PAGE 55

1. Bennett Ncwana is the man who in 1949 contributed unwittingly to the defeat by Mrs. Margaret Ballinger by thousands of Professor Schoeman in the election for the Cape Eastern seat in the House of Assembly. It was he that wrote curious election literature which the professor and his Nationalist friends later repudiated.—C.K.

CHAPTER IV

I Meet Hertzog

BEFORE extending the movement further afield, another conference was held at East London which began on January 17,
1924. Professor D. D. T. Jabavu from Fort Hare opened this
conference. At this time the country was politically unsettled. In
May the African National Congress held its own conference in
Bloemfontein. I was ICU delegate to this conference. The issue
before the conference was whether to take a decision in support
of the then government led by General Smuts as Prime Minister,
or to support the opposition led by General J. B. M. Hertzog. A
long resolution in favour of the Smuts Government was moved
by the Reverend Z. R. Mahabane, chaplain of the African National
Congress, while the ICU representative moved a resolution in the
following words: 'That a change of Government was necessary
and would be in the best interests of South Africa'. It will be
recalled that at this time, the Africans in the Cape Province
enjoyed the common political franchise with the Europeans. In
speaking to the motion, I reminded the conference about the sins
of the government in power. I mentioned forcibly the shootings
at Port Elizabeth in 1920, the Bulhoek massacre, the calling of
troops to the Cape Town dock strike in 1919, and many other
acts too numerous to mention here. When the vote was taken
and declared by the 'Speaker', the ICU counter-motion was
carried by a large majority. This was my first major political
victory.

It was arranged in Cape Town that while in Bloemfontein I
should try to call on General Hertzog. I had not previously met
the General, though on July 21, 1921, he had written to me as
follows, when he sent his donation of one guinea towards the
Bulhoek Tragedy Fund:

'Dear Sir,

'I have received yours of 19th instant, for which please receive my sincere thanks. My only regret is that I could not contribute more liberally. The feelings expressed by you on behalf of your Union, I much appreciate, in connection with my endeavours in Parliament, and I sincerely hope that these may contribute to a proper and true realization of the intimate connection in which those stand who are represented by your Union and myself in relation to the common good of South Africa.

'It is for us by our common endeavours to make this country that we love so much, great and good. In order to do that we must not only ourselves be good and great, but we must also see that there is established between the white and black Africander that faith in and sympathy with one another which is so essential for the prosperity of a nation.

'It is my sincere desire that that faith and sympathy shall exist, and to that end I hope to exert all my influence.

'With best wishes,
'Yours faithfully,
'(Sgd.) J. B. M. HERTZOG.'

With Samuel Masabalala I met General Hertzog for the first time in his office in Maitland Street, Bloemfontein. He received both of us cordially. The General was interested to see me. He was also quick to appreciate the resolution adopted by the ANC conference, which appeared in the daily press. He arranged to have the resolution printed in thousands at the Nationalist printing press in order to have it distributed by the delegates. Arrangements were also made with Keerom Street (Nationalist headquarters) in Cape Town to receive me kindly, and that the general election issue of *The Workers' Herald* (official organ of the ICU) be printed by the Nationalist press. Ten thousand copies of our paper were accordingly printed gratis and were distributed freely throughout the Cape Province. The general election campaign was now in full swing. We had won a great victory at Bloemfontein. There was another conference to follow, which directly concerned the Native voters of the Cape Province. The Cape Native Voters' Convention was to assemble next at King William's Town. Both Masabalala and I had now no difficulty in finding our train fares. General Hertzog, with Mr. Arthur

Barlow, M.P., arranged this for us from Bloemfontein. At the King William's Town conference we had to encounter opposition from old African politicians. There were old intellectuals like Messrs. Pelem, Sabanisa and Dr. Rubusana, ex-member of the Cape Provincial Council—all conservative. On our side we had an old politician named Makalima, from Queenstown. Professor D. D. T. Jabavu was in the chair. The conference sat the whole day and throughout the night, with the exception of meal intervals. At this conference we had the pro-Smuts elements who supported him because he was an ally of the British and who condemned the Nationalists because they happened to be born Boers. We argued that the decision of the conference should not be influenced by what the old Boers did to the Africans; for in the game of exploitation of the Africans, the English on their part did likewise by exporting the Africans to be sold in the slave market of the New World, which resulted in the presence of the Negroes in America. We urged the conference to follow the lead given by the African National Congress in Bloemfontein, and to be guided by the European electors who desired a change of government. In the early hours of the morning we challenged a division on the two motions. Our motion for a change of government, as adopted at Bloemfontein, won the day.

Jubilant and strengthened by these two political victories, I returned to Cape Town, where an enthusiastic reception awaited me from all sections of the population. In the closing stages of the campaign I became an important figure in Cape Town. During lunch-hours I addressed open-air meetings in support of the Nationalist-Labour Pact candidates. Wherever a Pact speaker, generally a European, got a bad hearing or heckling, I was sent for and rushed to the scene. One day at a meeting in Greenmarket Square, I was heckled by a son-in-law of J. W. Jagger. In my reply I told him to leave politics alone and go back to his firm and pay civilized wages to his non-European workmen.

I was one of six speakers at a meeting at the Strand in support of the Pact candidate there. The Labour Party and the Cape Federation of Labour Unions arranged this meeting. I went to the Strand first, before others who got there by cars. I was first required to canvass Native and Coloured voters at the Dynamite Factory. In the evening I joined the main party for the big meeting. The speakers from Cape Town were composed of three groups, Europeans, Coloured and the ICU representative as an African. The meeting was held in a large bioscope[1] hall, and was very disorderly from the outset. The chairman, who was a bit deaf, was howled down when he attempted to open the meeting. Speaker after speaker was howled down. While sitting in my chair, I wondered what would be my fate when called upon to address the meeting. All European speakers, including a Cape Malay, were refused any hearing. The chairman called upon me to address the crowd. Some shouts came from the gallery, some reference to 'swart mense' (meaning 'black men'). I began my speech challengingly in order to silence the opposition, appealing at the same time to the European electorate to give me a hearing as I had a special message from the African electors who had just met at Bloemfontein and King William's Town. With this dramatic announcement I captured the meeting, and thus became the chief speaker of the evening. After I had sat down, a vote of confidence in the Pact and the local candidate was carried unanimously.

On June 12, 1924, the General Election results were made known. The Pact between the Nationalist and Labour parties had won a decisive victory at the polls. After a week's rest in Cape Town, I obtained a railway ticket which covered all the four Provinces, in order to spread the new trade unionism to the African masses. Port Elizabeth, King William's Town and East London were visited. From East London I sailed by boat for the Garden Province of Natal.

In the middle of July 1924 I arrived in Durban by mail steamer. With other passengers I was taken to the Immigration Office, where I was not long delayed, as it was found that I came from Cape Town and was a parliamentary voter there. I was a total stranger to Durban and Natal generally. My only acquaintance there was J. T. Gumede of the African National Congress, who lived in Pietermaritzburg.

On my arrival in Durban I went direct to Ghandi's library, where a tea room was situated, and ordered breakfast. At first my order was refused, as no African had ever been served there with meals before. I informed the Indian waiter that if I was good enough to stage a meeting at the Grand Parade in Cape Town for Mrs. Sarojini Naidoo, at which I presided, I saw no reason why breakfast should not be served me. While this argument went on, a young Indian man, who had seen me in Cape Town, corroborated this statement. I had come to Durban to organize African workers, but on the first day I found there was another job for me to do there, and that was to bridge the gap existing between the various non-European races. Eventually this artificial colour-bar was smashed, and I was served with breakfast. In the course of my stay in Durban, I took meals at this tea room. At times I brought in fellow-Africans who had previously stood aloof.

While in Durban I stayed with a Zulu minister of the Lutheran Church, the Rev. Lamula. He and his wife were kind-hearted persons. The church house was not a big one, so I was accommodated in the sitting-room and I slept on a hard sofa. The minister advised me to obtain permission to address any meetings in Durban. I must admit that my first impressions of Durban and the Zulu people were very disappointing. All seemed to be so tame and ready to submit to anything the official European suggested to them. Being a stranger, I accepted the minister's advice and tried to obtain permission. This was refused me for fully six weeks. I then got into touch with J. T. Gumede, who eventually came down to Durban from Pietermaritzburg in order to assist me in obtaining permission. I approached the manager of the Native Affairs Department in Durban, but was directed to see the Chief Native Commissioner at Pietermaritzburg. I tried every avenue to surmount the difficulty in my way. I got into touch with a European who was reputed to be a friend of the Natives. He, however, asked whether the ICU was recognized by the Government. While on this tour, I was armed with copies of correspondence between the various government departments and the ICU. Among these was one from General Hertzog, which accompanied his donation of one guinea towards the Bulhoek Tragedy Fund. This so-called European friend, without permission, made copies of these documents, which apparently at a later stage were passed to Mr. J. S. Marwick, M.P. for Pinetown. In this way the famous 'Hertzog letter to Kadalie' became publicly known. It was first fired at the Prime Minister by the honourable member for Pinetown.

While permission to address meetings of Natives in Durban was being refused, Marwick put a question to the Prime Minister in the House of Assembly, to which Tielman Roos, then Minister of Justice, replied that the Government was aware of Kadalie's presence in Durban. He went on to say that there was no law in South Africa prohibiting the Natives or other non-Europeans forming themselves into trade unions. Thus a bitter dose was first administered to the reactionaries of Natal by the Pact Government. The ICU action in supporting the Pact candidates in the General Election just held was vindicated without any delay. Notwithstanding the Government declaration made by its Minister of the Crown in Parliament, the Natal slave-drivers did not yield easily.

For the six weeks during which I was refused permission to address meetings in Durban, I set myself to other work. Every evening, workers engaged at the Point, Durban Harbour, particularly wagon-drivers, came to see me at my temporary headquarters, and were enrolled as members of the ICU. My presence in Durban became a public question. Every newspaper in the country wrote about me.

Durban at this time happened to possess in its midst some finer elements, among them an English woman, different from the hypocritical Natalians who at this time were in ascendancy in the Garden Province. One morning I received a sympathetic letter from Mrs. Mabel Palmer, who afterwards did a lot for the ICU behind the scenes. At our first interview she expressed her sympathy with my predicament. She also informed me that she was a friend of the Webbs, who jointly wrote a book on the history of British trade unionism. She seemed to have taken a great interest in the ICU mission. At this time the Parliamentary Empire Association delegation from England, headed by the Right Hon. J. H. Thomas, M.P., was visiting South Africa. The delegation had just landed at Cape Town. After visiting Port Elizabeth and East London, they were coming to Durban. Mrs. Palmer suggested that the ICU should write to Mr. Thomas as Dominions Secretary, particularly mentioning his important position in the British trade union movement. J. H. Thomas was then the general secretary of the Railwaymen's Union in Great Britain. Mrs. Palmer suggested that I should inform him of the refusal of the

Durban City Council to permit ICU meetings, and should ask for an interview with the ICU representative on his arrival in Durban.

Acting on this advice I addressed a long letter to the Dominions Secretary, care of the mail steamer at Port Elizabeth Harbour. A telegraphic reply came which read as follows: 'KADALIE MILNE STREET, DURBAN. MR. THOMAS WILL SEE YOU TOMORROW AT TIME AND PLACE TO BE ARRANGED BY MAYOR OF DURBAN'. The telegram was a great relief. With haste I went to a printer for handbills for a meeting in a big Indian bioscope in the afternoon of the day Thomas was due in Durban, which was a Saturday. With the telegram in my pocket, I went to the City Hall to see the Mayor. As usual, I was flatly told that the Mayor would have nothing to do with me. Armed with the telegram in my possession, I informed the Town Clerk that this day the Mayor was bound to see me, whether he liked it or not. The Town Clerk went into the Mayor's Parlour. After some little delay, I found myself for the first time standing before the Mayor. Without any formalities I passed on the telegram to the Mayor. After reading it excitedly, he offered me a seat and inquired, 'How do you know Mr. Thomas?' My reply was that was not the contents of the telegram. He then got busy telephoning. Finally, it was arranged that I should meet Mr. Thomas at the residence of Sir Liege Hulett, the sugar magnate, in Berea on the day of his arrival.

On the following day, with J. T. Gumede and Chief Mini from Pietermaritzburg, I was privileged to meet the Dominions Secretary. The Chief Native Commissioner for Natal and the Mayor of Durban were also present. When we entered the big reception hall Mr. Thomas rose from his chair and warmly shook hands with us all. He spoke first. After mentioning my letter, he warmly complimented me on having set to work to organize my fellow-men. He asked about the ICU membership, which information was given him. Gumede also spoke, and in doing so got at loggerheads with the Chief Native Commissioner about some native land in Zululand.

After thanking Mr. Thomas for receiving us, we retired, and I had to rush to the bioscope where a great meeting was awaiting me. This was my first meeting in Durban. We inaugurated the ICU in the Garden Province. The official opposition was crushed.

This was a great victory, for both myself and the ICU, a victory that was bound to have beneficial repercussions in Natal. On the recommendation of J. T. Gumede, Alexander P. Maduna, who was residing at Pietermaritzburg, was installed as first secretary of the ICU in Natal. Maduna was left in full charge with an executive committee to carry on the good work.

NOTE TO PAGE 61

1. Cinema.

CHAPTER V

The Golden City

AFTER the triumphant hoisting of the ICU flag in Natal, there was yet another great fortress requiring my attention. Early in September of 1924 I found myself in the heart of Johannesburg. The stupidity of the Durban municipal authorities, backed up by the honourable member, Mr. Marwick, in Parliament, in trying to prevent me from addressing meetings of my fellow-men down at the coast, had given me the widest publicity. This was bound to assist in my work. This is how the Johannesburg *Sunday Times* welcomed me to the Golden City:

'Clements Kadalie, the well-dressed Nyasaland Native, who is conducting a propaganda tour of South Africa in the interest of the Industrial and Commercial Workers' Union of Cape Town, has been addressing meetings regularly in Johannesburg during the past fortnight. He now terms himself 'the apostle', a title with a curious fascination for Natives. He has also adopted the plan of prefacing his address with an apology for speaking in English—which he describes as a "foreign language". His difficulty is, of course, to address the houseboys and others whom he is anxious to rope into his Union in their own tongues, for he only speaks Swahili and English, the latter with a slight American accent. Kadalie is an astute speaker. He never transgresses the laws regarding public speaking, and is never inflammatory in a sense that would bring him within the law. His addresses are devoted to creating a black industrial alliance, and collecting black members for the ICU all over South Africa. He has established branches in Durban, Johannesburg and elsewhere, and is undoubtedly achieving a good deal of success among the Natives. "We shall experience in a few years the effects of his activities," said a well-known Pretorian police official yesterday, "and then we can look out for unpleasantness".

'Kadalie and Professor Thaele were educated in America. They achieved some prominence as speakers to Coloured peoples, and it is believed that their activities are being supported from the United States. Kadalie was due to address a considerable meeting in an eastern suburb of Johannesburg last evening in the interest of what, as far as the whites are concerned, is certainly a mischievous movement.'

So I was a missionary adventurer with a new gospel! And from America! As I travelled deep inland, I had to make friends for myself. I had known R. V. Selope-Thema, who was then the general secretary of the African National Congress. When the Congress sent a deputation to Cape Town, I had arranged for the welfare of the deputation, and had entertained them while in Cape Town. I naturally therefore expected some kind welcome from Congress leaders in Johannesburg. But the contrary was the case. Thema introduced me only to young men, like Stanley Silwana, Thomas Mbeki and Nimrod Tantsi. With these young men I started work in Johannesburg. Accommodation was found for me at the American Methodist Church in Philipps Street, City and Suburban.

The first opposition in Johannesburg came from the officials of the African National Congress, led by Makgatho, the President. Makgatho contended that the ICU invasion of the Transvaal was not sanctioned by him as the head of the Congress. He must have read in the press of the ICU fight and success in Durban, and he was apparently afraid of his position if the ICU got a foothold on the political field of the Transvaal. The ICU ignored Makgatho and took notice only of the officials of the Congress who did not oppose my presence in Johannesburg. Mvabaza, Mabaso and the Reverend Ngcayiya, also officials of the Congress, cordially welcomed the ICU and rendered me some assistance. While the Congress leaders were divided amongst themselves with regard to the ICU's uninvited intrusion into the Rand, I gathered together my young band consisting of dynamic Thomas Mbeki, Stanley Silwana, Tantsi and Mazingi. (Some years after the ICU was properly established in Johannesburg, the latter was found to be in the pay of Marshall Square Police headquarters.) With these young men we staged meetings at the various locations during workdays.

But the campaign was too slow for my taste. We decided therefore to print handbills and stage our meetings in the centre of the city, in order to let the workers know of our presence and mission. With this end in view, meetings were held in the Market Square of Johannesburg, where now stands the Public Library building. African workers came in their hundreds every afternoon for three days. The ICU and its organizers had now become a chief attraction in the Golden City. Europeans also came in to hear us addressing meetings. Enrolment of membership for the ICU was going on at a rapid pace.

The exploiters of African labour were disturbed by this new gospel being preached in the heart of Johannesburg. Something had to be done to stop it, but perhaps they were afraid of the 'multitudes'. Major Trigger, who was chief of the Criminal Investigation Department, sent for me one day while the meeting was in progress on the Market Square. When the crowd was told by Mbeki that I had gone to Marshall Square, it was decided to abandon the meeting, and a march to Marshall Square was undertaken at once to find out the intention of the police. While I was upstairs with Major Trigger, we heard a big noise outside. The modern slaves were in revolt, and shook the police head-quarters. Mbeki and others demanded that if Kadalie was being charged and locked up, they, too, should acompany him to gaol. The Rand had not been properly settled after the miners' revolt of 1922. The police were therefore apprehensive lest some European elements might take the law into their own hands to interfere with our meetings in Market Square. At least, this is what we were told. Major Trigger advised us to abandon holding meetings in the Market Square. But he was too late. Our purpose, to let the modern slave-dealers know that the time for eternal exploitation of the African had passed, was accomplished by these Market Square meetings.

During this my first visit to Johannesburg, I was privileged to meet Archie Crawford, who was connected with the South African Industrial Federation. I found from Crawford that he was not opposed to the organization of the non-Europeans into their own trade unions. As the ICU representative was a new missionary, he called also at the Trades Hall to see for himself what would be the reaction of the official European trade unionism towards his mission. Here he found a mixed welcome accorded him.

After fully two months spent in Johannesburg, I found that the branch had become established firmly with a membership of over a thousand. Branch officers and an executive committee were appointed. Being satisfied that good work had been accomplished, early in November 1924 I left the Rand for Bloemfontein, where meetings were addressed.

The progress made in Bloemfontein bore fruit in the following year, when the Wage Board sat there to determine the wages of the non-European workers of that city. The result was that a minimum wage of 21s. per week was legally fixed for Bloemfontein, and this act made the ICU more popular in the Orange Free State and was consequently an incentive for African workers to enrol in large numbers as members of the Union. It should, therefore, be noted that it was the ICU which first utilized the machinery of the Wage Board as soon as the Wage Act of 1925 became law. This splendid achievement helped our union to organize other branches in the Free State Province. Keable 'Mote and Simon Elias were prominent propagandists of the Union in this province. They had able and good branch secretaries in the persons of the twin brothers Nhlapo at Bethlehem and Reitz, as well as Robert Dumah in the western Free State. These able men did a lot to stir the central province to action.

From Bloemfontein, I touched at Kimberley and De Aar, and then went on to Upington. We had had a branch at Upington since 1924. It was arranged by headquarters that I should visit this centre to see things for myself. At our conference held at East London early in 1924, a delegate from Upington reported on the deplorable conditions prevailing there among both the Native and Coloured population. From De Aar I entrained for Upington, which I reached with only five shillings in my possession. This I used for sending telegrams to Cape Town headquarters and East London appealing for funds.

The location at Upington was nearly four miles from town. I was put up by our branch secretary, who could hardly express himself in the English language. Most of the non-Europeans in these parts speak only Afrikaans, of which I did not understand a word at that time. The secretary had a large family, including his aged mother, reputed to be over 100 years old. They lived in a grass-thatched house. It was so low that it was impossible for me to stand up while inside it. Water was also another problem, as this was fetched on donkey-driven carts from the Orange River about five miles away and sold at the location. This water was so dirty that on the first day I could not recognize a dirty tin put at my side for me to wash myself with. I spent most of my time at the post office in town waiting for replies to my telegrams, while at the same time availing myself of drinking water from the post-office tap. At 5 o'clock when the post office was closed, I returned to the location without any replies to my telegrams. In the evening I was taken to a small church for a meeting. I must confess that by this time I was so hungry that it was impossible for me to speak clearly at the meeting, which was in any case not well attended.

After two days and two nights, drinking water only at the post office, I joined a train from South-West Africa back to De Aar. I had hoped I would meet, say, a European traveller from Cape Town, to whom I could appeal for some food; but this was not the case. The following day I was back in De Aar. I could hardly cross the bridge to the location where a kindly Coloured woman, who was an ICU member, treated me with a light meal at first as if I were an invalid. I had almost lost my proper sense because of hunger. In due course I returned to East London, where I gave Lujiza a first-hand account of the opening-up of the three Provinces for the ICU.

The first round trip through South Africa took exactly six months. In December 1924 I returned to Cape Town, where the National Council welcomed its representative enthusiastically at a reception in the AME Church in Hanover Street. My report, furnished to the National Council, seemed to satisfy every member. I added in the report that it was essential for me to return to Johannesburg early in the New Year, in order to supervise the work personally on the Rand while it was yet in its infancy. This permission was granted. So, early in January 1925 I returned to the Rand, visiting Port Elizabeth, East London and Bloemfontein branches *en route*. On the morning of January 12, 1925, I reached Bloemfontein, and in the afternoon a big meeting was convened by the branch. At this time the location in Bloemfontein was in Waaihoek, close to the town. Thousands of African workers gathered to hear the ICU representative. I planned my campaign carefully, having decided to embark upon a nation-wide campaign which would give a direct lead to the oppressed peoples. The press and the police were well represented at this meeting.

For two hours I held the huge audience spellbound. I attacked every form of oppression which the African endured. The Chamber of Mines came in for some severe censure. European churches also were rebuked for their practice of hypocrisy, for the ministers did not follow the teaching of the Master who sided with the poor and not with the rich. I also planned to test the English-speaking people by calling them hypocrites. I declared that 'I would not trust an Englishman, even if he and I were found in Hell together. I should watch him for fear he left me there while he found a way out for himself.' I told the people to make 'such a hell of noise that the white man cannot sleep', meaning, of course, the white capitalist. I also said that 'Parliament must tremble'.

The occasion was big, and I planned to exploit it to the full. It was a big occasion necessitating a big speech for the first time in the history of Native affairs in South Africa. I realized after I had spoken that some history had been made, and that if the speech were reported in the press, the journey to Johannesburg might be interfered with. I decided, therefore, that I should entrain for Johannesburg the same evening, which was done. On arriving at Germiston station at 7 a.m. the following day, I saw the *Rand Daily Mail's* poster: 'Kadalie's outburst at Bloemfontein'. I bought a copy of the paper and read it casually as the train steamed in at Park Station. The *Rand Daily Mail* also published that I was on my way to Johannesburg. On arrival at the ICU office at 25 Fox Street, I took charge of the work. In the course of the day, a message came from Mr. Taberer of the Chamber of Mines, asking me to call on him. I hesitated to accept the invitation, but, as a brave man, I went to see him.

Mr. Taberer received me alone in his office and showed every kindness. He said that he had read with interest the speech in the *Rand Daily Mail* delivered in Bloemfontein, and that he was in sympathy with my aim to organize the Natives. He pointed out, however, that my attack on the Chamber of Mines was not justified, as the mining industry treated its African employees well, and much better than other employers. He offered to take me underground at the Crown Mines and to the compounds to see things for myself. After eulogizing me, he finally asked me to withdraw the statement I had made against the mines in the course of my speech, and suggested I should send a statement to the press. I totally refused to publish such a statement.

On the day the speech in Bloemfontein appeared in the daily press, questions were hurled at both the Prime Minister and the Minister of Justice in Parliament. It was the English members of the House who demanded my blood from the Government. This was also the first time the country as a whole knew that Kadalie was once arrested for deportation to Nyasaland. The honourable members, led by Mr. Marwick, seemed to have neglected their legislative duties in the House. Perhaps I had rightly prophesied when I declared, 'Kick up such a hell of a noise that Parliament must tremble'. For a long time the 1925 session of Parliament was devoted to discussing Kadalie's presence in South Africa, when charges and counter-charges were hurled at each other by the Government and the Opposition members. The Government was pressed for my deportation, while news-paper men came to interview me in Johannesburg in this connection. I was elevated to the status of a 'hero' of the land, as the publicity given me in the daily press equalled that accorded to the Prime Minister himself. It was during this time that the 'Hertzog-Kadalie letter' was made public, as it was prominently quoted in the House by Natal members. It is not out of place here to characterize the 1925 session of Parliament as the 'Kadalie Session' or, in other words, 'the ICU Session'.

The ICU propaganda had now become a national matter. On the mines, particularly the Crown Mines, we had enrolled a good number of members, including some African clerks. A. W. G. Champion was also employed there as a clerk at that time. Champion was connected with the first Native Mine Clerks' Union.

With my presence in Johannesburg the ICU membership rapidly increased.

The fifth annual conference of the ICU was now due and on my suggestion it was held in Johannesburg from April 13 to 17,

1925. Champion attended on one occasion as a distinguished visitor. It was during this time I first met Champion, who impressed me as having some qualities for the ICU work. I informed him of Mr. Taberer's offer and my refusal, which Champion described as a correct one. He then arranged to show me the Crown Mines on an agreed date one Sunday. Thus, without the knowledge of the Chamber of Mines, I visited the Crown Mines one bright Sunday morning. Champion introduced me to many native miners, including some African clerks who were very much interested in me, as they had already read in the press of my activities. This act of Champion proved that he was an able and brave man. It was at this time that he was offered work in the ICU, which he willingly accepted, resigning from the Crown Mines.[1]

By this time the ICU propaganda was being rapidly spread through the medium of *The Workers' Herald*. African intellectuals, who hitherto found no channel to voice their grievances, joined the ICU. Men like A. M. Jabavu, son of John Tengo Jabavu and editor of *Imvo*, joined the movement during this period. The Johannesburg conference was decidedly an improvement on previous conferences. The Mayor of Johannesburg, who was a Labour politician, officially opened our conference. Some white trade unionists came in to see how the new trade unionism was functioning. Among public questions which the conference discussed and took resolutions upon were the 'civilized labour policy' of the Union Government, the Pass Laws, the native recruiting system, registration of the ICU under the Industrial Conciliation Act of 1924, etc. In regard to the registration of the ICU under the Conciliation Act, we interviewed the Secretary for Labour in Pretoria (who was a Mr. Cousins at the time) on many occasions. Mr. Cousins was very sympathetic with our efforts in organizing African trade unionism; as a matter of fact, he was helpful in many ways to us.

It was customary for the ICU to stage a public rally at the closing of every conference. A mass meeting was therefore arranged in Eloff Street Extension on an open space opposite the old Inchcape Hall. The meeting was a huge success. At ICU public meetings it was an acknowledged practice for me to speak last, as no other could command the attention of the audience

73

after I had spoken. At this demonstration I delivered another powerful oration. As a matter of fact I was exceptionally vehement. Some delegates had left the previous evening for their centres, including those from Bloemfontein.

The residents of the Bloemfontein locations, led by local ICU officers, had organized a demonstration, with the result that public disturbances took place. Some leaders were arrested. For reasons unknown to anyone, these cowardly local leaders publicly alleged that Kadalie instigated the unrest. Of course, at this period it could be expected that any unrest in the country would be associated with my activities, as my name was at the zenith of national fame. When the arrested men came before the Supreme Court they were acquitted. With the rapid growth of the ICU throughout the Union, it was quite evident the Government was not going to sit idle while in office. The ICU ramifications and its vigorous agitation for improved economic conditions of the non-Europeans were of such a terrifying nature that they demanded immediate attention if catastrophe for the capitalists and the Government were to be avoided.

The Pact Government in its second year of existence appointed an Economic and Wages Commission. The Chairman of the Commission, Mr. S. Mills, C.M.G., and Professor H. Clay, M.A., came from overseas, but most of its members were South Africans. Among them were W. H. Andrews and Advocate F. W. Lucas, K.C. On behalf of the ICU I prepared our case for presentation to the commission at its sittings in Johannesburg. Champion and Tyamzashe accompanied me when we placed our case before the commission. We were well received by the members of the commission, including the chairman. As was to be expected, I was the centre of attraction at the commission. Our evidence, which was carefully prepared, covered a wide field in the economic life of the African workers. In submitting our evidence-in-chief, we gave detailed lists showing the cost of living of an African civilized family, giving five centres in particular, viz., Johannesburg, Port Elizabeth, King William's Town, Bloemfontein and Durban. The resolutions which were adopted by our annual conference that year were incorporated in our evidence-in-chief. In view of the importance of the resolutions at the time, I am anxious to have them recorded in this work.

74

'That this Conference most respectfully requests the government to recognize its decisions to exclude agricultural labourers and domestic servants from the scope of the wage bill, and to acknowledge the injustice of such exclusion and the overwhelming claims of agricultural labourers to the advantages sought to confer upon the workers in general under this bill. Further, this conference submits that the agricultural labourer is the hardest worked servant in point of length of working day, and should therefore come first for consideration in any scheme for improvement of wages and conditions of employment. And further that this conference elect a Wages Committee to proceed to Cape Town with a view to give evidence before the Select Committee of the House of Assembly, and that the Minister of Labour should be acquainted with this request.

'That this Conference congratulates the Government on the introduction of the Wage Bill now before the Parliament and which augurs as well for the future of all industrial workers, but we would humbly suggest the necessity of so amending the provisions of Section I of the bill as to categorically define industrial spheres to which the Act will apply and to insert an enabling section for the minister to extend its scope by an amending act, thus according an opportunity for full discussion of the merits of the measure from time to time in the interests of those concerned. Should the Bill become law in its present form, the conference fears that party political considerations may act as a brake upon the Minister in his exercise of the powers conferred by Section (I) of the Bill.

'That while fully realizing that replacement of Natives by Europeans in State undertakings is the settled policy of the government, and therefore without entering into any futile discussion of the pros and cons of the policy, this conference of the organized African workers most respectfully submits to the government that in the absence of a definite scheme of land settlement as a compensatory measure the enormity of injustice indicated upon the victims of this one-sided policy is incalculable and will positively provoke a deep-seated sense of resentment which the country can ill afford to ignore.

'That this conference of the Industrial and Commercial Workers' Union of Africa, requests the employers of labour in the dock areas throughout the union ports, to introduce a scale of wages with that which prevails in the Cape Town Docks. Further, that employees in the docks be paid accordingly, since the custom at present in vogue of engaging labourers in the Cape Town docks and discharging them at any moment, and paid for hourly and one-quarter day, is determined to the interest of the workers in those areas, whose work is mostly that of serving the general public, and that this conference authorizes the Executive Council to approach the Minister of Labour with a view to obtaining his support in bringing about the proposed condition.

'That this Conference of organized Native and Coloured is the opinion that Passes, no matter what shape or form, are nothing more or less than an institution of the present capitalist system of government to reduce the African workers to a state of abject servility so as to facilitate their utmost exploitation, and further, this conference condemns the proposals of the joint council of Europeans and Natives intended for submission to the prime minister, but in the opinion of this conference the only alternative is abolition of the Pass System.

'That this Conference requests the Government to introduce into the House of Assembly a short Bill so amending the Industrial Conciliation Act No. II of 1924 as to include Native Miners and Colliers in the definition of "Employee". Further, the conference considers it a grievous wrong to keep those workers entirely out of the pale of the Act while other classes of labourers are having the benefit of the machinery provided thereunder for consultation and conciliation and in the event of a clash of interest arbitration and meditation.

'That in view of the fact that there are so many complaints from the Natives about the Natives working under contracts in the Mines, the position of a recruited Native working under contract being no better than that of a convict who is not in a position to choose his working place, his class of work, his sleeping place, his kind and quality of food and his wages, this conference considers that the time has arrived when the government should consider the amendment of the Native Labour Regulation Act, of 1911, in so far as it affects recruiting systems. This conference requests the Minister of Labour to arrange for a conference with the representatives of this Union with a view to arriving at a system by which the natives should be enabled to reach the working centres, and further, this conference views with alarm the practice followed by the mine companies of compelling the voluntary Natives to work under contracts as though they were recruiting workers.

'That while desirous to avoid embarrassing the government in its laudable attempts to devise effective means of settling industrial disputes in times of emergency, this conference wished to call the attention of parliament and the public to the fact that the powers conferred on the Minister under Section II (I) of Emergency Powers Bill are constitutionally too enormous, and virtually obviates the necessity of an Indemnity Bill, which affords an opportunity, if not the only constitutional means known to modern democracies, of examining in detail the actions of a Parliamentary Executive on occasions of public disorders; indeed the section constitutes the sapping of the foundations upon which rests the constitutional doctrines of the rule of the law.

'That this Conference of organized Natives and Coloured workers gratefully records its appreciations of the material improvement of compensation benefits to the Native mine workers contemplated under Section 35 of the Miners Phthisis Acts Consolidation Bill, but we wish to draw the attention of the Minister to the urgent need of increasing the amount of compensation payable on death from the paltry sum of £10.'

In the history of South Africa we think this was the first occasion when the African case was ably placed before a Government Commission by representatives of the people concerned. Hitherto, the officials of the Native Affairs Department had the monopoly of stating the Africans' case. Our evidence was somewhat of a new explosive, so that officialdom became restless. Both the Director of Native Labour at the time, who was Major Cooke, O.B.E., and the officials of the Native Recruiting Corporation of the Chamber of Mines, were very indignant about our exposition. The daily press gave wide publicity to our evidence, which exposed for the first time the obnoxious recruiting system upon which the mining industry had built its cheap labour force. The Director of Native Labour, together with officials of the Chamber of Mines, did not sit comfortably in their offices in Johannesburg. They worked hard, following the Commission to other centres in order to refute the ICU evidence.

As I have pointed out elsewhere in this book, my presence on the South African political scene was a mystery to many, including officialdom. Of the three of us who gave ICU evidence before the Commission, A. W. G. Champion was known to have worked as a clerk on the mines. My connection with the mines was obscure to many. Before I came to the Union, I had worked as a clerk in two leading mines in Southern Rhodesia, where I watched the evils of the recruiting system. I resolved not to continue to be employed in mine compounds. It should be added that it was the systematic torture of the African people in Southern Rhodesia that kindled the spirit of revolt in me. As it was, I nearly forgot the good missionaries in Nyasaland, at my college in particular, who taught me the Christian faith that all men were equal and that their lives were valuable. Champion's experiences in the mines of the Rand, together with my own experience in Southern Rhodesia mines, were evidence too strong to be discarded by a government commission, which had a chairman from overseas and two Labour politicians of South Africa.

Our office at 25 Fox Street, Johannesburg, was converted into a new centre for African trade unionism, and Thomas Mbeki was appointed Provincial Secretary for the Transvaal. He was quite young, but extraordinarily brave for his age, while he was also a good platform speaker in both English and Xhosa. Henry Daniel Tyamzashe (later nicknamed 'Oupa' by my private secretary, Abe Phoofolo) also joined the ICU early in 1925. He became a member in this manner. By trade Tyamzashe was a first-class printer. He learned his trade in his early days at school at Lovedale. When the ICU reached Johannesburg, he was employed by an Indian printing firm, who dispensed with his services when the proprietor found he could not pay Tyamzashe the trade union wages in terms of the existing determination in the printing industry. Tyamzashe approached me in this connection. After we had exchanged views on the matter, a telephone call was put through to the offices of the Typographical Union. An appointment was fixed with the secretary. The result of the interview was successful, as Tyamzashe received back pay from his Indian employer. This was the first ICU victory in Johannesburg, and it led to long and close collaboration between Tyamzashe and me. Immediately after this victory Tyamzashe enrolled as a member of the ICU, and was later appointed Provincial Secretary for the Transvaal.

By 1925 the ICU had become a real national trade union movement, and, as such, it had to plan its activities objectively. Its

National Council decided that an attempt should be made to tackle the burning question of the day, namely, the pass laws, which were at the time being used against ICU officials throughout the country. Many branch secretaries, as well as provincial secretaries, were prosecuted under the pass laws. On the joint initiative of the assistant general secretary, La Guma, and me, the National Council sub-committee decided to call a general strike throughout South Africa as a protest against these laws. It was agreed, however, that to make the issue a real national affair, the co-operation of the African National Congress should be obtained, since that body had already made some bold attempts for the abolition of the pass laws on the Rand in 1920 in the abortive strike there. I was therefore delegated to meet the leaders of the African National Congress about the matter. It was agreed that if the general strike was to succeed, the ICU must have the full co-operation of the African National Congress, since the matter was somewhat of a political nature. An agreed telegraphic code was circularized to all provincial secretaries timing the day for action when this should be agreed upon. While in agreement with our proposal for a general strike, the Congress leaders, however, showed some reluctance to embark upon such a gigantic programme of action. The ICU headquarters in Cape Town was accordingly informed by telegram. The telegram so despatched was sent in the code we had designed for the purpose of secrecy.

While in Johannesburg in 1925 I received an invitation from America to attend the first Negro Labour Congress, which was held in May of that year in New York. This invitation was a great honour as it was now apparent that an international association was being forged for me as well as for the ICU. Before this invitation I had contributed some articles to an American Negro magazine, *The Messenger*. Through these articles my name and that of the ICU became internationally known. Immediately on receipt of this invitation, an application was made to the Department of the Interior for a passport to the United States of America. An acknowledgement was received from the department, but no passport was issued at the time. The ICU National Council gave me the necessary leave of absence to proceed to America, but the Union Government did not issue the passport.

The first invitation to proceed overseas did not therefore materialize. After I had forgotten all about going overseas, in December 1925 a registered package was delivered to me by post, and this happened, to my great surprise, to be a passport to America and England. Although the passport came too late for its purpose, it became in any case useful on another occasion, since it was of five years' duration.

My advent on the political scene in South Africa was somewhat of a mystery to many people, including the authorities. During my early days in Cape Town, some people thought I was an American Negro, since I could not at the time speak any South African native dialect. Probably for this reason, the Government wanted to establish beyond any shadow of doubt the origin of my birthplace. On reliable information, I was told that the Union Government had approached the Nyasaland Government, which in turn furnished the latter with my real origin. After having satisfied itself that I was a British subject by birth, the Union Government decided to issue the passport.

While our membership was of a general nature in terms of our constitution, it was decided to get one section of workers well organized in Johannesburg. At the Kazerne Compound, catering for the South African Railways and Harbours, ICU activities were concentrated. A healthy membership was quickly established here. The European contractor to the Railways Administration—a Mr. Glyn—was somewhat friendly towards the ICU. This, we found later, was due to the fact that he attended school at Lovedale Missionary Institution in the early days, when the colour-bar was unknown in this fair land of ours. Without many formalities we were permitted to enter the compound, where we addressed African workers on the ICU organization. Women members belonging to this compound became very active. With their own collections they raised funds with which our new offices were furnished up to date. Our telephone became one of the busiest in the entire city. Reporters from the *Star*, *Rand Daily Mail* and the *Sunday Times* sought interviews with us frequently and openly.

The year 1926 could be truly described in these pages as a very important one in the annals of the ICU, in view of the fact that the Rand nobly responded to our organizational efforts. The fifth congress was again held in the Golden City, and was attended by a bigger delegation. The press gave us further welcome publicity.

At the 1926 conference it was decided to remove the head-quarters of the ICU from Cape Town to Johannesburg. During my temporary stay in Johannesburg in 1925 I had found that the European trade union movement was stronger on the Rand, and it was here where European trade unionism was most antagonistic towards the non-European worker. However, in Johannesburg I had also found out that some European trade unionists were friendly towards the non-European worker generally. As chief executive officer of the union, I was respon-sible for setting up the agenda of our conference, which had to be circulated to all branches many weeks before conference took place. When the item of removal of headquarters from Cape Town to Johannesburg appeared on the agenda paper, the majority of the members of the National Council in Cape Town apparently were not in favour of this move. At this time my influence in the ICU was great. Consequently the Cape Town members of the National Council assumed that conference would agree on the removal of the headquarters from Cape Town. They therefore decided, without my knowledge, to boycott the removal by transferring all the ICU accounts in the bank to the Cape Town parent branch. At the bank at headquarters we had two accounts, viz., Current and Fixed Deposit, which were trans-ferred to the Cape Town Parent Body account without my knowledge as general secretary of the ICU. Our financial system was centralization of the union's funds at headquarters. The majority of the members of the national council in Cape Town were Coloured men and residents there. They felt that, as Cape Town was the mother of the ICU, it would be improper to remove its headquarters.

The financial secretary of the union was Eddie J. Khaile, an African, a Mosuto. He naturally did not approve of this arrange-ment by Cape Town to transfer accounts. He therefore decided to communicate the fact to me as general secretary, and requested that I undertake in advance not to divulge my informant's name during meetings of the National Council or conference. While communicating this information, he used a private address instead of our office. In reply Khaile was given an undertaking not to divulge his name as my informant. He was instructed, however, to bring to Johannesburg all books at headquarters, which he willingly brought along with him.

Before conference began, the National Council met in the Workers' Hall, which the ICU in Johannesburg, on my initiative, had acquired on lease. It was at the opening session of the council that some dramatic revelations came when conference agenda was being discussed. The bone of contention was the item of removal of headquarters from Cape Town to Johannesburg. Before members of the council came to Johannesburg, some of them, upon whom I relied, were informed in advance about the situation at headquarters in Cape Town with regard to the secession movement and the union's funds. It was during the discussion on the removal of headquarters that the big bombshell was dropped.

In a quiet and unsuspecting voice, I asked the president, J. G. Gumbs, and the assistant secretary, James La Guma, to inform the council whether all the financial affairs of the union at headquarters were in good order. After some hesitation the assistant general secretary informed the council that the accounts had been transferred into the Cape Town Parent Body account as a safeguard against the removal of headquarters by conference. Fierce and heated debate ensued, which kept the council sitting up the whole night. Eddie Khaile all along was afraid that I should give the game away. When asked by the president as to my informant, I replied that, as Cape Town was my home, I had many friends there in the Union who were loyal to me and who furnished me with the doings at headquarters.

A motion was tabled there and then for the arrest of all members of the National Council for Cape Town for fraud and theft. It was a dramatic moment, as the motion was bound to be carried by a large majority of the council. Men like Champion, Jabavu, Maduna and Doyle Modiakhotla rose to their feet one after the other demanding that the General Secretary should proceed to Marshall Square (police headquarters in Johannesburg) to lay the charge on behalf of the National Council. We sat the whole night until 7 o'clock in the morning, when some delegates to the conference came to the hall wondering why the ICU

National Council had sat up the whole night. La Guma made a strong plea direct to me as the leader of the Union to save the awkward situation. Whereupon I moved as a counter-motion that all members of the National Council from Cape Town should undertake in writing that, should the removal of the headquarters become an accomplished fact at the conference, they would not recommend the secession of the Cape Town Parent Body from the ICU. This motion was carried by a big majority. Thereafter Cape Town councillors attached their signatures to the resolution moved by me. At about 8 o'clock in the morning the historic meeting of the National Council was adjourned.

The conference was opened at 10 a.m. by the Mayor of Johannesburg, who at the time was a member of the South African Labour Party. As observed somewhere in these pages, the ICU was suspected of Communistic tendencies. We learned afterwards that Marshall Square actually had an informer on our National Council. What had transpired in the heated debate in the Council was consequently passed on to the authorities. Immediately the National Council rose, members rushed for breakfast, which was served in the ICU tea-room in the Workers' Hall. A cousin of mine was engaged as a chef in our tea-room, where first-class meals were served at a nominal charge. The opening of the conference brought to the Workers' Hall a distinguished crowd of Europeans. We met the conference as a united National Council; we pledged ourselves not to divulge the proceedings of our Council meeting. The ICU was now forging ahead; the second conference in Johannesburg took resolutions on many subjects, including one seeking affiliation with the International Trade Union Federation, which had its headquarters at Amsterdam, Holland. Our application was accepted, thus the ICU became the first national trade union centre in South Africa to affiliate with international trade unionism.

At this point I should like to say something about how we were spied on by the Government. Spying on the ICU in those days was a refined government speciality. I remember once when I left Johannesburg Park Station for Durban how I entrained alone in a 'reserved' coach, one specially set aside for non-Europeans in accordance with the Government's segregation policy. All along the journey I did not see any of the Johannesburg secret service men on the train, and I knew them all. But directly I arrived at Durban, I saw a well-known Johannesburg African detective. He alighted from the European section of the train. He must have been hidden in the European carriages all the way from Johannesburg. They were hiding and spying on a harmless, law-abiding subject of the country, just because there was such a wicked and unnecessary colour-bar between the Africans and the Europeans. Therefore I, as an organizer and chief executive officer of a legitimate non-European trade union, must be shadowed as if I were an ordinary felon and escaper from constitutional law and order. There is hardly any difference between the South African law in its application to Africans and the law of Hitler in its application to Jews. This spying must also have been applied to other ICU officials, but possibly most of these officials did not then appreciate the position. When I used to travel on any line, detectives were posted at all important stations to look out for me. This innovation was carried so far by the Government that, when the ICU provided me with a motor-car for travel on union business, the police took the trouble to record officially the number of our car, which in turn was circularized to all police stations in the country.

With the removal of our headquarters from Cape Town to Johannesburg the ICU definitely entered a new plane in the world of South African trade unionism. Our affiliation with the Amsterdam International was accorded wide publicity in the daily press in this country. The ICU, as it grew from strength to strength, had to contend with a dual allegiance amongst its leading officials. The Communist Party, which always plays the opportunist role in every country outside Russia, found in 1926 that within the ICU its active work had begun. Hitherto I had not expressed any public pronouncement about Communism, either for or against. The big employers of labour throughout the country, and, probably, the Government, suspected me of Communistic tendencies, while the Communists themselves looked upon me as bourgeois. In the National Council of the ICU, the assistant general secretary, La Guma, the financial secretary, Khaile, and two other leading officials, John Gomas and de Norman, were members of the Communist Party. There was also Thomas Mbeki, young, energetic and a good platform speaker.

The Communists were certain among themselves that they would eventually capture the ICU. Of course, I was the stumbling-block to their machinations, as they were not so sure about my allegiance.

While the Communists were carrying on their battle to capture the ICU, there were other factors behind the scenes. In South Africa there were certain European women, I am bound to acknowledge here, whose advice and help led me to adopt a middle course. One of them was Mrs. Etheldreda Lewis, the novelist. She was at this time resident in Johannesburg, and she introduced me to many distinguished people, amongst them being Miss Winifred Holtby, Dame Sybil Thorndike, the actress, and Miss Margaret Hodgson (now Mrs. Margaret Ballinger, but at the time a lecturer at the University of the Witwatersrand). These distinguished European women visited the ICU offices and the Workers' Hall run by us in Market Street, directly opposite the big Native Pass Offices. My meeting with Miss Winifred Holtby in Johannesburg was such a blessing in the following year during my visit to Geneva and in Europe generally, where she helped me tremendously, as will be recorded later in this book.

The rapid growth of the ICU in Johannesburg could be attributed to our foresight in acquiring the Workers' Hall in Market Street, where the social side of the African people was catered for. The hall, which had been used as a bioscope, had to be altered to suit modern requirements. The floor was altered accordingly. A young Coloured man named Scott, small in stature, was in charge of the artistic paintings, which attracted many leading Europeans to visit the 'ICU Hall', as it was commonly known to many on the Rand. On its walls were painted artistically an African miner, as well as international slogans of the labour movement, such as 'Workers of the world, unite!' etc. Distinguished Europeans made special visits to look and to admire the artistic paintings of the hall. At nights, dances or concerts were arranged. Men like Dr. Gow, of the AME church from Wilberforce Institution, gave us first-class concerts in the hall. The Chinese population of Johannesburg used our hall for their bioscope shows twice a week. In its minor hall the ICU fixed its library as well as a first-class tea-room. In a word, the ICU revolutionized the life of the African proletariat of the Golden City through its Workers' Hall.

While the social side of the African people was being revolutionized in Johannesburg by the ICU, our prime object, to improve the conditions of our fellow-workers, was steadily forging ahead. It was at Messrs. Maythams Limited, tinsmiths and sheet metal factory, in Mayfair, that the first action by our members was taken. About 52 members of the ICU decided to stop work until the management conceded to the demand for an hour's respite in which to enable the employees to have breakfast. This strike the Johannesburg *Star* reported as the 'native trade union's first strike on white lines'. When the men came out on strike, they marched in a body to the Workers' Hall, where I took charge of the situation. The men were threatened with arrest. Despite this, on my suggestion they remained in the Workers' Hall for any eventuality, while we got into touch with the Department of Labour. The Inspector of Labour at the big Pass Office opposite our ICU offices did not help the men at all. With the inspector of white labour, who at the time was Mr. R. H. Miller, I went over to Maythams' factory. For the first time I boarded a public tramcar in Johannesburg through the courtesy of the inspector. The inspector's intervention secured an amicable settlement, by obtaining for the men a half-hour off from 8 a.m. to 8.30 a.m. for breakfast.

The year 1926 was a very important one in the history of the ICU. It was the year that marked me out as an outstanding agitator in South Africa. The Director of Native Labour, who was then Major Cooke, often called me to his office demanding that I should carry a 'monthly pass'. But he was informed that I, as leader of such a large organization, saw no reason to carry a pass, being well known to the police, not as a criminal but as a law-abiding citizen. I informed him also that as a registered parliamentary voter in the Cape Province there was no necessity for me to carry a pass. I was willing, however, to carry an 'exemption certificate', to which Major Cooke replied that that would make me more free to move about in the country. The Government, he told me, required me to carry a pass as an ordinary labourer, with a view to controlling my free movement about the country. The most interesting thing of all was the fact that the police knew perfectly well that I had neither an 'exemption' nor an ordinary 'pass', but they did not arrest me. Perhaps the police were afraid of the 'multitudes'.

During negotiations between the European Mine Workers' Union and the Chamber of Mines arising from the appointment of the Mining Regulations Commission towards the end of 1925 in which the white miners demanded the removal of all Coloured and Native drill sharpeners, and their replacement by Europeans, also as to locomotive winches and pumps, the ICU national council showed its strong disapproval of these demands and we consequently despatched the following telegrams to both the white miners and to the Chamber of Mines. Both telegrams were signed by myself in my capacity as the general secretary of the ICU:

> 'My union strongly protests against your demands for the removal of all Coloured and Native drill sharpeners on mines and their replacement by Europeans, also as to locomotives, winches and pumps. Your action in the opinion of my union is widening racial strife between white and black workers. For traditional trade unionism my union requests you to withdraw this obnoxious and selfish demand.'

To the president of the Chamber of Mines we despatched the following identical telegram:

> 'My union strongly protests against demands of Mine Workers' Union for removal of all Coloured and Native drill sharpeners on the mines and their replacement by Europeans, also to locomotive, winches and pumps. According to such obnoxious and selfish demands, your chamber becomes a party in widening racial strife between black and white of South Africa— strife that sooner or later must inevitably bring serious catastrophe.'

This protest culminated in the largest meeting which the ICU had organized in Cape Town and these resolutions were unanimously adopted.

NOTE TO PAGE 73

1. A. W. G. Champion has a different version of how he and Kadalie met and how he came to join the ICU. He states that at the time of Kadalie's visit to Johannesburg in 1925 he was

President of the Transvaal Native Clerks Association, an organization recognized by the Chamber of Mines. Besides playing an active part in other African voluntary associations in Johannesburg, Champion was a member of the ANC. Champion was asked by the General Manager of Crown Mines to attend ICU public meetings and report on them to the management. He claims that these reports were to be sent to the Chamber of Mines. Kadalie, at his meetings, Champion recalls, attacked the mines' system of recruiting African labour, of paying the African mine workers very low wages for arduous and dangerous work, and compelling them to live in grim all-male barracks. Champion remembers being impressed both by Kadalie's knowledge of conditions in the mining industry and by his denunciation of them. According to Champion he was at home one day when Kadalie paid him a visit. 'I was very much surprised', Champion reflects, 'because Mr. Kadalie was not supposed to come into mine property . . . He must have taken courage, and he came to my house, and greeted me as Comrade Champion . . . Kadalie informed me that he had come to appeal to me to join him in the big work he had undertaken to do, that of organizing the workers of my nation'. Champion states that he was uneasy about giving up a comparatively well-paid post with a free house, and asked Kadalie if he could have time to consider the offer. When Kadalie returned the following week Champion agreed to become a full-time official of the ICU. Champion transcript in my possession, p. 150.

CHAPTER VI

Challenging the Ban

IN 1926 the ICU had reached its greatest organizational strength. Branches were being opened up everywhere in the four provinces. Natal, with Durban as its headquarters, had now attained the role of leadership, both numerically and financially. It was here that the authorities feared upheaval, in view of the Zulu nation's past history. In Natal my name was now a household word. Hymns were being composed and sung in connection with my name. Whenever I travelled by car (the ICU headquarters had now provided me with a new car), teachers would bring to the roadside African schoolchildren waiting for my car, and these would greet me with songs. The ICU and 'Kadalie' became synonymous words.

Early in 1926 I was booked to address a big demonstration in Pietermaritzburg's Market Square, which I reached in the evening on a Saturday. A huge crowd welcomed me at the railway station, including Champion, and not forgetting the police. My colleague Champion had not informed me beforehand while I was in Johannesburg that a big campaign was being conducted in the Natal daily press, urging that I should be prohibited from addressing this meeting. The City Council had communicated with the Minister of Justice, Tielman Roos, in Cape Town, asking him to ban the meeting. There was a reception that evening in my honour in a certain hall. Before the time of the reception came, the police were already at the hall, and they called Champion aside. The District Commandant advised Champion to cancel the meeting, as it was too dangerous. This Champion did, with my concurrence. The house we lodged in that night was guarded by ICU members. It was in the evening when Champion informed me of the agitation to ban the meeting, producing newspapers at the same time for me to read for myself. I told Champion that whatever happened the following day (Sunday), I would speak in the Market Square. Long afterwards Champion told me that he doubted whether I would have the courage to face the threat. The day came. I had prepared my speech well by making some notes.

The Market Square was extraordinarily crowded with a large audience of all sections of the city. The Zulu workers came in thousands; Indians, as well as a large crowd of Europeans, were also there. The agitation in the press had evidently brought an unusual crowd to the meeting. Champion presided, briefly stating in challenging words: 'I shall call upon the Man of the Hour, my leader'. My name was mentioned. I spoke without hesitation. My first words were deliberately brave, for I expected some shot at me from any direction, since the press had anticipated it. Here again my English vocabulary was in excellent form. I threw down the gauntlet, reminding the rulers and exploiters of Natal about the Angoni tribe in Nyasaland, descendants of the Zulu, who, when brought to Lake Nyasa for the first time by my forefathers, saw the waves of the lake rushing ashore. They took their sticks to beat the waves back into the lake, but failed. I asserted defiantly that, whether they gaoled, shot or deported me, the onward march of the Zulus with the rest of their brethren in other parts of South Africa, would continue until they were free.

So that the reader may appreciate the importance of the occasion, I may mention that the Deputy Commissioner of the South African Police in Natal attended the meeting in person. I was also informed that the editors of both the *Natal Witness* and the *Times of Natal* came specially to report my speech, as if I were the Prime Minister of the country. I spoke for nearly two hours without any single interruption, as my oratory had apparently captured the mixed audience. Naturally, I ignored the threat of being shot at, for I had a holy mission to speak to the modern Pharaohs. Immediately I finished speaking, I was rushed by car to the railway station to join the mail train for Johannesburg, where I arrived the following day, feeling indeed proud of the successful meeting. The Natal daily press, particularly the *Times of Natal*, reported the speech verbatim. Europeans were flabbergasted and could not understand how I was permitted to address a huge meeting in the heart of Pietermaritzburg, the capital of Natal!

Immediately on my return to Johannesburg, I received a communication from the Secretary for Native Affairs, Pretoria, informing me that I was forbidden to enter Natal Province. I was banned under Law 48 of Natal. For five months the Native Affairs Department restricted my freedom to enter Natal. The notice preventing me from entering Natal was served on March 1, 1926. Sidney Bunting[1] obtained legal opinion from Saul Solomon, K.C. (afterwards Mr. Justice Solomon), who was well known to sympathize with the cause of the African people. We were informed that if I undertook to challenge the ban, I should be arrested and on appearing before the court would be convicted, rendering myself liable to deportation. The learned counsel went even further, and said that staying in Johannesburg without a pass was also a contravention of the law. In Natal, Champion obtained a different legal opinion from that of Mr. Justice Solomon. Our Natal solicitor gave us his definite opinion that I should win in the Supreme Court. Mr. George Findlay, now a K.C., and a judge in Pretoria, corroborated the opinion of our Natal solicitor.

At the ICU headquarters in Johannesburg, most of my colleagues thought that Champion's desire was to put me in trouble. They were, therefore, reluctant to agree that I should challenge the ban. About August, however, I decided to travel to Durban as a challenge. My Pretoria attorneys were instructed to inform the Minister of Justice of my decision. On August 17, 1926, at 9 p.m., I boarded the mail train at Park Station, Johannesburg for Natal, alone. I decided to occupy the top bunk as bed for the night. In the early hours of the morning the train crossed the border into Natal. The first station in Natal is Charlestown, where the train was boarded by a European sergeant, accompanied by an Indian and an African constable. The European sergeant, after enquiring my name, which was readily given, ordered me to leave the train. I promptly informed him of my mission to Durban, where I was due that day. I also informed him that I was still in my pyjamas and should not be interrupted from sleep. The train stopped at this station for a longer time than was ordinarily necessary. The sergeant urged that I should agree to his request so that during the day I could see the magistrate.

At every big station in Natal during that morning I expected to be arrested, but that was not the case. Instead, ICU officials and members flocked to the stations, as if they had to meet an important European personage travelling on the train. Gifts of all kinds were showered on me as if I were the late Chief Dinizulu of the Zulu nation. When I reached Pietermaritzburg station there was an even bigger crowd to welcome me with many gifts. It had been agreed with Champion that I should alight at Berea station instead of at the main station in Durban; but the train ran straight into the city. On the platform Champion was ready to welcome me. The police were there as well, but did not interfere. On reaching the ICU offices we at once made a telephone call to our solicitor, Major Cowley, who welcomed me enthusiastically. At once legal machinery was put into operation. An advertisement was drafted for the morning paper, the *Natal Mercury*. It stated briefly: 'Kadalie in Durban. Will address Public Meetings at Cartwright's Flats at 5 p.m. from tomorrow.' For a full week I addressed public meetings in Durban. They were attended by a special European detective named Arnold. His native nickname was 'Tshaka', for he happened to speak the Zulu language. During this time the authorities were busy taking counsel in Durban and Pietermaritzburg, the headquarters for Natal, and were in daily communication with Pretoria. The ban had been openly defied by an African for the first time in the history of South Africa. The modern Pharaohs were in a dilemma, while an African addressed huge crowds of over 5,000 people daily in the heart of Durban. After one week's stay in Durban it was decided that I should return to the ICU headquarters in Johannesburg.

After I had been in Johannesburg a month, it was decided that I should return to Natal to find out whether the ban was definitely removed. On September 24, 1926, I was back in Durban. This time I became ill, probably because the train I was on was delayed for many hours *en route*. Immediately on my arrival Detective Arnold came to the ICU offices and summoned me to appear in court, where a remand was ordered for the following day. The court house was well protected with additional police guards.

Hundreds of Zulu workers, mostly ICU members, and Indian citizens besides some Europeans attended the court. As was expected, I was convicted of entering Natal without a pass and was fined three pounds, or fourteen days. I cannot remember exactly who paid the fine there and then, whether the ICU or some Indian sympathizer. Our solicitor, Major Cowley, at once gave notice of Appeal to the Supreme Court.

Immediately sentence was passed, the Public Prosecutor was rushed in a car to the Durban Country Club, where he was fêted and congratulated for having scored a conviction against the 'notorious agitator', while on the other hand the Zulu workers heralded me as a modern 'martyr in the cause of African freedom'. I was carried shoulder-high from the court, the crowd singing the African National Anthem 'Nkosi Sikelela i Afrika', upsetting and disorganizing traffic, to the ICU offices in Leopold Street. It did not take long before a bigger blow was inflicted upon the authorities in Natal.

As we were anxious for a final decision, the appeal was set for hearing at an early date in the Supreme Court at Pietermaritzburg. It was arranged that a full bench of judges would sit to hear the appeal. I travelled specially from Johannesburg to Pietermaritzburg for the occasion. The ICU engaged Advocate Hawthorn, K.C. (later to become Judge-President of the Natal Provincial Division of the Supreme Court). The Zulu workers, again, went to Pietermaritzburg from many parts of Natal to be present at the hearing of the appeal. Curiously enough, the majority who listened to the legal arguments in the Supreme Court did not follow the proceedings, but the reader will understand that among the Zulus at this time my name was held in reverence. The judgment was postponed, and I had to return to Johannesburg to await the verdict.

It was not long after my return to headquarters that one afternoon a trunk telephone call came through from Durban direct to me. Major Cowley told me that I had won the appeal and was again free to enter Natal without any hindrance. It was another bitter pill for both the Union Government and the Natal authorities to swallow. It is fitting here to record in these pages the full judgment delivered by the late Mr. Justice Tatham, K.C., which reads:

'The appellant was tried and convicted upon an indictment which charged the offence of contravening Rule 26, Part III, of Government Notice 120, framed under the Natal Law 48, 1884, as read with proclamations Nos. 6, 20 and 26 of 1885, in that on or about September 24, 1926, at Durban, he, being a Native of a neighbouring Colony, state or territory, was found to be in the Province of Natal without a pass as provided for by the rules published in Government Notice 120, 1910, Natal. The relevant facts were as follows: The appellant is admittedly a Native within the meaning of Law 48, 1884, and the rules published under its authority; and it is not said that he is not a person to whom the Act relates. His occupation is that of National Secretary of an organization of Natives known as the Industrial and Commercial Workers' Union, which functions throughout the Union of South Africa and particularly in Durban, but his own residence is in Johannesburg. In August 1926 the appellant visited Durban, and after a short stay there he returned to Johannesburg. On his arrival in Durban, on August 19, 1926, he applied to the proper officer in Durban for a pass in compliance with Law 48, 1884, and the rules framed under it. The officer to whom he applied, and to whom he paid the prescribed fee, informed him that he would not issue the pass without express instructions from the Native Affairs Department of the Government of the Union. The appellant returned to Johannesburg without having heard any definite refusal or grant of the pass. On September 24, 1926 (about a month later), he returned to Durban from Johannesburg, and was immediately charged with the offence already described, and was convicted.

'The third ground relied upon stands on different footing, and I think it succeeds. It is said for the appellant that upon a proper construction of Rule 12 (f) of the Rules promulgated under Law 48, 1884, he was entitled to freedom from prosecution upon a charge of being in Natal without a pass on September 24, 1926, because he had entered the Province for a purpose coming within the exemption created by the words "For the purpose of trade, etc.", and he had not been in Natal more than seven days (the extended period fixed by the amending Rule of June 18, 1917). The Rule 12 (f) provides: "Any Native living in Natal, or in a neighbouring state adjacent to the inland borders of the Colony, requiring to cross and recross the border on a short visit for the purpose of trade, etc., shall not be required to take out a pass". Section 127 of the Criminal Procedure Act, 1917, seems to throw upon appellant the onus of showing that he was entitled to the exemption. The evidence shows that the appellant is the paid secretary of the Industrial and Commercial Workers' Union, and that his visit to Natal was undertaken, *inter alia*, in the auditing of the accounts of the Durban Branch of the Society. It is not said that this purpose can be described as a "trade" purpose, but that it is within the "etc." I have no recollection of ever having seen the phrase "et cetera" in an Act of Parliament or in regulations having statutory force, much less do I think it likely that it has ever occurred in the abbreviated term of the "etc.". It is not surprising, therefore, that Counsel have been unable to find any direct authority as to its meaning when occurring in a statute. As the Statute is one restricting liberty it must be construed in favour of the subject where it is ambiguous . . . I think the intention of the rule was to permit a Native to visit Natal for business reasons if his stay did not exceed seven days, and that appellant's presence in Natal on September 24, 1926, was for a business purpose. It is said, and not denied, that this was the primary object of his visit, and if he also had in mind an intention to test the validity of efforts to exclude him, he was nonetheless in Natal for his business purpose of auditing the books of the Durban Branch of the concern of which he is paid secretary. It has been suggested for the Crown that the real object of the appellant's visit to Durban was to engage in political activity. This may or may not be the case, and whatever I may think about this I am bound by the evidence led in the Court below, which does not establish that fact. As he had not been in Natal for seven days on September 24, 1926, he had not on that date offended against the Statute. The appeal must be allowed, and the conviction and sentence set aside, and a verdict of acquittal substituted.'

The acquittal in the Supreme Court at Pietermaritzburg, with the consequent smashing of the ban on my free movement, increased the popularity of the ICU in the Garden Province. Natal now rallied to the ICU on an unprecedented scale. Zulu workers in Durban and Pietermaritzburg, as well as in adjacent towns, flocked to the ICU banner. To exploit the occasion to the full advantage, Champion leased a big property in the heart of Durban, which was used as offices and a club for our members. Dances in modern styles hitherto not practised among the Zulus were inaugurated in the 'Workers' Club'. The Borough authorities, particularly those who professed to be friends of the Africans, were alarmed at the meteoric rise of the ICU in Durban.

Having put our two heads together—literally speaking—Champion and I decided to test the legality of the compulsory dipping of Africans by the Borough Council authorities. It was customary in Durban at the time that any African coming to the city for the first time was subjected to dipping with his or her belongings in disinfectant, as if he or she were an animal. The result of the test case in the Supreme Court was successful. Thus another humiliating by-law in the leading city of Natal was squashed. This victory Champion exploited to the utmost, and it helped him to swell the ICU membership in Durban and throughout Natal. Just as was happening in the other provinces, young men, particularly teachers, flocked to the ICU, where they occupied remunerative positions in various branch offices at better wages than they received as teachers. In many cases, I regret to record, these young men were not all well equipped or trained for elementary trade union work. At this time in the offices of the ICU in Durban alone there were employed about a dozen clerks, who used to work as late as 9 p.m. daily, enrolling new members, as well as receiving membership dues, which sometimes ran into hundreds of pounds daily.

In Natal we had one notable provincial secretary in the person of Sam Dunn, who had joined the ICU in its hectic days. Sam Dunn was a Coloured person, his father being a European of that name, who in the early days had kept many Zulu wives, including Dunn's mother. It will be seen at once that Dunn played the part of Zulu or Coloured as the occasion demanded. He was an excellent platform speaker in either English or Zulu, and was rather more proud when he used the latter language in addressing meetings. He was nicknamed 'Zulu kwa Malandela', for he always used this expression when in the course of his great oratory he appealed to the inner feelings of the Zulu people. At times, in the course of his orations, tears would flow from his eyes, with some electrifying results on the Zulu audiences. I once addressed a huge meeting of about 5,000 with Sam Dunn at Bethlehem Location in the Free State early in 1927, and from that occasion Dunn was marked for higher promotion in the ICU movement.

With the advent of the powerful Sam Dunn in Natal, it was soon evident that another bull had appeared to challenge the authority of the reigning bull in the person of A. W. G. Champion, the Provincial Secretary. When rivalry between these two officials became apparent, I decided to transfer Sam Dunn to headquarters in Johannesburg, thus leaving Champion without a rival in Natal. At headquarters Sam Dunn did not stay long, for it was soon found that his temperament was not conducive to good discipline. Full credit must, however, be given to Sam Dunn for his organizational achievements, for it was he who was responsible for the opening-up of many branches of the ICU in Northern Natal and Zululand. On one occasion Sam Dunn arranged for me to address a public meeting at Vryheid in Northern Natal. We motored to this centre from Johannesburg. Admittedly this was the largest meeting I ever addressed in Northern Natal. Many came to the meeting from as far as Zululand itself. Some Europeans of this important Northern Natal town were alarmed when they saw thousands of Zulus streaming into Vryheid from all directions on horses as well as horse-drawn vehicles. Notwithstanding wild rumours, the meeting passed off quietly without any incident. This account is recorded here to prove that Sam Dunn was a capable organizer, in contrast to his rival, Champion.

The ICU having captured Durban, it was now clearly apparent that the Indians had to take some recognition of its leaders. The Indian leaders and some merchants became very friendly towards the ICU, more particularly with us. Whenever I visited Durban, Indian merchants would offer me their beautiful cars for the day as it suited my taste. I remember once I was accommodated in a large mansion in Berea, a suburb of Durban. I attributed my popularity among the Indians to two things: firstly, my work in championing the cause of the African proletariat was identical with the struggle in India waged by its leaders there; secondly, some merchants thought their association with the ICU leaders would benefit them in capturing our members as customers in their establishments. Before the advent of the ICU in Durban, I had already established my political association with Indians in Cape Town. During the visit of Mrs. Sarojini Naidoo to Cape Town, the ICU staged a big demonstration which was addressed by her at the Grand Parade and at which I presided. I had also met their first Agent-General, the Right Honourable Sastri, P.C., also in Cape Town. It may as well be acknowledged here that among the first members of the ICU in Durban were three Indians. Two of them I can still count as my friends up to the time of writing.

As already mentioned in this work, in 1926 the Communist Party decided to exert all its powers to capture the ICU. Through its press and propagandists definite action was undertaken by its branches. In Cape Town the Communist Party was fortunate in having secured the membership of La Guma, assistant general secretary of the ICU. Eddie J. Khaile, financial secretary, and John Gomas, provincial secretary. In the Transvaal, Thomas Mbeki was also an adherent, but he was rather pliable. Mbeki, a young man in his twenties, was one of the first recruits to the ICU when I invaded Johannesburg in 1924. Young Mbeki was a good platform speaker in both English and Xhosa. He also spoke Afrikaans, though not fluently. In his zeal to improve himself, young Mbeki took private studies in night school classes provided in the twenties by the Communist Party in Johannesburg. It is well to record in these pages that young Mbeki could have risen to higher achievement in the African trade union world if the bad associations which surrounded the young man had not overpowered the young man. It was a treat to hear him address big audiences. I vividly remember when I visited Middelburg, Transvaal, early in 1928 on the invitation of Mbeki himself, who was the provincial secretary for the North-Eastern Transvaal. A meeting was arranged in the location at which I was the chief speaker. We travelled by car from Johannesburg. On reaching Middelburg we put up in town with an Indian supporter. We arrived on a Saturday evening. Africans who attended this meeting came from all parts of the North-Eastern Transvaal. When we got up on Sunday morning, we saw all sorts of primitive vehicles, such as donkey-carts, and horses in large numbers, conveying Africans to attend the meeting. The town was somewhat alarmed at this African pilgrimage. I also was on the alert, in view of the fact that the local police authorities had mobilized their forces. At 2 p.m. sharp young Mbeki mounted the wagon platform defiantly. With his wide, ugly mouth he opened the huge meeting with 'Nkosi Sikelela i Afrika'—God bless Africa. The local press estimated the crowd that attended the meeting at 5,000. Notwithstanding rumours that trouble would eventually crop up, the meeting passed off quietly. I think this was due to the bravery of young Mbeki. When I was appointed by the ICU National Council to proceed to Geneva at the Durban conference in 1927, it was felt by some delegates that Thomas Mbeki should have been appointed as Acting National Secretary in my absence overseas. His age precluded him, since Africans judge individuals by age and not by qualifications. When the ICU split came about in 1928, Mbeki was found on the side which followed me. Unfortunately for Mbeki, liquor had mastered him early in age, thereby affecting his mentality. It is not clearly known to me how Thomas Mbeki died during the last war. It was rumoured he joined the army at the time.

In the Western Province of the Cape we had John Gomas, a young Coloured man, as provincial secretary, who was a tailor by trade. He was succeeded by R. G. de Norman, an Indian, after his expulsion from the ICU due to his Communist affiliations. Although not an outstanding organizer, Gomas was however an able speaker on the platform. During his period at the Cape, the ICU slowly declined. In Griqualand West, with headquarters at Kimberley, the ICU had Doyle Modiakotla as its provincial secretary. Although a capable man, Modiakotla was a complete failure as a trade union organizer. Kimberley and district did not show any real enthusiasm in the work of the ICU under his leadership. He rallied, however, faithfully to the side which followed me when the split in the ICU took place.

To return to our dispute with the Communist Party: the ICU policy was now and then criticized by the Communist organ. The president of the ICU, James G. Gumbs, who was West Indian by birth, was nationally minded. He was an out-and-out 'Marcus Garvey' who had the slogan 'Africa for Africans'. He was naturally opposed to anything in which Europeans were in the ascendancy, as was the case with the Communist Party in South Africa. My policy was, of course, the middle one between the two views. The struggle for ascendancy between the two groups was inevitable sooner or later. I was approached personally to define where I stood, and I averred that it was a matter for the

National Council of the ICU to decide. Their decision I was bound to respect. The two conflicting theories were, however, very unhealthy in a movement which was bound to grow, with probable implications for the future shaping of African native policy. It was therefore decided to convene a special meeting of the National Council. This was held in Port Elizabeth in December 1926. The members of the National Council, numbering twenty-one, all turned up to attend this special meeting.[2]

For a full day and half a night we discussed the question on the agenda, whether paid officials of the ICU should be permitted to remain members of the Communist Party. A full debate was permitted by the president in the chair. Very late at night, by a large majority, the National Council adopted a resolution calling upon all officials of the Union who were members of the Communist Party to resign from the Party, as their dual allegiance jeopardized the success of the ICU, failing which to accept their expulsion forthwith. The assistant general secretary, the financial secretary and the provincial secretary thereupon refused to comply with the resolution and were consequently expelled from the ICU. The decision of the National Council was communicated to the daily press, receiving a good reception. The Communist press thought otherwise. It heralded the news as the road towards the disappearance of the ICU from the political scene. As usual, I was severely maligned by the Communist press as well as by its leaders on the platform. The Communist Party press and its European leadership did not understand the African psychology at the time. Instead of the ICU heading towards its doom as foreshadowed by the Communists, after that memorable decision by its National Council the ICU grew from strength to strength, culminating in another revolutionary stage in the following year, 1927.

The decision of the National Council, declaring publicly its policy against Communist dictatorship, won for the ICU immeasurable support from liberal European public opinion, as was observed in the following year—the year which may be truly chronicled as the turning-point in South African native policy. In April 1927 the ICU held its seventh annual congress at Durban. This was another history-making congress on the part of the ICU, for two important decisions were taken, namely, (a) nominating its National Secretary, the writer, as a delegate to attend the International Labour Conference at Geneva; (b) adopting the following resolution:

'That in the opinion of this congress, we consider the time has arrived when both white and black workers of South Africa join in one national trade union movement, with a view to presenting one united front against a common enemy—namely, the arbitrary and unlimited power of capitalism—and that this resolution be telegraphed to the South African Trade Union Congress, now in session at Cape Town.'

I record here with pride that for the first time the organized European workers of our common country reciprocated our gesture for solidarity in the following resolution, which was telegraphed to us at Durban:

'That this Congress instructs the incoming National Executive to invite all workers' organizations, irrespective of colour, to affiliate to the South African Trade Union Congress; and that Congress instruct the National Executive Council to arrange a meeting with the Executive of the Industrial and Commercial Workers' Union of Africa for the purpose of discussing matters of mutual interest.'[3]

NOTES

1. (p. 91) Sidney Bunting, a Johannesburg barrister, was a leading member of the South African Communist Party. Bunting led the group within the Communist Party which believed the African, not the White workers, to be the real proletariat in South Africa. After 1924 this view prevailed in the Party.
2. (p. 100) Roux, in *Time Longer Than Rope*, p. 163, and Johns, 'Trade Union Political Pressure Group or Mass Movement?', Typescript, p. 33, cite contemporary sources claiming that there were only 13 of the National Council's members present.
3. (p. 101) Roux thought Kadalie mistaken in believing this resolution was passed by the conference of the South African Trade Union Congress. The resolution was held over for discussion in the co-ordinating committee of the SATUC and the Cape Federation of Labour. Ultimately the SATUC offered to meet the ICU informally to discuss matters of common concern.

CHAPTER VII

My Trip to Europe

B EFORE I could devote my time to preparing for departure to Europe, there were two important matters requiring my attention. From the Durban conference I was called away a day before closing to proceed to Bloemfontein to attend the first sitting of the Wage Board, where the case of the unskilled workers was presented by me on behalf of the ICU, being the only active and recognized trade union in that centre at the time. On my return to headquarters in Johannesburg I had to instruct my attorneys to sue the Native Commissioner in Pretoria for refusing to issue me with an 'Exemption Certificate' from the pass laws. The case was argued in the Supreme Court at Pretoria while I was aboard the *Windsor Castle* bound for Southampton *en route* for Geneva. The judgment in my favour was delivered during my absence, and I am bound to record here with pride that I won the case and was awarded about £150 costs against the Union Government. I shall refer to this matter again later.

On January 19, 1927, the ICU National Council forwarded my name to the Minister of Labour as a candidate to represent the organized non-European workers of South Africa at the International Labour Conference at Geneva. This application was acknowledged by the Secretary for Labour on January 26, 1927, and this was followed by another letter on February 2, 1927, asking for detailed information on the ICU. The information sought by the Government was promptly forwarded, and this was followed by our financial statement duly audited by a European accountant. The Government duly acknowledged these, but remained silent for a considerable time, until we saw from the press reports that the Government was anxious to appoint only one European delegate with one white adviser from the South

African Trades Union Congress of the Transvaal and the Cape Federation respectively. Unfortunately for the Government, these two bodies were not prepared to divide the representation; the South African Trade Union Congress claimed to be the more representative organization of the two, and consequently refused to allow their delegate to take part in the representation. In the meantime we wired to the Minister of Labour and asked what was being done about the ICU application for representation. We received a reply to the effect that the matter was under consideration. The Government then tried to arrange a meeting between the officials of the two white federations, but the South African Trade Union Congress declined to participate. Thereupon the Government decided to nominate no one. We eventually sent a telegram to the Minister of Labour to ask if he would nominate the ICU representative, and we received the following telegram from the Secretary for Labour: 'RE YOUR TELEGRAM. MINISTER OF LABOUR CANNOT REGARD ICU AS THE MOST REPRESENTATIVE INDUSTRIAL ORGANIZATION IN SOUTH AFRICA AND IS NOT PREPARED TO NOMINATE ITS NOMINEE FOR GENEVA.'

The decision of the ICU conference at Durban was to the effect that its National Secretary should proceed to Geneva regardless of the ruling of the Minister of Labour not to send any workers' representative. The underlying motive of my proceeding to Geneva was to present the ICU case before the bar of the International Labour Office, thus to expose for all time the colour prejudice of the Union Government. With this mandate of the conference, I got ready to proceed to Geneva, but there was another difficulty to overcome before my mission could materialize. My passport to Europe was of course ready, but the question of getting a passage on the mail-boat was another difficulty requiring solution. It was arranged that our official in Cape Town should obtain the passage for me. R. G. de Norman, ICU provincial secretary—an able Indian—approached the Union Castle Mail Steamship Company about the matter, but without avail. Our solicitors, Messrs. Dichmont and Dichmont, also of Cape Town, were approached to assist to obtain the passage. In Johannesburg I was suffering from slight pneumonia, but with determination I decided to proceed to Cape Town, where I was well known by the two managing directors of the Union Castle

Company. Accompanied by my private secretary, who at the time was Abe J. Phoofolo, I entrained for Cape Town. On arrival at our office, I immediately put through a telephone call to one of the directors of the Union Castle Company. I was offered first-class accommodation in the R.M.S. *Windsor Castle*. Thus on May 13, 1927, at 4 o'clock in the afternoon, I sailed from Cape Town docks as a 'missionary in reverse', with a new mission to Europe. I went on board recuperating from my illness, and on the first day aboard the *Windsor Castle* my health had greatly improved.

In 1927 the ICU was still publishing its official newspaper *The Workers' Herald*. I decided as a journalist to keep the readers of the paper and the public generally in South Africa well informed about the progress of my European tour. But before quoting from *The Workers' Herald* I am bound to insert in these pages what the official white trade union journal thought of the adventure to Europe. *The Monthly Herald*, edited by Archie Crawford, once secretary of the South African Industrial Federation, wrote eulogistically, while at the same time painfully, about my mission to Europe:

'The Significance of Kadalie

'No excuses are necessary for returning to the subject of Kadalie and his visit to Geneva. It is the most outstanding event that has occurred in this country since Union, for it marks the first clear and incisive step of the native races of this country in the direction of racial and national development, and a conscious and unreserved acceptance of the obligations and implications imposed by civilization. Besides this momentous fact, the racial wrangle on the Flag and Nationality Bill pales into insignificance. It is not less curious that these two events should coincide—that the hour which saw Mr. Clements Kadalie step aboard the *Windsor Castle* as the first elected representative of the coloured workers of this country to the International Conference was that which the white man dedicated to the accomplishment of his division. Obvious and fatal as is the division between the two white races, it is still more obvious and still more fatally apparent between the coloured and white races. It is conceivably more fundamental, for it is based upon discriminations which are more explicitly defined and more implicitly developed. Now, the most startling and significant aspect of Clements Kadalie's first-class European tour is that it signalizes his determination to express and develop this division, not on a national and racial basis but on an international and economic basis. He is not prejudicing European sympathy and support in his attack on the white man's predominance in this country by assuming a racial and coloured standpoint. On the contrary, he has adopted the converse attitude, he has taken an international standpoint and has thrown himself into alignment with the working-class movement—the greatest movement the world has yet seen, and which undoubtedly will be the governing and determining factor in national and international policies in the future . . . Now, do we rightly appreciate the significance of this? It is so portentous that, if it is an achievement of conscious cerebration on the part of Kadalie, it stamps him as one of the most able men this country has yet produced.'

Referring to the disunity of the South African white Labour movement and their inability to agree on a delegate to represent them at Geneva, Crawford concluded his article:

'Mr. Kadalie, in a first-class suite, passes over to Geneva as the only recognized Labour representative of the workers of this country. The irony of it—and, yes, the stupidity of the Labour Party and all those inconsequential extremists who destroyed but could not rebuild.'

During the voyage to England, the majority of white passengers from South Africa behaved most inhumanly towards me. I vividly remember one lady who, if she happened to spot me on the deck, immediately turned her back to avoid me. The fourteenth day brought us to Madeira Island, where, since the *Windsor Castle* stopped for two hours, I had an opportunity to go ashore. To break the monotony of so many days at sea, I hired a car and was driven through the town, which was wonderfully beautiful. Afterwards I breakfasted at an hotel, and to my great surprise found nothing of the spirit of the colour bar prevalent. This was the beginning of quite a different feeling on this matter, which I have since discovered everywhere I have been in Europe. White men in Europe, generally speaking, have little or no prejudice against the black man merely on account of his colour.

We were now fast approaching Southampton. We had first, however, to pass through the Bay of Biscay, and really rough sea. During the day it was cold and poured with rain, and every-thing was generally unpleasant. I sent a wireless message through to the Independent Labour Party in London, and the day before landing I received a reply from Fenner Brockway, political secretary of the Party, assuring me of a good welcome and telling me that a Southampton comrade would meet me at the docks there and Miss Winifred Holtby would meet me at Waterloo Station, the London terminus. This message relieved me of the minor anxieties one commonly feels on arriving in a strange land. The seventeenth day seemed interminable, but night fell even-tually, and the steward informed me that by midnight the lights of England would be visible. I determined not to sleep, and when I went on deck discovered that we were anchored at Southamp-ton. Day soon dawned, and at 6 a.m. on Monday morning, May 30, 1937, the *Windsor Castle* was berthed on the quay.

While we were awaiting the scheduled time for going ashore and I was watching for the ILP comrade who was to meet me, an elderly lady came up to me. I had previously noticed her a good deal during the voyage, and the fact that she always greeted me when we met on deck. She told me that her name was Lady Aisler, that she came from Scotland, and that she had wished before we disembarked to express her admiration of the way I had behaved during the voyage, despite the bad manners of the white passengers from South Africa, who had left me in complete isolation, and had been as rude as conventions permit. This courtesy, as sincere as it was kindly, was very pleasing after the seventeen days of unpleasantness to which I had been subjected.

After passports had been examined and stamped, I landed finally on English soil. Compared with the docks at Cape Town, the Southampton docks were tremendous. The dock workers were white, and were doing all the work which in South Africa is described as 'kaffir work' by the white population. The contrast was indescribable. On my departure from Johannesburg, a white porter had refused to carry my luggage. At Southampton the colour bar had absolutely vanished, and everyone was helpful and very friendly. At 8.30 a.m. the boat train left for London, the ILP comrade and I having missed each other in the tremendous crowd. There was no nonsense now among the white South Africans who came up to London on the same train. A gentleman from Turffontein, a suburb of Johannesburg, was in one compartment with me, and we ate and drank from the same table. At midday we arrived at Waterloo, a huge station crowded with human beings. The deportment of the white South Africans seemed to have undergone a still further change. On the steamer they had attempted to behave as beings from another plane. Here they were just ordinary people, rather worried about their luggage and not at all concerned about their inherent superiority as white men. In the crowd I had some difficulty in discovering Miss Winifred Holtby, who was meeting me, and I stood for some time waiting for her. While I was waiting, a rather transparent young man, who had quite obviously come from Scotland Yard, but who didn't realize that the fact was obvious, made conversation with me, and was very anxious for information about Clements Kadalie, the work he was doing in the ICU and so on. But in the middle of the conversation Miss Holtby discovered me. The South Africans who still surrounded me were greatly astonished to see the tall young Englishwoman rush up and shake hands with the black man whom they had all barred on the voyage, and see her drive off with him in a taxi! We drove to the ILP headquarters at 14 Great George Street, Westminster.

'South African Native Leader Clements Kadalie in London' was the heading of a special news item in the *New Leader*, an important weekly of the Independent Labour Party. It read:

'An interesting visitor to London this week (June 3, 1927) has been Clements Kadalie, secretary of the Native Trade Union organization in South Africa. The Imperialism Committee of the ILP has for some time been helping his union in a number of ways, and Kadalie's first action on reaching London was to visit the ILP headquarters at Westminster. He is a splendid-looking man, six feet high and broad, and the smile of his white teeth with the background of his ebony face and hair is dazzling. He speaks perfect English, and one has only to be with him a short time to understand his success in building up the largest union in South Africa.

'Kadalie was only in London 24 hours, and left on Tuesday for the ILO conference at Geneva, which he is attending as an official delegate, but he is returning to this country in July, when he hopes to address meetings throughout the country under the auspices of the ILP. In August he will attend the meeting of the IFTU in Paris and, after studying the Labour movement on the Continent, will also visit America. Can the IFTU perform the difficult task of healing the breach between the South African white and coloured unions? The effects of the breach are disastrous both in Africa and internationally. The British Labour Movement might also do something. Next year the Commonwealth Conference is to meet in London. I believe that at the last conference two years ago, only the white labour movement of South Africa was represented. Cannot an effort be made to get representatives from both for the gathering next year.'

At the ILP offices Fenner Brockway, the political secretary, a tall, slender man in his thirty-ninth year at the time, welcomed me very cordially and made me feel that I was amongst friends and comrades. He was a conscientious objector during the first World War, and had served a long term of imprisonment. During the time I spent in his office, he impressed me with his great powers of organization. Within half an hour of arriving at his office, my immediate programme was arranged. It had been settled that on the day of arrival, I was to address a meeting of the Women's International League, at which Mrs. Rheinallt Jones from South Africa was also speaking. In the interval before the meeting, I lunched with Miss Winifred Holtby, booked my passage for Geneva and met a number of other people. Then we went on to the meeting, where I spoke, and the address made a very good impression on the audience.

On Tuesday, May 30, 1927, I crossed the English Channel for France, and on the following morning reached Geneva. At the hotel I was told that the officials of the International Federation of Trades Unions had called twice for me, so I immediately joined them, and we went on to the Conference Hall. I was asked to join in a photograph which was being taken of the Workers' Group. (There were three Groups at the International Labour Conference, viz., the Government Group, the Employers' Group and the Workers' Group. The members of each Group held conferences among themselves to discuss the Agenda and appoint speakers for the Plenary Assemblies.) Entering the Conference

Hall, I became the centre of attraction. I was the only black man at that great assembly. There were, of course, Indian, Japanese and Chinese delegates at the conference, but these have been associated with Geneva ever since the inception of the League of Nations. Africa had been talked of in the past, but no African had ever been present at the conference. For the first time, Africa had sent its own son to plead its cause.

My presence was welcomed by nearly every delegate, with the exception of those from the South African Government, who were obviously disturbed and displeased at my presence. They had never expected me; they thought that the resolution passed at the ICU Congress at Durban was merely bluff. On my second day at Geneva, I was invited to address the Workers' Group of the conference. This was an extraordinary opportunity of winning the representatives of the workers of all countries to our side, and I think I can say that the object was achieved. After my speech, nearly every workers' delegate interviewed me, and long accounts of the work of the ICU and the non-European workers of South Africa appeared in the European press as a result. I mixed freely with the various delegates and journalists from all the countries of Europe, England and America—and delegates from Canada and Australia also sought interviews with me. During my two weeks' stay at Geneva, I was invited to every official function, except one. The South African delegates, with the honourable exception of William Freestone, who was Inspector of Labour at Cape Town, did not appreciate the welcome I received. I presume that since the ICU delegate had no official status at the conference, they had expected me to be isolated, but in that they had made a great mistake—the South African attitude would not do at Geneva. The president of the conference at the time was himself an Indian.

To counteract my success, the South African delegates carried on an underhand current of propaganda against me personally and the ICU generally. The delegates were told that we had a membership of only 6,000 throughout South Africa, and that I was not a British subject, having come from the Belgian Congo. All this, however, had very little effect on the continental delegates. The Geneva mission was to bring all races together, whether they came from the Belgian Congo or the Sahara desert! To some extent the propaganda affected the British delegates, who were of the older school, but apart from this it did me almost no harm. Next came the incident of the Empire photograph, in which I, together with six other unofficial delegates, was included. The South African delegates, with the exception of William Freestone and the Employers' delegate, Hannick, demanded that I should be cut out, giving as their excuse the fact that I was not officially a delegate. However, as there were six other unofficial delegates in the photograph, it was quite obvious that their reason for demanding my exclusion was on the grounds of race. Contrast their attitude with that of the Right Honourable Arthur Henderson, M.P., and the Right Honourable George Lansbury, M.P., who, far from objecting to appearing in a photo with a black man, were photographed, at their request, with me at the House of Commons, and asked specially that the photo should be reproduced in *The Workers' Herald*, which was done.

I think that the importance of my presence at Geneva cannot be exaggerated. It dramatized for the conference the whole problem of the African natives, and gave life to what had been in the past merely academic discussion of the subject. In my unofficial delegacy at Geneva, I think I can safely claim that a great deal was learnt by me in the art of lobbying, which afterwards helped my mission tremendously when I returned to England later. Among the civil service of the International Labour Office itself, the heads of the various Sections welcomed my mission. The head of the Colonial Division, Harold Grimshaw, took a personal interest in my mission, for he undertook to advise me during my three weeks' stay at Geneva. Whatever success I had as the first African ambassador at Geneva was due largely to his advice. I remember at times I had to sit up very late at nights with Mr. Grimshaw studying the Conference Agenda and Reports, while he helped me to draft various memoranda in connection with my mission. This high official of the International Labour Office also scrutinized and made some suggestions for inclusion in the ICU Constitution, which later was properly redrafted by Arthur Creech-Jones, M.P., later to become Secretary for the Colonies in the pre-war British Labour Government. The revision of the ICU constitution was not completed at Geneva, and later we had to meet and sit up again with Mr. Grimshaw one whole night in one of the first-class hotels in Berlin. Two other officials who took a keen interest in my mission were Mr. and Mrs. C. W. H. Weaver, both English, who were so kind that they invited me to dine with them one evening at their residence. I was specially asked by Mr. Weaver to wear an evening dinner suit, for which I was well prepared.

On my return to South Africa the majority of the ICU members and the public generally did not realize that the mission to Geneva had been of value, and was not merely a waste of money on a pleasurable adventure. My presence at Geneva influenced the Director of the International Labour Office to insert the following in his Report to the Tenth Session:

'The parties most interested in the application to the Colonies of the decisions adopted by the Conference are the workers themselves, who, up to the present, have not been represented. It would appear, however, that in certain cases, where industrial organization has developed to some extent, the desire to seek representation at the Conference has been awakened. The office has been informed that this is the case with an organization of native workers in South Africa. The British Commonwealth Labour Conference suggested in 1925 that in suitable cases, native advisers should be chosen to accompany the workers' delegation. It will be recalled also that at the eighth Session of the Conference the South African Government delegate drew attention to the problem, saying that he did not "suppose that this Conference could ever take to itself the position that it represents the whole world while it ignores, or appears to ignore, countless millions of the great continent of Africa, and that this was a position time would have to remedy". Evidently, it will be for the governments, the employers and the workers to examine what steps can be taken. Nevertheless, it can undoubtedly be stated that it would be well if time found some remedy before the conference is called upon to deal with native labour problems in the form of Draft Conventions or Recommendations. It seems clear that the decisions of the conference would lack the moral authority they have so far been able to claim if in its body were represented not only experts on native labour problems, but also those who can claim to speak in the name of the natives themselves.'

In one of my memoranda to the conference I stated that the South African Government with its anti-black bias never intended nominating a delegate from the ICU, no matter how good our case was, so there was no other alternative for our organization but to delegate one here with a view to making our appeal direct to the International Labour Conference. We were not as selfish as the white trade unions to demand that we alone had the right to nominate, but we did claim that we had the right to nominate at least one delegate, and we based our claim on the following three facts:

1. The ICU was the only industrial organization affiliated to the International Federation of Trade Unions, with headquarters at Amsterdam;
2. We had a larger membership than the SATUC, and the Cape Federation of Labour Unions combined;
3. We were the most representative because our members were working in every trade and calling, including the agricultural workers, marine workers, waterside workers and general workers.

We were the only organized body in South Africa who could represent all these workers. According to the Government Official Year Book, in 1924 there were 97 white trade unions with a total membership of 87,147. On the other hand, we had a membership of over 80,000, and our membership was increasing every day (thanks to the Government's anti-black legislation). In round figures we could divide up our membership in occupations as follows:

Agricultural workers	16,000
Building workers	5,000
Municipal workers	8,000
Mine workers	5,000
Marine workers	2,500
Railway workers	13,000
Warehouse workers	2,500
Transport workers	6,000
Waterside workers	7,000
General workers	10,000

The vast majority of our members belonged to the native races of South Africa, but we also had thousands of Coloured men and women in our organization, also many Indians and a few

Europeans. Our constitution laid down the principle that all workers could join the ICU irrespective of race, creed or colour, and we had always shown willingness to affiliate with our white brother workers, but had always been refused or shown the cold shoulder. We had done everything possible to bring about closer relations between white and black workers so that all might get proper representation in Geneva, but were treated with contempt by both the Government and the majority of organized white workers, so we had no alternative but to appeal direct to the International Labour Conference and ask for their co-operation so that justice might be done to this large, influential and most representative body of workers in South Africa.

The result of my visit to Geneva, where I protested against the non-inclusion of a native workers' representative in the South African delegation to the International Labour Conference, may best be summarized in the words of Harold Grimshaw, in a letter addressed to Fenner Brockway:

'Kadalie leaves for London tonight, and I think it may possibly be useful for you to have my opinion upon the value of his visit here and my impressions as to its probable influence on matters in which we are both interested. In the first place, his "Protest" in connection with the South African workers' delegate to the Conference was technically out of order. His letter of January last protested in advance *in the event of the appointment of a white worker*. Since no white worker was in fact appointed, his protest naturally fell to the ground. On the other hand, the white unions of South Africa protested against the *non-appointment of a workers' delegate*, and their protests were therefore in order under the circumstances, were considered by the Credentials Committee, and were published as official documents of the Conference . . .

'As to the more general aspect of Kadalie's visit, I should say in the first place that it has aroused very widespread interest. He has been well received, particularly, of course, by the Workers' Group, and has undoubtedly made a favourable impression and secured a personal success. I have heard very favourable comments on the modesty and moderation of his proposals and procedure, and this in spite of the fact that an attempt was made to prejudice his case and to discredit him personally. In sum, he has prepared the way for a very favourable reception of representations of black workers, who will undoubtedly be present at future conferences, and for a favourable hearing of their demands.'

After three weeks' stay at Geneva, I returned to London on June 16, 1927. Fenner Brockway became my immediate and personal adviser during my stay in England, and he arranged an office for me in the building occupied by the Independent Labour Party, for which I had to pay rent. While at Geneva I had been in regular communication with the Imperialism Committee of the ILP and with Miss Winifred Holtby, and when I reached London I found that an extensive programme had been mapped out for me. On the first day I was besieged by newspapermen—English and American—and by the second day of my stay a large proportion of the newspapers, Labour, Liberal and Tory alike, had published accounts of my mission. My work began and continued in a glare of publicity.

An odd coincidence took place on the second day of my stay. Quite by chance, while in a hotel lounge in company with H. N. Brailsford, editor of the ILP paper, the *New Leader*, and Winifred Holtby, I met the two Warner sisters, both professors of Oriental languages at London University. One had been in Africa, and as far as Nyasaland, and both spoke many African languages, including Swahili, Zulu, Nyanja and others. We carried on a long conversation in my native tongue, which here in the heart of London was interesting by reason of its very unexpectedness, and on the following day I spent my afternoon with them at their residence outside London.

I spent most of my first Sunday in London in Hyde Park, and found it, with the exception of the Zoo, quite the most amusing spectacle in the city. It is in fact a sort of human Zoo. I found meetings of every description in progress. There were atheists, vegetarians, Salvation Army folk, Communists, people demanding the 'clearing-out of the Reds', anti-vivisectionists and Nonconformists, all concentrated into the space of a few hundred yards. The size of the audience of each seemed to depend on the capacity of the speaker for shouting; for if the Salvation Army speaker managed to drown the voice of the fiery old Tory holding forth on the adjoining platform, all the latter's audience who were being encouraged to sing 'God save the King' would go over to join the Salvation Army speaker's crowd, and sing 'Washed in the Blood of the Lamb' with every appearance of enthusiasm. And if one watched long enough, some other speaker with a still louder voice was sure to turn up and capture their enthusiasm for the cause of Jewish nationalism; and the same process would be repeated all over again, the Salvation Army spokesman being deserted! If it had not been so funny, it would have been pathetic. After Hyde Park I dined with some friends in a queer little restaurant in the Italian quarter of London (every nationality had its own colony in London, and certain districts and groups of streets which it had selected as its headquarters) and journeyed to the East End of the town, a huge poverty-stricken area surrounding the London docks.

No bigger contrast could be imagined than the contrast between the squalid streets of the East End and the scene in Hyde Park, no more than a couple of miles away. Here one realized Hyde Park as nothing more than a bad joke, a sort of by-product of civilization, and knew that these poverty-stricken streets, stunted and pathetic human beings, the great factory chimneys which rose to the sky, and the queer, uncouth foreign sailors who slouched by one, were the bedrock and reality on which Western civilization was built. Western civilization has accomplished things of infinite magnitude. It has built great bridges and machines and spanned the world with steamships and railroads. It has awakened in mankind the thirst for knowledge and power, and it has planned and foretold the course of the stars. But still it has not learned that while great masses of its children go hungry and barefoot, and while the very thirst for knowledge which it has itself awakened is stunted and denied to a large proportion of its men and women, it carries its own failure inherent within itself. All these things are to be learned as well in the East End of London as in the slums of Johannesburg and in the poverty and squalor in which the African workers are forced to live.

On Monday began a big campaign of propaganda which scarcely slackened during all the time I was in Britain. Fenner Brockway had arranged that I should meet most of the leading men and women in the British trade union and the labour movements, and visit the offices of all the various unions to study their methods of organization. My time was so fully occupied that to get through my work I had to secure the assistance of a typist who ably helped me in my activities during the whole of my stay in London, and was paid from my own funds £3 17s. 6d. per week. At Eccleston Square (the headquarters of both the British Trades Union Congress and the Labour Party) I was very cordially received by the general secretaries of both the political and industrial movements, who gave me every facility to study their general and office organization, and I was a constant visitor to the House of Commons. On my first visit there, David Kirkwood, M.P., showed me round the whole House. As a matter of fact, during my stay in London I was guest of the Labour Party, who were then the official Opposition, and as such I had some special privileges whenever I visited the House of Commons. I sat for a while in the Dominion Gallery, immediately behind the son of the Governor-General of South Africa.

All the Labour members were anxious to get first-hand information on the situation in South Africa; a great many asked me to the House of Commons as their guest, and I had long informal talks with several groups of them. I was also invited to address a meeting of the Empire Group of the Labour members. This Group includes all the Labour M.P.s specially interested in Dominion and Colonial affairs, which in fact means practically the whole of the Parliamentary Labour Party. The veteran Labour leader, George Lansbury, presided at the meeting, and J. R. Clynes, Arthur Henderson and other leading members of the Labour Party at the time were present. Henderson moved a vote of thanks for my address, and asked me to convey to the members of the ICU his assurance that the British Labour Party would do everything possible to assist us in our fight for freedom. During my first three weeks in London I visited the headquarters of the Co-operative Movement, and of most of the big trade unions. I also spoke at two week-end schools organized by the Imperialism Committee of the ILP, where I renewed acquaintance with Edward Roux, then a student at Cambridge. I met a great number of interesting and influential people.

Besides my programme in London, the ILP had arranged a big campaign of meetings for me in the Provinces, and on July 11,

1927, I journeyed to Glasgow. I travelled by the fastest train in the world, namely the 'Royal Scot', which left Euston Station, London, at 10 a.m., reaching Glasgow a few minutes before 6 p.m. At 8 p.m. I was addressing a big crowd in a square in the centre of the city. King George V was visiting Scotland at the same time, and had been received in the same square in which I spoke at noon the same day. It was a humorous situation, and I greatly enjoyed the opportunity of drawing the attention of the people of Glasgow to the exploitation of the King's subjects in South Africa. I only wished that His Majesty had remained for a few hours longer to listen!

From Glasgow I went to Perth, Aberdeen and Dundee, and finished up the Scottish tour at Edinburgh. My visit to Scotland created a double interest. By the Scottish Labour Movement I was received as an African labour leader, but the chief interest of a great number of people was that I was a product of the United Free Church of Scotland's African Missions. In Glasgow I met Dr. Donald Fraser, and also spoke for a short time to the David Livingstone Memorial Committee. At Edinburgh I was met at the station by the Reverend Cullen Young, who was one of my teachers at Livingstonia Missionary College in Nyasaland, and later in the day I met his wife, whom I had also known while at College. Cullen Young took me round sight-seeing in Edinburgh and, curiously enough, I was shown the historic St. Giles Cathedral of which he taught us at Livingstonia College. I saw the famous Stool of the church, associated with the outbreak of war between England and Scotland. Having completed the Scottish tour I went on to Yorkshire, where I addressed meetings in eight cities. I had a successful meeting in Hull, and on the following day was taken by local comrades to Wilberforce House, the birthplace of Bishop William Wilberforce. I was shown the room in which Wilberforce was born in 1759, and a large number of objects kept in memory of his career and his brave fight against slavery—photographs of slaves chained together by iron collars, slave whips, and placards announcing the sale of 'Hannibal, about thirty years old, an excellent house-servant'. It was a great privilege to be allowed to pay homage at the shrine of the memory of the great saint, and I wished for the rise of another Wilberforce in Africa, brave as he was, and strong to denounce the modern slavery as he did the old. Before I left Hull I visited also a great famous chocolate factory, owned by a family renowned for their consideration of their employees' welfare and happiness. All that I could see of the organization of Cadbury's was shown me during the half-hour of my stay there, and when I left the Managing Director presented me with a huge box of chocolates, which I saved and brought to South Africa where it was shared with my comrades.

I went on to Bradford, where the ILP at the time was stronger than anywhere else except Glasgow. I spent one day and two evenings there, and spoke at six meetings, including a gathering of small children at the Socialist Sunday School. Very bright and eager the young audience was; they sang socialist songs and listened attentively to what I had to tell them about the boys and girls of Africa. I meant, of course, non-European children at home. Questions were showered upon me, and I left the school with a Socialist Sunday School badge on my coat which a small boy pinned there, and a determination to see whether something like this Socialist Sunday School could not be started among our boys and girls at home.

From Bradford I went on to Leicester, where I addressed another enthusiastic meeting. The ILP was strong in Leicester also, and the city was once represented in Parliament by Ramsay MacDonald, the first Labour Prime Minister. The Leicester meeting was followed by other meetings at Rugby and Nottingham, and at the latter place I met Comrade H. G. Swindell, an Englishman who had spent some months in South Africa and who was a regular reader of our *Workers' Herald*. At Nottingham also I found a fellow African who lived in the city and was a member of the ILP branch there. He was greatly liked by the Nottingham comrades and was very happy in the work he was doing. I had to go on to London for a few hours the next morning, and from there journeyed to Leamington, where I addressed another meeting. Every meeting at which I had spoken so far had been well attended and enthusiastic. The Leamington meeting was also well attended, but there I encountered a new phenomenon—a Tory churchman who heckled me. He misrepresented my speech as being an attack on Christianity, and created a disturbance until a very placid and impartial policeman ordered him out of the meeting. Then I got on with my speech, and the rest of the audience was extremely sympathetic and enthusiastic. From Leamington I went to Birmingham, where I finished my three weeks' lecturing programme, and then having returned to London and gathered up my papers, I proceeded to Paris to attend the International Trades Union Congress.

My second visit on the Continent was in connection with this Congress in Paris, which was held from August 1-6, 1927. The way for my cordial reception was smoothed by the fact that I had already made contact with the officials of the International Federation of Trade Unions at Geneva. Apart from these personal contacts, accounts of my invasion of the international scene had already appeared in many continental newspapers. The ICU by this time was affiliated to the International Federation of Trade Unions. Thus I attended the Conference as an accredited representative with all the privileges enjoyed by other delegates. As was the case at Geneva, I was again the central figure of attraction for the continental delegations. When my time came to address the congress, nearly every delegate was present, notwithstanding the fact that I spoke in English. My speech, which was brief, was officially reported as follows:

'Clements Kadalie, who represented the Industrial and Commercial Workers' Union of Africa, one of the new national centres admitted to the IFTU, said that he felt extremely gratified in being present at the International Trade Union Congress for the first time. The affiliation of his organization to the IFTU was received with overwhelming satisfaction by the coloured workers in South Africa, who saw in it that it would create such a favourable atmosphere which was bound to break colour prejudice which exists in his country between white and black workers. The white workers having refused to recognize his organization, it was found necessary to open up international correspondence. The General Council of the IFTU accepted them in January last.

'Clements Kadalie then went on to refer to the rapid industrialization of the African Continent, and this meant to him new problems for the international trade union movement. He laid strong emphasis on the awakening in the Far East and Africa, and he hoped that the IFTU would do all in its power to bring into its ranks the organized workers in China, India and Asia, for he thought that if these workers were not brought into the international trade union movement, they were bound to become a menace to the European workers. Capitalism, as they all must now realize, was not only organized nationally, but internationally as well. He reminded the delegates that France, Belgium, Italy, and not the least Great Britain, had large possessions in Africa in which millions of coloured workers toiled at very low wages. The low wages paid to these workers there would no doubt in time react on the wages in Europe generally. The duty of the IFTU in his opinion was now to make a bid for capturing the colonial workers, and in doing so they would be really building up a real international trade union movement, which would recognize no frontiers, race or creed.'

It is customary at the workers' international gatherings to set a day free from meetings so that the delegates may go sightseeing. Versailles was chosen as the venue for this purpose. Each nationality was conveyed in a separate bus. For all purposes I was classified as part of the British delegation, since the Union of South Africa is a member of the British Commonwealth of Nations. The journey to Versailles was very interesting indeed, for it afforded me an opportunity to see French life at its best, while at the same time I saw the English men and women on their social pedestal. Many of the leading delegates brought their wives to Paris. The women delegates treated me kindly. In the bus the spirit of real internationalism prevailed. Here one saw Will Thorne, M.P., Benn Tillet, George Hicks, M.P., and the Right Honourable Walter Citrine, at the time general secretary of the British Trade Union Congress, all participating in singing aloud. We had Connolly, an Irishman, who demanded that I should sing him an African song, which I accordingly did. Versailles was beautiful to see. We dined in the large hall where the Peace Treaty of 1919 was signed. I saw and actually touched the table where the Treaty was signed. After a full day's sightseeing, we returned safely to Paris to continue the deliberations of the Congress.

The speech I delivered at the Congress was published in many continental newspapers as far afield as Sweden. It was at this time that my association with Ido Fimmen, who was then the general secretary of the International Transport Workers' Federation, was actually established. Fimmen extended an invitation to me to visit Amsterdam, Holland, where his headquarters were, together with that of the IFTU. It was at the Paris Congress that I made the ICU name, together with my own, internationally known. Here I met delegates from China, Mexico, India, etc., besides those of Europe. The Mexican delegates specially arranged for a banquet in honour of the colonial delegates, where I was the chief guest. At this banquet toasts were proposed and drunk for each country. I was specially popular because socially I held my own. J. H. Retringer, a delegate from Mexico, presented me with a copy of his book, *Tierra Mexicana*, with this inscription: 'To Clements Kadalie—this description of the fight and sufferings of another oppressed race. In real friendship. August, 1927.' I also met another delegate, Professor Lo' from China. When I went back to England I was privileged to meet Lo' again in London and Edinburgh. We lectured about our respective countries at week-end summer schools in England.

Notwithstanding the limited time at my disposal, I fixed in a week to visit Holland during the month of September 1927. I visited Amsterdam as an official guest of both the IFTU and also of the International Transport Workers' Federation. In Amsterdam I addressed a good meeting which was well attended. On a Saturday afternoon we motored to Utrecht, where another excellent meeting took place. The chairman of this meeting was a member of the Dutch Parliament at The Hague. There were members of the Dutch Parliament in the audience. I informed them that it would look ridiculous for an African in my country to address an audience of Dutchmen, for it was the South African Dutchmen who proclaimed in their Boer Law that there was no equality between white and black men in all spheres of human activities. I stressed the fact that most of the opposition we encountered in South Africa was initiated and perpetuated by the Dutch in South Africa. My visit to Holland was therefore in the nature of an appeal to them to come to Africa's aid by interesting themselves in South Africa. The speech was enthusiastically applauded. The President assured me that as Dutchmen they did not approve of any colour distinction, and strongly condemned their South African brethren for perpetuating the colour-bar. He praised my efforts for getting the Africans organized industrially, and assured me that both the political and industrial wings of the Dutch movement would from henceforth take an active interest in South African affairs. The meetings ended, after I had answered some questions put to me by the audience, with a warm vote of thanks to me.

During this visit to Amsterdam arrangements were made for me to visit Moscow. Ido Fimmen arranged to get me into Moscow whenever I was ready to go. It was planned I would journey through to Poland and on to the border, where the Soviet Government aeroplane would fetch me into Moscow. The secret would never have been known in South Africa of my having visited Russia. The reader will appreciate that at the time I went to Europe I was suspected by the Union Government and part of the European public of having some connection with Moscow. I, however, failed to visit Russia because time was so limited. I also had an engagement to tour the United States. Owing to the short time at my disposal, I had to choose which country to visit before returning to South Africa. However, at this moment I received disturbing news that the affairs of the ICU at home were in a chaotic state and required my personal attention. My visit to Holland was limited to a week-end, as from there I had to proceed to Berlin, for a hurried visit. The trip was undertaken towards the end of August 1927.

I reached Berlin about sunset, and was met at the railway station by officials of the German Federation of Labour, who warmly welcomed me to the German capital. I was taken to the Trade Union Club, where I was quartered. On entering the hotel, which was crowded at the time by the working-class people, I was the attraction of everyone. I took my first meal there, and was surrounded by a number of people who were anxious to get a close glimpse of my person. In the evening I addressed a well-attended meeting and was accorded a cordial reception. The following day I visited some trade union offices where I was also well received. By midday I left Berlin for London. The train passed through Brunswick, Essen and Hanover. It was about dusk when the train crossed the Rhône into Holland, passing through Rotterdam on the Hook of Holland. I had made some purchases in Berlin which were bound to pass through the customs officials for declaration. Whether it was on account of my dark colour or my daring in walking straight from the train, the terminus of which was quite close to the quay, is not known, but I found myself aboard the steamer without rendering dutiable goods or declaring anything. The following day I was back in London.

CHAPTER VIII

On the International Stage

O N my return from Germany I resumed my tour of the provinces, and visited Derby, where I met Dr. Norman Leys, a staunch supporter of the African cause who had spent some twenty years as a doctor among the natives of Kenya. His book on Kenya had created a great sensation among the authorities. I addressed meetings in Derby and also lectured at the ILP Summer School which was held at Mickleover Manor, a few miles away. Before I left the district I was taken to the Rolls-Royce Engineering Works, and shown the whole process of the manufacture of motor and aeroplane engines. A fascinating experience it was. Most of the employees took me to be an Indian prince.

While at Mickleover ILP Summer School I came into contact with a young Scottish socialist named Sam Leckie, who became friendly with me. He was a very bright and intelligent young man. I suggested to him that he should volunteer to go out to South Africa to act as an ICU adviser. Leckie willingly agreed to come out to South Africa, but I was advised by my ILP friends that Leckie was too young for such a big job, while at the same time his health would not stand up to the African climate. In my album Sam Leckie inscribed as follows: 'To Clements Kadalie, with very best wishes for great success to the ICU. Vukani m'Africa.' I was so impressed with him and concluded that he would prove to be a very good adviser because in the short space of about three days of our association, at the Summer School, he was able to pronounce and write the African language as quoted above. I shall return to the question of the ICU adviser in the course of this work.

For over two months I was engaged in delivering speeches

throughout England and Scotland—nearly every day at that. It was inevitable that my health should break down. At Mickleover Summer School I became indisposed for the first time since my arrival in Europe. I was taken in a motor-car to Dr. Norman Leys. I had previously visited Derby during my tour and stayed with Dr. and Mrs. Leys at their residence. Dr. Norman Leys had taken me in his car to Mickleover at night. A Southampton comrade drove the car. When we reached the junction of two roads, the driver was unable to decide on the correct road to the doctor's house. An argument arose between the driver and his friends about the right road. Whereupon as a stranger from Africa I directed the driver into the correct road which took us safely to the doctor's house, much to their bewilderment. When the doctor was told of this, he remarked that Africans had wonderful memories. He eulogized in particular the East African natives, my own tribe being in the lead, who were cleverer, he said, than any contemporaries he had ever seen while in Africa. It was indeed another great compliment for Africa worth recording in these pages.

It is impossible to state definitely whether any other African or colonial visitor to London was ever accorded privileges similar to those presented to me while in the Empire's great capital. My ambassadorship was officially recognized by both wings of the British Labour and the Trade Union movements. The doors of Eccleston Square in particular, where the Labour Party had its headquarters, were flung open to me. At Eccleston Square the officials of the British Labour Party were extraordinarily kind to me, particularly its chief, Arthur Henderson. Arthur Greenwood, the tall ex-schoolmaster, helped me to study the up-to-date methods in research work carried on by the British Labour Party.

During my visit to England I found that far away in Nyasaland, where I was born, my fellow-countrymen were also suffering under the iron heel of imperialism. As a result of my representations the Labour Party (through the person of Mr. Wallhead) again raised in the House of Commons the question of the sentence of three years' hard labour imposed upon Isa Macdonald Lawrence, a native of Nyasaland, for importing into Rhodesia six copies of the *Negro World*, published in Philadelphia, and two copies of *The Workers' Herald*, published in Johannesburg. Mr. Wallhead said:

'I should like to know why the Rhodesian authorities prevent the formation of branches of the Industrial and Commercial Workers' Union, and why they take the line which they do take against allowing the natives to organize themselves in protective bodies in order to improve their conditions and standard of life. I wish to know if there is any chance of a revision of this sentence, which seems to be a particularly harsh one for the offence of taking into this district a few newspapers.'

I was told on my return to South Africa that, as a result of my representation in this case, Isa Macdonald Lawrence was released from prison. The same applied to Robert Sambo, another ICU agent, who was deported from his Nyasaland home. His case also was presented by me to the British Labour Party with that of Macdonald Lawrence. When I was being tried with others in the Supreme Court at Grahamstown in 1930, following the East London general strike, I silenced the Solicitor-General by mentioning the above cases when he asked what I had done for Nyasaland natives instead of stirring up strife in South Africa, as he alleged.

In 1927 the Native Administration Bill was being debated in the South African parliament. I vigorously fought against its enactment while in Europe. Writing for the English press, I said:

'We have as Africans a twofold battle to fight in South Africa. We are not only struggling against British Imperialism, we have also a tremendous fight against the prejudice of the South African Labour Party. I am reluctant to say anything against the South African Labour Party at this juncture, for immediately before I left South Africa it seemed, from the fight they put up on the Native Administration Bill on our behalf in Parliament, that a change had taken place in their attitude. I cannot claim full knowledge of the development of events since I left, but it is absolutely certain that in spite of their original attitude, all but three members of the Labour Party finally voted for the Bill in a form very little different from the original, and the following resolution passed by the Executive of the Party has just reached me:

"That the British Labour and Independent Labour Parties be advised not to interfere with or express uninformed opinions upon the burning question of colour in South Africa. After years of struggle, the South African Labour Party has succeeded in establishing the principle of acceptance of the Coloured man on terms of equality with whites (that is, equal work, equal pay). The native, however, who is still in a state of semi-savagery, has not yet been accepted, and any outside interference will be, we are sure, a great hindrance to any forward march, but will tend to excite feelings that are undesirable."

'The resolution undoubtedly refers to my presence in this country. I came here to arouse the International Trade Union and Labour Movements to a sense of their responsibility towards the native races in the various colonies in Africa. While Britain has two-thirds of the African continent under its dominion, I consider that it is the British Labour Movement, political and industrial, that must take the initiative in demanding the liberation of the native workers from political and industrial slavery. The British Labour Movement has a great responsibility to the people of these British Islands, and also to the millions of people of subject races under British rule. My people, like the Hebrews of old under Pharaoh's yoke, are crying for help, and their need is urgent and imperative. Soon it may be too late. Our oppressors are the oppressors of the workers the world over. They are organized both nationally and internationally, and unless the workers exert their strength internationally, they are doomed to defeat.'

Much of my time and energy while in London was spent in the fight against the Native Administration Bill (now an Act of Parliament). Correspondence on this subject was voluminous. I wrote to the press as well as to the British Labour and Trade Union movements.

Many influential men and women came to our assistance. After they obtained information from my office, they contributed articles to the press on the subject. Others sent their articles to the Continental press in order to let all Europe know about the reactionary legislation that was being placed on the Statute Book of South Africa. The *Manchester Guardian* wrote editorially in strong condemnation about the provisions of the Bill. Public men and women, to mention only a few like Lord Olivier, Dr. Norman Leys, Miss Winifred Holtby, as well as A. Fenner Brockway of the ILP, and a host of other eminent writers, wielded their pens in indignation over the measure. In mobilizing all the democratic forces we could command in opposition to the Bill, legal opinion was obtained from an eminent English barrister, Mr. Holford Knight, K.C., who wrote to say that he was willing to give help. He informed me that he once fought for Dinizulu in Natal, and for Ghandi and Gokhale, the Indians.

But the climax of our fight was the big meeting in Memorial Hall, in the East End, on October 13, 1927. I was told that the Memorial Hall has been associated with great causes in the history of England, and that eminent public men, including prime ministers of Great Britain, made their big orations there. The handbills convening the meeting read: 'Is South Africa to be a slave state? Come to the Memorial Hall . . . to protest against the Native Administration Act of South Africa. Speakers: E. Lewis Donaldson, Canon of Westminster; Clements Kadalie, secretary, Native Trade Union organization; J. W. Brown, ex-secretary, International Federation of Trade Unions; Winifred Holtby, author and journalist; chairman, A. Fenner Brockway.'

I received a great ovation on rising to address the distinguished gathering. In the audience there was E. Rayner, an aged Englishman who, with A. F. Batty, attended the first meeting in Cape Town at which the ICU was inaugurated. He specially came to the meeting to meet me, as he had read in the press about my presence in London. After the meeting we went together to my hotel where we renewed our early days in reminiscence in Cape Town. He expressed his astonishment that the twenty-four members of the ICU at Cape Town in 1919 had been destined to make such admirable history by sending me to Europe. The meeting was indeed a great success. Many messages were sent and read to the meeting, including one from Lord Olivier, who said:

'I should have been glad, had I been able to attend, to assist in making clear in this country what is happening in South Africa: for the same tendencies infect the policy of the Government of Southern Rhodesia . . . the South African Government has now definitely taken up the line of declaring that the natives have no rights in the land, in the control of their tribal institutions, of public meetings, or of criticizing the views of Europeans, with regard to dealings with natives. For this last is what will no doubt be the application liable to be given to the provisions of this new Act inflicting penalties on

any expression of opinion intended to promote "hostility" between natives and Europeans. The action of the South African
Labour Party in supporting this special anti-Native legislation
is disastrous and contemptible.'

After the London public meeting on the Native Administration
Bill, I resumed my continental tour passing through Paris, with
a stop at Geneva, where I had an engagement with Mr. Harold
Grimshaw. We sat throughout the night examining and redrafting
the ICU Constitution. Mr. Grimshaw and I had to compare and
examine the draft made by Creech-Jones, which was posted on
to me by my secretary in London. The reader will note, therefore, that the revised constitution of the ICU which I brought
from Europe in 1927 and ratified by a Special Congress of the
Union held at Kimberley in December 1927, was passed by effi-
cient brains whom the writer contacted in Europe.

At the time I attended the International Trades Union Congress
in Paris, personal contacts were established with the leaders of the
Continent, who in turn invited me to visit their respective countries. I received invitations as far afield as from Spain and Denmark.
In September 1927, however, I accepted the invitation of the
Austrian Trades Union Congress with headquarters in Vienna.
After having taken leave of Mr. Harold Grimshaw at Geneva,
I set out for Austria. Perhaps another person would have hesitated
to penetrate so deep into the heart of Europe unaccompanied, but
for me I left my fears behind in Africa. My duty was now to
penetrate alone, if need be, through Europe to tell the story of a
New Africa in the making. On the train I met a refined lady from
Paris, who joined in conversation with me and who was on her
way to Constantinople. She was, I think, a millionairess, since
she gave me to understand that she periodically travelled between
Paris and Constantinople for climatic reasons. She ridiculed the
white Americans whom she had met in Paris on account of
their colour prejudice. This voluntary statement by the lady was
somewhat refreshing, for it gave me more enlightenment on the
colour feeling on the Continent.

It was on September 29, 1927, when I reached Innsbruck, the
first town in Austria. At the station I was warmly greeted by the
officials of both the trade unions and the Socialist Party, who
afterwards drove me to an hotel they had arranged for my stay.

My official interpreter, Franz Huttenberger, who spoke English, was there to take care of me. In the evening I was taken to a crowded hall where I delivered my first speech in Austria about our conditions in South Africa. The interest in my visit was great, as elaborate publicity was given in advance by posters as well as through the medium of newspapers accompanied by my photograph. As was the case in England, I was advertised as a 'Great Negro Orator', and one can imagine the thoroughness of the continental socialists in espousing a specific cause. Innsbruck being my first place to deliver an address in Austria, it was of the utmost importance for me to make an impressive speech if my lecture-tour was to be successful. The interpreter told me after the meeting that I succeeded in my object. As was expected, I answered some questions to the satisfaction of the audience. After the meeting I was taken to many amusements, including a dance-hall where I danced.

As an ambassador of new Africa, it was my duty to show Europe that we did not neglect the social side in our onward march to a higher civilization. I went to bed in the early hours of the morning, and as a result overslept. A number of officials of the socialist movement came to my hotel in the morning to see my departure for the next stage in Austria, which was Salzburg, where I was due to address my second meeting the following day. On telephoning the railway station, I found that there was no local train between the two cities that day. The only available transport was by aeroplane. In this first week of my Austrian tour there was a big air tragedy in Europe in which some distinguished people lost their lives. Because of this tragedy and because I had never before travelled by 'plane, I was reluctant to agree to go by air. Another enquiry was made at the railway station when it was found out that a special train would be running that afternoon. This was the famous International Express which used to run from Paris through central Europe to the Far East. I was privileged to travel by this most luxurious train.

On October 1, 1927, I reached Salzburg, where another very cordial reception was accorded me. Probably the speech I delivered at Innsbruck had been read there, thus paving the way for an improved reception for me. Salzburg city was somewhat different from other cities in Austria. Here I found many churches, almost all Roman Catholic—which reminded me of the many churches in our urban locations in South Africa. I saw many priests when I was taken round the city, and I was informed that an African priest brought to Austria by the Roman Catholic church from North Africa gave rather a bad impression of Africa. It was felt that my mission as a trade unionist was the correct one. Another interesting spectacle witnessed here was a mannequin parade on a Sunday accompanied by the latest music and dances characteristic of the Austrian people, in spite of the fact that the town possessed so many churches and priests. Of course, the interest of it all was that I was witnessing European civilization at its best!

It was on October 3, 1927, that I penetrated deep into the heart of Austria when I reached Linz, the city lying on the great River Danube. Linz is the second city in Austria, and the socialist and trade union movements were, therefore, powerful, second only to Vienna, the capital. I reached the city in the afternoon. At the station I was met by a representative gathering of the socialist movement. Elaborate arrangements were made here by the Party to make me feel that I was really visiting friends. I spent two days here enjoying myself to satisfaction beside the blue waters of the Danube. The Linz gathering was a tremendously successful one, as the large hall where it was held was crowded to capacity. On my entry into the hall with the president, I heard the loud sound of a bugle from a gallery, and the audience stood to attention as one man. I must admit that this was something new to me. I was told afterwards that the bugle sounded to welcome me heartily to the city. The president made a beautiful speech welcoming me to Linz, while at the same time assuring me that the Austrian trade union and socialist movements were in full sympathy with our struggle for a better and higher life in human civilization. Here, I think, I delivered one of the best speeches on the Continent, which made a big impression upon the audience. The next morning the socialist papers published the speech in full with my photo.

After this successful meeting I was taken to a social banquet where I was the guest of honour. In the small hours of the morning I went with the president to his house where I was accommodated. An interesting incident, although at the time a sad one, occurred in the house at the breakfast table. The smallest child of the house, about three years old, was brought to breakfast. On seeing me the child wept frightfully, as if something had hurt it. It was an awful spectacle to behold, for I feared that the child might collapse immediately. On enquiry from the parents as to the reason for the child's demeanour, I was told that he had taken fright from seeing a black man's face for the first time. Eventually the child stopped crying after the parents had explained things to him. Thereupon we continued our breakfast in a calm and friendly atmosphere. Immediately after breakfast I was driven to the Party's offices, where everyone was anxiously waiting to shake hands with me. In their curiosity some comrades, particularly the women and children, would ask permission to feel my hair and shake hands with me. They did this not with any mark of disrespect but to make sure of my being human. At the Party's offices arrangements were made to take an official photograph. In the afternoon I was taken across the great River Danube at the bank of which was a cable railway up the mountain, the top of which we eventually reached at noon. We had lunch there. From the top I viewed the blue waters of the Danube below. It was a magnificent panorama, to see the great river and the city below. We returned to the city in time to enable me to join the train there for Vienna, which I reached about sunset.

As was the case at other centres, socialists and trade union officials welcomed me at the station. Two full days were spent here addressing meetings, visiting trade union and socialist movements, studying their office systems. In the evening of October 5, 1927, I addressed a public meeting. This is what I wrote at the time to Miss Winifred Stidolph, my secretary in London: 'Last night's meeting in Vienna was excellent. There must have been 800 people who cheered me throughout my address. I consider it was one of the best addresses I have given in Europe so far. The socialist papers are full of it this morning with my photograph.' After the meeting I was taken round the city of Vienna, and what a beautiful sight to behold at night. I visited many places of interest, including some grand opera houses for which Vienna was internationally famous. I was shown some historical buildings and places. Yes, I enjoyed every minute of my stay, including a bright evening in Vienna, not easily to be forgotten. In the morning I had an interview with the socialist mayor, Herr Karl Sertz. He received me in his beautiful parlour at the City Hall, and I had a good time with him. He asked me some questions about South Africa, and also for a copy of the Colour Bar Act, which I asked my secretary in London to forward to him. He presented me with a book of photographs, showing the old and new Vienna. This book is still in my possession.

I was then taken to the headquarters of the Austrian Trade Union Congress, where I was shown everything of interest. A photograph with the officials of the movement was taken here. In Vienna my hosts arranged accommodation for me in a first-class hotel in one of the main streets of the capital. In continental Europe there is no colour-bar. The next day I was taken to an adjoining town, known as Wien-Neustadt—New Vienna—where I addressed another successful meeting. A member of the Austrian Parliament was my host here, and he presided at my meeting. I was taken for a visit to a socialist co-operative store. The manager asked me to select anything I fancied to keep as a memento of the new Vienna. I selected a very beautiful and attractive sweater which had a belt to match, and which I kept for a long time at home in South Africa. After the meeting we returned to Vienna. I ended my Austrian tour with another big meeting at Graz in Styria, where the socialist comrades enthusiastically welcomed me.

The Austrian Trade Union Congress allocated the sum of £50 as my fees for the lectures I made during the tour of their six cities. When I left Vienna on October 7, 1927, I felt indeed satisfied that my mission had been more successful than I had expected. The case of African trade unionism had now been brought to the knowledge of the labour and socialist movements in Central Europe. The Mayor of Vienna expressed the hope that the socialist and trade union movements would do all in their power to render us assistance whenever some international channel presented itself.

After my successful tour of Austria I reached Berlin on a second visit on October 9, 1927. The train from Vienna passed through Prague, the capital of Czechoslovakia, between about 9 and 10 o'clock at night. The city looked beautiful from the train window. On reaching Berlin I was cordially met at the railway station by the representatives of the German Federation of Labour.

The second visit to the German capital was well timed and planned. I was accommodated in a big workers' hotel where I was comfortably cared for. At the station my official interpreter, Comrade Franz Wendell, was there for my comfort in the matter of conversation. After my supper I was taken round the city. I was shown the Reich Chancellery as well as the ex-Kaiser's palace. I was shown a special street which, I was told, was used, before the 1918 revolution in Germany, exclusively by the Kaiser and his wife. Further on I found myself beside the Reichstag, the German parliament—a magnificent building to see at night. About midnight I retired to bed. The second day I was accompanied by a middle-aged German to the headquarters of the German Federation of Labour where I had to join my interpreter. We could not speak or understand one another's language, so on our way we employed signs to converse. As we crossed one street after another, at a certain point we were stopped by a passer-by, who unexpectedly greeted me in Zulu, saying 'Sakubona' (meaning 'Good morning'). I had to stop in order to talk to him, as I was absolutely surprised that in the German capital I could be greeted in Zulu. When I asked him in English, which he spoke also fairly well, how he happened to speak Zulu in Berlin, he said that he had lived in Johannesburg, and had his business in Commissioner Street. As an alien he had been deported after the outbreak of the 1914-18 war.

On arrival at the headquarters of the German Federation of Labour I was warmly greeted by the officials of the movement. I was taken throughout the building, visiting every department, culminating in having a photograph taken. I studied here the methods of affixing denomination stamps on a member's card for every subscription paid into a trade union as a check against unscrupulousness. This method satisfied me entirely, so that on my return to South Africa the system was introduced in the ICU organization, with good results. From the headquarters of the German Federation of Labour I was taken to the Printers' Union Offices. Here, again, I saw trade union organization at its best. One would think you had entered a Prime Minister's office when you are ushered into the President's office. His desk and chair were too beautiful to describe by pen. The building itself was huge and impressive. It was not a wonder to hear later after Hitler had taken control of Germany, that he had liquidated all the assets of the trade unions. After I was shown all over the building, the President handed me a beautiful table clock as a present from his union for me to take away to South Africa.

I finished off the afternoon sightseeing by visiting the central Berlin aerodrome. Here was another very fascinating spectacle to see! Bands were playing, while refreshments were being served. Every five minutes or so, you hear the announcer telling you by loudspeaker that an aeroplane is landing from London or another is leaving for Warsaw, etc. Others would go up to have an aerial view of the city. I must admit here once again that I was not keen to board an aeroplane while in Europe.

It goes without saying that my second meeting in Berlin was another climax in my continental tour. The hall where the meeting was held was crowded. The president in the chair in welcoming me stated that the gathering was composed only of leaders of the various trade unions and socialist organizations. There were over 800 people, all keen to listen to my address, which I delivered for an hour and a half. Immediately I sat down, those who were on the platform came forward and shook hands with me in congratulation. As an ambassador of my country I had been well advised in advance that the Germans had some influence with some members of our Government, in view of their ancestry, and that my pronouncement about South African affairs in Berlin might have some beneficial results on our behalf as subject races. In consequence of my speech an influential German woman presented me with a copy of a book, *German Colonization—Past and Future*.

On my return to London I received a letter from my interpreter, Franz Wendell, in which he said:

'Dear Comrade Kadalie,
    On Wednesday last I posted two copies of *Vorwärts* with the report of your meeting. In reference to the resolution it says in this report:
    "After a lengthy discussion the following resolution was adopted unanimously: 'The representatives of Berlin workers

listened with greatest interest to the lecture of Comrade Kadalie. They condemn the attitude of his white fellow workers of South Africa. The representatives convey to the latter their sympathy, send them brotherly greetings and wish their endeavours the best success.' " '

In pursuance of our previous meeting at Geneva I was again privileged to meet Mr. Harold Grimshaw in Berlin in a first-class hotel. The draft of the ICU constitution from London also reached me, which we jointly examined and approved. I went sightseeing and visited Potsdam. I saw the huge bedroom used by the Kaiser and Kaiserin. The beds were adorned with diamonds distinctively marked 'from Kimberley, South Africa'. I was amazed to witness South African diamonds and gold lavishly displayed by a foreign monarch.

My second visit to Berlin was wonderfully successful. The continental socialists knew how to make a stranger feel happy when in their midst. After the meeting, the German Federation of Labour voted a sum equivalent to ten pounds in our currency for entertaining me. I was taken to so many places of amusement in one night, as was the case in Vienna. I danced throughout the night. So many interesting things I witnessed that night, besides enjoying German beer with comrades. As an ambassador of my country I was careful not to take too much of the intoxicants, notwithstanding the fact that the comrades would insist on saying through my interpreter that I was not playing the game by preserving my beer mug too long while they had theirs refilled many times. We broke up the party in the small hours of the morning.

After my meeting in Berlin I returned to London and then went to Edinburgh, Scotland, to attend the Annual Conference of the British Trades Union Congress. I was anxious to attend the Congress as a fraternal delegate of my country, South Africa, but there were some international obstacles in the way. The majority of the members of the British Trades Union Congress belonged to the old school, and as such they were not at all at ease to accept me willingly as a fraternal delegate to the Conference. Acting on the suggestion of my advisers, I cabled home to South Africa that the ICU headquarters should at once cable the British Trades Union Congress General Council appointing me as a fraternal delegate to the Conference. A large volume of correspondence passed between by advisers in London, the leading members of the General Council of the Trades Union Congress and myself on the subject. At the ICU headquarters in Johannesburg the acting national secretary, Champion, finally sent the desired cable, which reached me just before I left for Edinburgh. The cable read: 'The national council Iseeyou sends fraternal greetings appointing Clements Kadalie fraternal delegate Trade Union Congress Edinburgh'. The following correspondence will give the reader an idea about the reactionary set-up of the officialdom in the British Trades Union Congress at the time, whenever matters affecting the subject peoples in the British Empire confronted them. Miss Margaret Bondfield, who was Minister of Labour in the first Labour Government under the Rt. Hon. J. Ramsay MacDonald, wrote to Fenner Brockway this way:

'I have had talks with several people about Clements Kadalie, and while I think that he is doing splendid work in South Africa, there will be very serious difficulty in the Trades Union Congress General Council giving him the position of fraternal delegate at Edinburgh. I will talk the matter over with Mr. Citrine, but Congress must be careful not to do things through sheer sentiment which will in the long run antagonize or upset other sections of the trade union movement with whom they are in association, and Kadalie's Union is not yet affiliated to the South African Trade Unions. Although there is a movement, I think, in the direction of recognition on the part of certain sections of the white trade unionists.'

The reader will clearly gather that I did not succeed in attending the British Trades Union Congress as a fraternal delegate, but was cordially welcomed to the conference itself. I was given every facility to mingle freely with delegates. I had the privilege of meeting Ramsay MacDonald, the leader of the Labour Party.

In July 1927 I began making arrangements to go on a tour of the United States. The organizers in America even went so far as to issue a pamphlet describing me and the ICU, but in September, after I had booked my passage on the *Berengaria*, I received an unexpected cablegram from New York cancelling the tour. The reason given was that the delay in starting and the short stay contemplated made the tour impracticable. This was the first blow I had encountered since I landed in Europe.

During my stay in England I discovered that our trade union movement in South Africa was far behind in the equipment of its officials, the majority of whom hardly knew anything about the elementary history of trade unionism. In my sojourn overseas, I was privileged to attend as well as to lecture at various summer schools. In most offices I was given the opportunity to study trade union routine, freely discussed with officials of the movement. At Oxford I lectured at Ruskin College to students on our movement in South Africa. I discovered that most of the students there were studying economics, including trade union history. It was arranged with the principal, Barratt Brown, that the College could take about half a dozen men from the ICU to study there. I also arranged for two or three students from the ICU to study at one of the Quaker Colleges near Birmingham, and Fircroft was chosen. At the International People's College, Elsinore, Denmark, I was also able to arrange for another six scholarships for the ICU. The principal of the People's College, Denmark, wrote *inter alia*:

'The students will have to choose among the subjects of English, German, French and Danish languages, History, Geography, Sociology, study of the Labour movement, international and racial problems. A special course was offered on the Danish folk school and co-operative movements. It was understood that students should, after their stay at Elsinore, go on to study at a folk high school or a college or university in Denmark, Germany or England. They could study economics at the University of Copenhagen without any fees.'

Before I left England, I went into the question of securing an adviser for the ICU. I felt strongly that an adviser from England was a great necessity for our young movement. Sam Leckie, a young man whom I had met at Mickleover Summer School, was considered to be too young for the post. Creech-Jones was suggested, but he was out of the question as he then held an important post in the Transport and General Workers' Union, while on the other hand the ICU was not in a position to pay his full salary if he came out to South Africa. As my time to return to South Africa was approaching, it was agreed that the matter of an adviser be left in the hands of Fenner Brockway, my chief adviser in London, together with Miss Winifred Holtby, who would advertise in the press the post after my return, pending of course the National Council of the ICU's concurrence in the suggestion.

The reader knows perfectly well now that I was born outside the Union of South Africa. In 1920 I was under arrest for deportation to Nyasaland, but the deportation order was squashed by the authorities. The agitation for deportation was again raised in 1925 and in 1926, both in Parliament and in the press. Having left the country temporarily in 1927, although on an important mission, I was mindful that permission to land back in South Africa might not be easy. It was imperative, therefore, that I discuss this situation with my advisers in London before embarking for home. I had a long interview with the officials of the Labour Defence Council in London. The Labour Defence Council aims 'to assist trade unionists throughout the world when persecuted by capitalist governments for their working-class activities'. W. T. Colyer, the secretary, gave me a good deal of advice, which he put into writing. Fortunately my return to South Africa was not opposed by the Union authorities, and I had no need to make use of this material.

During the early part of October 1927 I began to take stock of my mission to Europe in preparation for my return to South Africa. I was satisfied that much had been accomplished on behalf of the African people during the limited time at my disposal. My advisers and sympathizers, who had now grown into a respectable number, felt concerned about my additional heavy responsibilities arising from the European missions. Charles Roden Buxton wrote to me to say:

'In case I do not see you before you leave for South Africa, I should like to say how very pleased we are that you have been able to make this visit to Europe, and how much I hope you will be able to accomplish really good work on behalf of your people. I am sure you feel that very great responsibility which rests upon you now, and how absolutely essential it is to avoid injuring the prospects of the ICU at this critical stage in its development. I know you will exercise the greatest care in accuracy of statements, in moderation of policy, and in strictness with regard to accounts. Your opponents will be on the watch for any failure in these points, and will make the very most of it, if it occurs.'

Another true friend of Africa, the late Miss Winifred Holtby, wrote in this manner:

'All good wishes go with Clements Kadalie. The work which he is doing is of vital importance, not only to South Africa but to the civilized world. The problems of South Africa today will be the problems of the world tomorrow. By raising the standard of life for the workers in South Africa he is taking the first step towards securing that unity of race and colour which is a condition of true civilization. His friends in England wish him strength, courage and wisdom, for his difficult but splendid task.'

Similar farewell messages were received from Arthur Henderson, Sidney Webb, Walter Citrine, A. Creech-Jones, Fenner Brockway, John Fletcher, A. Barratt Brown, H. N. Brailsford, Norman Leys and many others.

On October 28, 1927, I left my hotel for the ILP headquarters at 14 Great George Street, Westminster, London, S.W.1, to shake hands with many friends at the offices of the Party which was largely responsible for the success of my mission. From there I motored to Waterloo railway station to join the boat train for Southampton. Friends were there to see me off. The English wintry weather was now setting in. Before noon the boat train moved off from London where, for about five months, I had made my headquarters. My mission to Europe had now ended. I must now return home to South Africa to work harder than ever before. To me it now appeared I was in the role of the Biblical Moses, who had gone to Mount Sinai, returning with the new commandments to the children of Israel below. To Africa I must now return with new ideas to further the cause of the new trade unionism. My mind and body were now full of vigour. On the afternoon of October 28, 1927, the mail boat left Southampton for Africa, amid the sound of beautiful music.

During my European tour, which lasted about five months, my total expenditure came to about £570. In this figure is included affiliation fees of £40 to the International Federation of Trade

Unions; wages of my secretary totalling £45 19s. 6d.; printing and stationery being £12 13s. 2d.; cables and telegrams £23 13s. 10d. The money earned from my lectures in Germany and Austria amounted to £50—which was included in the grand total expenditure.

CHAPTER IX

Back in South Africa

A FTER seventeen days at sea the *Balmoral Castle* landed at Cape Town early on the morning of November 14, 1927. A number of ICU officials, including the president, J. G. Gumbs, and my brother Robert, were at the quayside to welcome me back. The Cape Town branch of the ICU had arranged in advance to accord me a civic welcome during the evening, a function which I had to decline as my plans were to make my first official pronouncement at headquarters in Johannesburg. I joined the 'Union Limited'—the fast mail train which ran between Cape Town and Johannesburg. I was probably the first African to have travelled by this luxurious train on the South African Railways. At Johannesburg I was met by my family and the officials of the ICU, who were all so excited to see me back home looking spick and span. To welcome me back to South Africa, the ICU National Council was convened to meet in Johannesburg on the day of my arrival. A public reception was therefore arranged at the Workers' Hall. The affair was elaborately organized, and a number of leading Europeans were invited. The Johannesburg *Star* in reporting the meeting had this to say:

'During the course of his first public utterance since his return from Europe Mr. Kadalie, general secretary of the ICU, speaking at the ICU hall, Johannesburg, last night, attacked the three Labour ministers for having sold themselves to capitalism. He predicted the destruction of the South African Labour Party. In reference to Colonel Creswell, Mr. Madeley and Mr. Boydell, the speaker said:

"We helped to place them in power and now they have sold the principles of international trade unionism and the spirit of the ICU. They have sold themselves to the sweaters of labour.

Is it not time for the rank and file of the Labour Party to realize that they should cut out of the Labour movement parasites who are helping the capitalists to bleed the workers and start afresh an organization which will not recognize any colour, race or creed? At the next general election the South African Labour Party is going to be out of existence, and General Smuts will come back into power. There are statements," he went on, "emanating from unknown quarters to the effect that the white workers were not going to recognize the ICU. I want to utter one warning. If they do not recognize the ICU, an organization which does not stand only for black and coloured, but has become international, they will find that the workers overseas, particularly those of Great Britain, will have nothing to do with the South African Labour Party or with the South African Trades Union Congress." '

It is noteworthy that at this meeting W. H. Andrews, who at the time was secretary of the South African Trades Union Congress, was present and spoke, saying that it was certain that in time to come the great ideal of Karl Marx would be realized and workers the world over would unite.[1] At this meeting the national council of the ICU presented me with an illuminated address, which still hangs conspicuously on the wall of my sitting-room, an address which I cherish with unbounded pride. It reads:

'We the undersigned officers on behalf of the members of the Industrial and Commercial Workers' Union of Africa, on your arrival from Europe, wish to place on record our deep and sincere appreciation of the great, noble and everlasting work you have done for the African workers during the past eight years. In the year 1919 you realized the appalling conditions of the great army of unskilled and semi-skilled workers of Africa, and at Cape Town you started for them the Trade Union which is now popularly known as the ICU, and by your determination, energy and outstanding ability you have not only spread the organization throughout the length and breadth of the African sub-continent, but won for it recognition and appreciation throughout the whole world of trade unionism. We marvel at, and admire your force of character which has helped you to overcome the most appalling obstacles such as no trade union leader in any other part of the world has had to face because, while recognizing that the ICU has no colour bar, you have had a constant fight against the prejudices and opposition of the majority of the white workers against your efforts to organize the black man who forms the vast majority of the unskilled workers of Africa and therefore the vast majority of the members of the ICU. You are still a young man, and with God's blessing we trust that you will live long enough to see the edifice completed of which you have laid so good and true foundation, of which you are so worthy a corner-stone. May your dreams be realized and in the completed edifice may we all see the industrial, political and social emancipation not only of the African workers, but of workers of all the world.'

Sixteen members of the ICU national council attached their signatures to this address.

Less than a fortnight after my return from Europe in November 1927 a letter was received in my capacity as general secretary of the ICU from the All-Indian Trades Union Congress, inviting me to attend its annual conference which was to be held in Madras at the close of the year. As I had just returned from Europe and had to attend to ICU affairs at home, which were then pressing, the invitation was turned down. Fraternal greetings were, however, transmitted to the conference. In passing I must express here my deepest regret for missing such opportunities offered in 1927 to visit three important countries, namely, the United States of America, the Soviet Union of Russia, and British India, as it was then known.

During my absence overseas, the new Native Administration Act, with its 'hostility clause', had been promulgated. The Secretary for Native Affairs notified our headquarters of the provisions of the Act. Special reference was made to the clause relating to the promoting of unrest between white and black, and the letter stated, *inter alia*, 'It would, I think, be desirable that you should invite the attention of the propagandists of your association to the terms of Section 29 (1) of the Act.' On receipt of this letter a circular was sent to all our secretaries and branches, telling them to realize that something very near martial law had been proclaimed against Africans. The section of the Act to which the attention of the ICU was officially called read as follows: 'Any person who utters any words, or does any other act or thing whatever with intent to promote any feeling of hostility between Natives and Europeans, shall be guilty of an offence and liable on conviction to imprisonment for a period not exceeding one year, or to a fine of £100, or both.' When the acting national secretary, Champion, was interviewed by the press at the time, he made the following comment: 'It is evident that the Government is contemplating some action against the ICU. But we shall go on as we have been doing until some charge is laid against one of us. I can only say that it is not the intention of our organization to put Africans against white people. Our intention is to create the better feeling between master and servant which has long been missing. It is admitted that the existence of our organization is the result of a long-standing grievance of Native workers of this country. In my own opinion it is to be regretted that the Government seems to be persuaded by a certain number of employers to legislate against our free movement for the reason that they are afraid that one day we shall compel employers of labour to pay us a living wage.'

In spite of the Native Administration Act, the ICU grew from strength to strength, and branches were opened up in nearly every urban centre as well as in rural areas of South Africa. Our membership also increased considerably while funds swelled the coffers of the union. Our wage bill trebled as we had to keep a large staff to run the affairs of the union all over the country.

In Southern Rhodesia, Robert Sambo, an African of Nyasaland, had begun to organize for the ICU. He had succeeded in building a branch in Bulawayo. As a result of the formation of branches in Bulawayo and Salisbury in Southern Rhodesia, the neighbouring governments were always on the look-out for the ICU agents. Consequently we were debarred from entering Basutoland and South-West Africa, where we had two branches. The South African Government debarred us from the Transkei, our largest 'Native Reserve'. Even in Lourenço Marques a watchful eye was set upon us. The Africans were on the march, while the authorities were restless at this awakening of the toiling masses of the sub-continent!

Political war having been declared by the government of the day, it did not hesitate to use the machinery of the Native Administration Act. As was expected, I was the first victim, as a result of a speech I delivered in Pretoria, an account of which appears somewhere else in these pages. Simon Elias and Keable

'Mote followed in the Orange Free State province, and general prosecution under the Act became the order of this period. With my acquittal in the Pretoria Magistrates' Court and other acquittals which followed my own, the Government realized the ineffectiveness of the Native Administration Act. It consequently brought into Parliament another Bill which was also passed and was designated the Riotous Assemblies Amendment Act of 1929. Notwithstanding all this, we maintained our union's activities as before.

My public utterances, as well as my trade union activities amongst the African workers and other non-Europeans, did not earn for me any blessings of officialdom. To most officialdom my advent in organizing the oppressed workers was unwelcome. The establishment of the ICU headquarters in Johannesburg, directly opposite the big Pass Office, was a matter that left a very sore spot with officialdom. I was often summoned to his office by Major Cooke, the director of native labour, who drew my attention to the fact that I was residing in Johannesburg illegally, as I did not possess any kind of 'pass'. To this I retorted that I was not a criminal but an ICU chief executive officer, and as such a respectable public servant. I was advised, however, to obtain a monthly pass contract which I refused to do. However, I was willing, I said, to carry an 'exemption certificate'. To this Major Cooke replied that the Government desired to know of my movements each time I left Johannesburg in the course of the ICU activities. He further threatened that I was inviting arrest for residing in Johannesburg without any kind of pass. When finally the Department of Native Affairs refused to furnish me with an exemption certificate, it was decided on the advice of the ICU's legal advisers to sue the Sub-Native Commissioner of Pretoria. All this happened before my trip to Europe. My petition was accompanied by numerous letters in support of my application for exemption. Among those who testified in writing to my good character were Cecil Frank Glass, Julius First, W. H. Andrews and Henry Pereira. A considerable amount of correspondence passed between our attorneys (Messrs. Findlay and Niemeyer) and the Sub-Native Commissioner. The judgment of the Supreme Court was delivered while I was abroad. The judgment itself is an extremely lengthy document, and I do not propose to weary

the reader with all the legal details. In his concluding remarks
the senior judge (Mr. Justice Feetham) said:

'When a man is applying for some privilege or benefit which,
on proof of certain facts, he is entitled to have granted him,
and a public body or an administrative official has to act in a
quasi-judicial capacity for the purpose of deciding whether or
not he has made out his case, it is the duty of such body or
official to give the applicant a fair opportunity of presenting
his case. Where, in order to give the applicant a fair opportunity
of presenting his case, it is necessary to give him information
of points which are being made, or are being taken into account,
against him, he is entitled to have that information if asked
for. I do not think it can be said that the decision of the Sub-
Commissioner was fairly arrived at, owing to his failure to give
the applicant the opportunity for which he asked of fully
presenting his case, and therefore I think it must be set aside.
It is hardly necessary to add that this decision involves no
expression of opinion as to whether the applicant has succeeded
in his application for the grant of a certificate or registration: it
may be that, even if he had the further opportunity of representing his case to which I think he was entitled, the decision
would still have gone against him, and it is not for this Court
to express any opinion as to whether or not he should be granted
a certificate. The Court is only concerned with the manner in
which the decision was arrived at, not with the correctness of
the decision itself. As we are setting aside the refusal of the
Pass Officer on the grounds of gross irregularity, I think that
the appellant is entitled to the costs of appeal, and also to the
costs of the original application, in accordance with the principles laid down as governing the award of costs against tri-
bunals acting in a quasi-judicial capacity in Klipriviersburg
Licensing Board *v.* Ebrahim, 1911 A.D. 458. The appeal is
allowed with costs, the respondent's refusal of the certificate is
set aside, and he is directed to consider the application for a
certificate afresh, the applicant being allowed to submit fresh
proof, the costs of the application in Chambers to be paid by
the respondents.'

Justices Krause and Gey van Pittius concurred in the judgment. As may be seen, as a result of this judgment I was given
the opportunity of making a fresh application for exemption
from the pass laws. I did not take any further action, however,

nor did the authorities on their part arrest me for failing to carry a pass. They just dropped me like the proverbial 'hot potato'.

Following the experience gained by me while overseas, new methods were introduced at the ICU headquarters early in 1928. Members' subscriptions were receipted by means of denomination stamps enumerated as follows: 2s. entrance fee for male members in urban areas, with 6d. weekly subscriptions; whereas female members' subscriptions were fixed at 1s. entrance fee, with 3d. weekly subscription. Week-end schools were run at various centres at which branch secretaries received lectures from the General Secretary on this new orientation. Some secretaries welcomed this new method, while some did not approve of it because it obviously interfered with free manipulation of union funds to their own private use. Contrary to a belief held by some members of the public, the financial side of the ICU was well managed. The Assistant General Secretary, James A. La Guma, was in charge of this department, and was afterwards superseded by Eddie J. Khaile, a qualified book-keeper. Our financial books at headquarters were well kept, and it was an established custom to take all such books to the conference, wherever it met, for the purpose of scrutiny or verification, should any intelligent delegate feel inclined to do so. We also engaged the services of European accountants to examine the books before these were submitted to our annual conferences. At all times our financial books remained available at headquarters for inspection by anyone who desired it. The national council regretted greatly when James A. La Guma and Eddie J. Khaile left the ICU on account of their Communistic allegiance in 1926, in accordance with the Port Elizabeth decision of the national council. After their departure a European, C. F. Glass of the Witwatersrand Tailors' Association, became our book-keeper at headquarters.

The reader will recall that at our Durban Conference in 1927, prior to my trip to Europe, we had decided to approach the South African Trades Union Congress on the subject of affiliation. The TUC showed itself not unwilling to discuss this matter. On my return from Europe I advised the National Council of the ICU to seek affiliation with the TUC. Accordingly on December 8, 1927, we applied for affiliation on the basis of 100,000 members. This came as a shock to the white trade unionists, who realized that the total strength of their combined affiliated membership was only about 30,000.

As a result of our application the question was placed on the agenda of the South African Trades Union Co-ordinating Committee, a body representing both the TUC and the Cape Federation of Labour Unions. It was actually on the suggestion of Mr. Robert Stuart, secretary of the Cape Federation, that this was done. The committee met in Johannesburg on December 28 and 30, and drew up the memorandum which is summarized below.

The memorandum began by declaring that 'a proposal so important to all sections of the South African workers as the affiliation of a Native labour organization which claims 100,000 members to the Trade Union Congress should not hastily either be turned down or adopted.' It went on to describe the penetration of African workers into industry, and stressed the fact that 'the Native worker very often finds himself doing identical work to that done by European workers, and receiving a very much lower rate of pay'. The Native workers had succeeded, after several false starts, in building up an important industrial organization.

The memorandum then went on to describe many of the disabilities suffered by black workers in South Africa:

'The Native worker, therefore, sees the only way to self-expression in industrial organization. Having reached this stage, in spite of the aloofness and in many cases hostility of the European worker and of the policy of ruthless repression by the authorities (Bulhoek, Port Elizabeth, Witwatersrand massacres), he asks for recognition at the hands of his European fellow-workers—his big brother, so to speak, as experience at any rate goes.

'What is the answer of the European trade unions? The European worker is haunted by the fear of competition from the great masses of Native labourers with their low standard of comfort, and consequent willingness to accept wages which to the European mean degradation, if not starvation. He knows instinctively, if not by observation and reading that the employing class is ever anxious to exploit the weak, whether women, children or Natives, to the detriment of those workers who have painfully, through generations of struggle, attained to a higher standard of living.

'Naturally this nightmare of the abyss yawning at his feet induced him to demand protection even sometimes at the price of gross injustice to those weaker than himself. Self-preservation is the first law of nature, and so the policy hitherto adopted has been one of "keeping the Native in his place" in order that certain of the higher-paid jobs might be retained as the special preserve of the European worker. If this policy had proved successful, there might be no need—outside the ethical aspect—to be discussing the question.

'Such is not the case, however; the Native worker constantly, if slowly, encroaches on these privileged positions. Mining has already passed to a great extent into the hands of Native and Indian workers. Agricultural work has always been almost exclusively performed by the same class. With the growth of industries and mass production, the highly-skilled worker is becoming a less important factor. He will never be eliminated, but the proportion of skilled to so-called unskilled and semi-skilled operatives is rapidly diminishing. On the other hand, in spite of all his handicaps, the Native worker is slowly but surely pushing himself into the higher and more responsible branches of industry, trade and even into the professions (doctors, parsons, lawyers).

'What section of the workers who are willing and able to take the longer view is already convinced that repression, segregation—either industrial or geographical—can only be partially successful, and then only for a time. They recognize that sooner or later the national trade union movement must include all genuine labour, industrial organizations, irrespective of craft, colour or creed. The question is, when and how? This brings us to the question immediately under discussion. Would it be in the best interests of the European and the Native organizations to grant the application for the affiliation which has been made by the ICU?

'The first objection is that the 100,000 members claimed by the ICU would on a card vote in any Congress out-vote all the other unions put together if a division took place, as is possible, on race lines.

'It may be argued, with truth, that this difficulty might be overcome by mutual arrangement, such as reducing the number affiliated to very much smaller proportions. In any case, it is doubtful if the ICU seriously proposed to pay affiliation fees on 100,000, which would be £5,000 per annum. Assuming that this was satisfactorily arranged and the voting strength reduced to, say, 5,000, which could never, without the co-operation of some European unions, dominate Congress, there still remains the danger that important sections of organized labour which may affiliate in the near future would remain aloof, and also that some unions which are now affiliated would secede. If this happens, the European unions would suffer, and the ICU would receive no benefit, they would again be as they were, isolated. It is the considered opinion of the Committee, therefore, whilst keeping in view the soundness of the principle that all bona fide trade unions and employees' associations should be linked up in a national co-ordinating body, and through the national body to the international organization, that a considerable amount of propaganda is needed among the Union membership before affiliation can take place with benefit to all concerned, and it recommends the meeting of Executives with the NEC to give careful consideration to these points of view.

'There is, however, another question which deserves careful consideration, and that is how far is it desirable, and, if desirable, possible to bring about periodical meetings between the two organizations for consultation on matters of common interest?

'These meetings would tend to inform both sections of their mutual difficulties and problems, and would pave the way for more formal relations in the future.

'It must always be borne in mind that the ICU or similar organizations which may possibly spring up from time to time, will seek and find contact with Europeans and European organizations as their strength increases, and if the workers' organizations refuse to associate with them and give them the benefit of their experience and superior knowledge of the Trade Union movement, the Native masses will find friends in the enemy's camp.

'The question ultimately is, are the Native workers to be friends or enemies of the European workers? As enemies they will be used to drag us down as nearly to their level as is possible. As friends they may assist us to maintain and improve our position by demanding and securing wages and conditions which will narrow the great gulf between the two sections and thus remove the nightmare which oppresses the European worker of being hurled into the abyss of Native wage and living standards.'

The memorandum was signed by R. Stuart and W. H. Andrews as joint secretaries.

NOTE TO PAGE 143

1. W. H. (Bill) Andrews was a former Chairman of the South African Labour Party and Member of Parliament for Benoni. After the Labour Party reversed its decision, in 1915, to oppose the European war, Andrews resigned from the Party. He became a member of the War on War group and the first chairman of the South African Communist Party which was formed in 1921. Although his political views were rejected by White workers he maintained wide support in the Trade Union movement.

CHAPTER X

The Kimberley Conference and the Natal Breakaway

I MUST now continue to chronicle in order the events after my return from Europe in November 1927. Before the National Council met in Johannesburg, the *Star* reporter interviewed me at our headquarters, and he summarized that interview in his paper dated November 16, 1927:

'In an interview with a representative of the *Star*, Mr. Clements Kadalie, national secretary of the ICU, declared that the National Council of the organization will consider changing the Constitution of the Union so as to make it a purely labour organization. A prominent member of the trade union movement in Britain will come to South Africa for six months to a year in order to place the ICU on a sound trade union basis, and five or six young men of the ICU will be sent to colleges overseas to study international labour movements in order to be of use to the Natives in South Africa. Kadalie has just returned from Europe and he will make these proposals to the Council when it meets tomorrow. Money to send these men overseas had already been donated in England, and it was proposed to send three ICU members to the International People's College in Denmark, two to Fircroft College in Birmingham; and possibly one to Ruskin College in Oxford.

' "The next meeting of the national council," said Mr. Kadalie, "is going to make definitely our movement a trade union organization. As the position is at present, some of our members do not realize that the ICU is a trade union movement, and that it must have the co-operation of the white trade union organization, both in this country and overseas. There has been justification in the past for a suspicion that the ICU is anti-white. This is due, of course, to our people not having had special training in the labour movement. Under the new organization our men are going to be specially trained and no Native is going to be tolerated who is anti-white. The ICU must be a true trade union movement. We do not abandon the idea, however, that our ultimate goal must be international socialism."

'The National Council was going to consider the changing of the constitution. The new constitution had been drawn up in England, after consultation with the leaders in the trade union movement. Under the reorganization proposed, great changes would be made, instead of having a national secretary at headquarters, there would be a general secretary, whose duties would be to attend to the editing of a new and more up-to-date newspaper for Natives. Under this general secretary would be an organizing secretary. There would be a financial secretary, and following on the English principles, the financial system would undergo entire reorganization on trade union lines. The ICU would have a research department, which in time would be regarded as one of the most important branches of the Union. All daily and weekly papers would be collated and all the speeches of the political leaders of the country would be collected and scrutinized closely, so that the information would be readily obtainable about the political and trade union outlook.

' "We want to have general statistics available for use at a moment's notice," Mr. Kadalie continued. "We want to know, for instance, what is the cost of living at Cape Town, the wages paid to the dock labourers and their general conditions. We must know the wages of the Native or Coloured worker in relation to the European worker throughout all the towns of the Union, and through all the urban or rural areas. We are also going to investigate the possibilities of industries being unable to pay higher wages to Native employees. We want to find out what are the profits as far as every business undertaking is concerned. A parliamentary secretary is also essential. His business will be to go to Cape Town and to listen to debates when every Bill dealing with any industrial question, or which has any relation to Native affairs, is being discussed. We want to see where the sympathies of the members of Parliament lie. We must know who are the progressive, the liberal members who support industrial progress, and, according to our information we will advise those of our members at the Cape who have the franchise how to vote."

'He added that in addition to other departments that would be formed there would be a legal department, which would be able to advise the organization exactly how it stood regarding enactments of parliament and ordinances passed by the provincial councils, particularly with reference to such matters as the colour-bar and the Native Administration acts. "While in London," he said, "I sought eminent legal advice on the Native Administration Act, and was told that there are loopholes in the Act. We intend to fight the Act until it is removed from the Statute Book, as it is contrary to the British principles of fair play and justice."

'The position of the provincial secretaries would be altered materially. Under the proposed Constitution, provincial secretaries would have to take up special branches of study in order to assist the movement in various parts of the country. One would have to investigate and make a close study of farming conditions, so as to be able to advise in such instances as had recently arisen in Natal, where farmers, incensed at the activity of the ICU, had taken to burning huts. The organization would do all in its power to help Natives placed in such a position by the farmers who did not thoroughly understand the aims of the ICU. Another provincial secretary would have to specialize on mines and mining conditions; another would have to deal with, say, dock labourers, employees in the building industries, and so on. In the end these specially prepared men would be stationed at head office, ready to be called upon when required, but at present they would have to undertake their work while provincial secretaries, because of the question of expense.'

Immediately on my arrival at headquarters in Johannesburg from Europe a special National Council meeting of the ICU was convened, and members attended in large numbers to receive a report of the European tour. The Council met from November 18-25, 1927. It was during this meeting that A. Butler, deputy director of the International Labour Office at Geneva, who was on a visit to South Africa, came in and was introduced by me to the members of the Council. It was also at this meeting that I was elected a member of the General Council of the International Federation of Trade Unions, which had its headquarters in Amsterdam, Holland, with A. W. G. Champion as my substitute. After the constitution was agreed to, the national council summoned a special congress to be held at Kimberley beginning on

Dingaan's Day, December 16, 1927. The accounts of the European tour were also presented to the council, which were adopted after some discussion.

I reported to the Council about the negotiation made while in England for the acquisition by the organization of a printing press. I also gave a report about the proposed trade union adviser from Great Britain. The National Council resolved to accept the principle of obtaining a trade union adviser for the ICU from London, and that the Imperialism Committee of the ILP be informed accordingly. The arrangements made with regard to the various scholarships offered to the ICU overseas were also presented to the National Council, and were adopted unanimously.

Our campaign against the Native Administration Act was discussed at length. I emphasized that the opposition to the Native Administration Act was strong in England, and that it was suggested that the matter should be tested in the law courts in South Africa, and, if necessary, as far as to the Privy Council. Financial support was promised in England and in other European countries.

This special meeting of the National Council occupied a full week, and on its conclusion it 'placed on record its highest appreciation and thanks' to me for my able report. As soon as I had outlined the new ICU policy to the press, messages of congratulation poured into our headquarters from many people throughout the country. The Right Reverend Walter Carey, D.D., the Bishop of Bloemfontein at the time, wrote the following letter to me:

'My clergy are very anxious to do their part in helping towards the causes of justice and welfare for the Bantu, but have been puzzled and weakened by some utterances. Your programme published today seems to put many of these utterances straight. If the Church does not help the poor and the oppressed it must die, and rightly, although the Church cannot identify itself with any political party, as you know.'

The Johannesburg meeting of the ICU National Council, having scrutinized and approved of the draft constitution brought by me from London, decided to convene a special congress to ratify it. This was held in Kimberley in December 1927 and was attended by large numbers of delegates from all over the Union and South-West Africa. When I left Johannesburg in the 'Union Limited', the fast mail train to Cape Town, I was booked in one compartment with my colleague Champion. The notice card on the compartment window read: 'Mr. Clements Kadalie and his private secretary'—meaning of course my colleague Champion, who naturally did not approve of the description. I only mention this incident to show the reader that at this period in my life my reputation was at its zenith. The railway authorities took special trouble to see that I was accommodated as comfortably as possible on the trains whenever I travelled, and instructions to this effect were issued accordingly.

The Kimberley conference mainly dealt with the consideration of the revised constitution, which was submitted for approval, and finally adopted. I was truly proud of this constitution, which was based on the model of the best modern trade unions in England.

At this conference we discussed also the burning question of the day in Natal, and the buying of land for our members, who were now being evicted in large numbers by European farmers. We had differences of opinion on this subject, but finally it was felt that the matter be left in the hands of our Natal officials to tackle the problem as best they could in the light of fresh information.

Another item that confronted the conference was the report to the National Council about a trade union adviser from England. We had a number of delegates who could not see their way clear for the appointment of an adviser who would be a white man. I reported to the conference that while in London I had employed a young English girl, who was very able and useful and knew the ICU work and needs perhaps better than many of them. My advisers in England would not approve of her coming to South Africa in view of the colour-bar difficulties, but eventually agreed to send us a male trade union adviser. A resolution for approval to obtain the services of an English trade union adviser was carried by a large majority. By this time, however, the name of the prospective adviser had not been given to the conference yet, as his selection was still being considered in England by friends of the ICU.

With the adoption of the revised constitution, the office of the National Secretary was converted into that of the General Secretary as 'the principal executive officer', while Champion assumed the position of Organizing Secretary.

At the Kimberley conference I reported to the delegates that over 400 books were brought by me from Europe for the ICU library at headquarters. These books were donated by several individuals and organizations in England. The books dealt with many different subjects. Special attention, however, was paid to the trade union movement, as well as the socialist and labour movements. The library was installed in the tea-room inside the Workers' Hall building, and subsequently became an interesting place for visitors to admire and members to use.

Hitherto all the ICU conferences were not blessed with the presence of the mayor of the city or town where our conferences were held. At Kimberley, however, the mayor officially opened our conference, and, as was expected, he exhorted the delegates to moderation. I was called upon by the president (in the chair) to respond to the mayor's speech; whereupon I vigorously attacked him for counselling moderation. I argued that moderation had led to the wholesale exploitation of non-European workers in South Africa. We were there in conference to sound warning to the modern Pharaohs to listen to the voice of the awakened worker whose duty was to demand a just share of the goods he assisted in producing.

During the proceedings of the conference an invitation from the management of the De Beers Company, which operates the diamond mines in Kimberley, was extended to the delegates to visit one of the mines, but this led to a heated debate. I led the opposition for the refusal of the invitation, for the simple reason that our agreement to visit the mine might be interpreted as the ICU's acquiescence in the continued exploitation of our African fellow-men. The motion to refuse the invitation was defeated by a majority vote of the conference, because it was felt that no harm could be done by our acceptance. The following day we were taken to one of the big mines by cars from De Beer's, where opportunity was afforded to the delegates to see those enormous works which produce more than half of the world's famous diamonds.

The Kimberley Conference and the Natal Breakaway

A good deal of the discussion at Kimberley centred round events in Natal, where our organization, both externally and internally, was facing a crisis. The European farmers throughout Natal province were incensed at the rise of the ICU, as their labourers flocked to join the movement in large numbers. Natal white farmers refused to have tenants who were members of the ICU, they 'smelled them out', felling their huts to the ground, burning out others, and throwing tenants on to the roads, confiscating at the same time their stock, if they did not leave quickly enough. Contributions dropped markedly. The European farmers went even further by attempting to burn ICU offices at Krantzkop, Weenen and Greytown. I remember vividly how these incensed farmers even marched into Pietermaritzburg, the capital of Natal Province, where they intended to set on fire the ICU offices and hall in Church Street, main thoroughfare of the city.

I happened to visit Natal at this particular period, and was ignorant of what was going on there. When we reached the ICU offices by car from Johannesburg, we found great excitement amongst our members and the general public. Before long an order was given by a police officer that everyone should vacate the ICU premises that evening as the 'Greytown Commando' was on its way to Pietermaritzburg to set fire to our premises. I immediately got into touch with police headquarters, where I was instructed to inform our members to leave the premises as they (the police) feared that the mob would set the place on fire. The Zulus refused to quit, as they decided that they were prepared to defend and protect the premises themselves. I was advised to go away with the car for safety, for if the European mob were to get information about my presence in Maritzburg, they would go all out to try to locate me. The mob came about 7.30 p.m. direct to the ICU premises. The police authorities had assured us that they would protect our property; and they placed a number of constables in front of our offices. When the mob arrived, the deputy commissioner of police ordered them to disperse. When the mob failed to go, the commissioner told them that if they refused to disperse he would order the police to shoot. The leader of the mob, after consultation with his men, eventually moved them off quietly. Thus the European hooligans were prevented from causing further damage to ICU property in Natal. The following day I sent a long telegram to the Minister of Justice in Cape Town, drawing his attention to this mob law in democratic South Africa.

The ICU's position in Natal was further complicated by certain internal troubles in our organization, which had shaken the confidence of our members, while our enemies made use of them against the union and its leaders. Our provincial secretary for Natal, Sam Dunn, had been sentenced by the Supreme Court for embezzlement of the ICU funds. George Lenon, a Basuto, who was at the time a member of the Durban branch executive committee, became dissatisfied with the manner in which the union's funds were handled, and consequently published a pamphlet accusing Champion of mismanagement of the ICU funds in Durban. The latter naturally took exception to this accusation. The climax was a Supreme Court case for libel against George Lenon by Champion. Champion lost the action with costs against himself.

The public press took advantage of the strong strictures made by the learned judge and published long accounts of it. This happened about a month and a half after my return to South Africa from overseas. I immediately made a public statement to the press to the effect that a thorough investigation into the Durban financial management of the ICU would take place. With this exposure of the ICU's financial chaos in Durban, the confidence of the general public in the organization became shaky. I was therefore compelled to make an immediate visit to Durban, where to my great surprise I found that there was no ICU banking account. All funds were deposited in the bank under the personal name of the provincial secretary. On my initiative the funds in the bank were transferred for the first time under the organization's name. Champion obviously did not fully appreciate this necessary and businesslike transaction, and from this time onwards some misunderstandings arose between headquarters and the Natal organization.

While in Durban on my first visit after my return from overseas, I discovered that the Durban branch had more than a dozen men in office drawing a large sum in salaries. In my capacity as chief executive officer I instructed Champion to cut down this large staff in order to save the Union's funds. He had some doubts about this, but finally acquiesced. Immediately on my return to headquarters in Johannesburg I put into effect the suggestion from Mr. Justice Tatham, who had delivered judgment in the Lenon *v.* Champion case, and advised the National Council sub-committee to appoint auditors to proceed to Durban. A Johannesburg firm of chartered accountants undertook the work. Meanwhile, an annual conference of the Union was pending at Bloemfontein during Easter of 1928, where it was expected that the auditors' report would be available.

This conference of the ICU in Bloemfontein was the largest ever held, as there were nearly one thousand delegates. Natal alone sent 300 delegates, who were divided in their loyalty to their leader, Champion. The delegates from the northern district of Natal were overwhelmingly anti-Champion, while Durban and Pietermaritzburg were for 'our leader right or wrong'. The auditors' report was delivered at the ICU headquarters just in time for me to take it along to the conference. It was a document of hundreds of pages. The feeling at the conference ran very high indeed. Various caucus meetings were in progress at soon as delegates reached Bloemfontein. The conference was under the able chairmanship of president J. G. Gumbs, who had a good loud voice and was well respected by all, since like myself he was free of tribal affiliations.

It took me a day and half to read the report to the conference. Immediately after I had sat down a resolution was moved by Alex P. Maduna, seconded by Doyle Modiakhogtla, for the arrest of Champion for mismanagement of the ICU funds in Durban. This resolution brought out bitter attacks against Champion by some of his enemies among the huge delegation. The debate continued for about three days, and it was quite obvious that the resolution to lay a charge against Champion would carry the day. Early in the morning on the last day of the debate, when the conference was to make its momentous decision, Champion walked into my room, for we happened to stay in one house. I saw at once that he was in great mental agony. He addressed himself to me as his 'chief' and colleague, pleading with me to save his face. It was obvious to me that he was the victim of circumstances and that others were to blame. I told him that personally I could not promise him anything as the matter rested entirely with the conference, and I was not a dictator, but that I would do my best for him. So after many delegates had given vent to their anger, I rose to address the house, which was electrified. For about an hour I analysed the auditors' report as understood by me. I warned the conference not to act hastily, and suggested that we should conform to the suggestion of the auditors to appoint a commission to proceed to Durban and in the meantime that the Durban authority should be suspended pending the investigation. I moved a resolution accordingly. It was duly seconded and adopted by a large majority of the conference.

From the foregoing narrative the reader will agree that I was loyal to Champion, who merited loyalty. But subsequent events were against us. When delegates returned to their respective constituencies, it was maliciously reported in Natal, particularly in Durban, that I alone had 'dismissed' him, which was absurd. My presence was demanded there to explain the true position.

Many good and some bad things have had to be said in this book about some of the ICU secretaries, but now I must give a personal account of the man who admittedly played a very important part in the history of the union. I now refer to Champion, A. W. G. Champion, who, while I was away in Europe in 1927, acted as national secretary in my place. Champion is a Zulu, and has all the characteristics of that great people. As is recorded somewhere in these pages, I met Champion at the Crown Mines on the Rand where he was employed as a clerk for many years before he joined the ICU. When he joined the union in Johannesburg in 1925, I first sent him to Bloemfontein to settle a branch dispute which he did to my satisfaction. I at once realized that as a Zulu he would do well in Durban among his people where Alexander Maduna had failed. Without hesitation Champion was transferred to Durban to succeed Maduna who, in turn, was sent to Bloemfontein. Immediately Champion took charge of Durban, the ICU flourished there beyond our expectations. The membership rapidly increased into four figures, and large funds came into the ICU. Durban soon became the stronghold of the union. With his forceful character he acquired for the union a big property in the heart of Durban which was used as offices and a recreation hall where modern dances were conducted every evening, including Sundays. He met strong opposition from the Durban City Council, but he succeeded in the Supreme Court against the Council, who had instituted action against the ICU. There is no doubt that Champion was a good organizer, for during his term as provincial secretary for Natal the ICU attained great influence among the Zulu workers, thus creating fear among the powers that be.

Champion was also a good platform speaker, particularly in the Zulu language. He was fearless as far as opposition was concerned. I have recorded how one day both of us stormed Pietermaritzburg, capital of Natal province, despite the fact that there was a threat to shoot at us in the market square. Champion used the courts of law to attain his ends, and in this he succeeded admirably. He worked in collaboration with a well-known legal firm, and in this connection thousands from the ICU funds passed into that firm, which did good legal work for the union. Champion, as a Zulu, liked power, but without him Natal could never have taken a leading part in the affairs of the ICU during the twenties and thirties.

In the course of my work as general secretary of the union, life was not at all easy. I once toured the Eastern Province of the Cape accompanied by the Cape provincial secretary, T. B. Lujiza, of East London, and the senior vice-president, Mac Jabavu, brother of Professor Jabavu and editor of *Imvo*. We addressed a meeting at Adelaide in the morning and from there went to Bedford, where we surprisingly encountered a well-organized mob of ICU women belonging to that branch. The assistant general secretary, James A. La Guma, had dismissed a secretary of the branch who was also a local schoolteacher. La Guma did this on strong representations made to him by the provincial secretary, James Dipa. I was stationed temporarily in Johannesburg at the time, and was not informed of the feud between the branch and provincial secretaries. It was assumed by the local secretary that I was responsible for his dismissal. We reached Bedford at 1.30 p.m. by car from Adelaide. As soon as we were ushered into a house which was used as an ICU office, women members surrounded the front door carrying stones in their shawls. These are commonly used by African women to carry various articles in default of other containers. Thus they awaited us; the atmosphere was tense. The women demanded my presence so that I could be stoned. Jabavu, the senior vice-president, knowing the area well and seeing that the danger was real and imminent, suggested that we abandon the meeting and retreat. Hastily we got into our car and left the place without addressing any meeting.

During my public life as leader of the ICU I experienced many such dark episodes, but nothing was so serious as that which befell me at Durban among the people I was supposed to lead. As I have said, after the Bloemfontein conference at which Champion was suspended from office pending a commission of enquiry into the financial affairs of the union in Natal, particularly those of Durban, a demand was made by the branch for my presence at that centre to explain the decision of the Bloemfontein conference. I readily agreed, and motored to Natal. We were unable to reach Durban the same day owing to bad roads due to heavy rains. We decided to stay overnight at Pietermaritzburg, which we reached late at night. A 'phone call was put through to our Durban office informing the officials there of our decision. This decision did not satisfy the officials of the Durban ICU, who sent a well-organized, quasi-military mob to Pietermaritzburg at midnight to fetch me into Durban by force. This mob, which left Durban by car, was accompanied by the European detective head constable Arnold ('Tshaka'), whom I mentioned in Chapter 6.[1]

The mob commanded me to proceed with them to Durban. We changed drivers, and I was bundled by force into the Durban ICU car, while our Johannesburg car was also occupied by some of these ICU 'soldiers', making sure that we did not abscond back to Johannesburg. On arrival at Durban at about 2 a.m. I was rushed on to the platform in the ICU hall, and I was jeered to scorn by the meeting, of over a thousand people, while other 'soldier' members threatened to strike me violently. I was ordered by an angry chairman to explain to the meeting why I had dismissed Champion. The delegates who had attended the Bloemfontein conference had maliciously reported to the Durban branch that I alone actually dismissed Champion. When I rose to speak I realized that death was certainly hanging over my head in those small hours of the morning. At one stage when I was making my statement that Champion was suspended by the ICU conference and not dismissed, one of these illegal 'soldiers' rushed forward with an instrument aimed at my forehead, but was immediately stopped by detective Arnold, who had been with this mob and had actually accompanied it to Pietermaritzburg, presumably to watch its proceedings when it went there to fetch me by force. This detective drew his revolver just in time; which prevented the man from attempting a perhaps fatal blow.

As it was nearing daybreak, the meeting decided that I should again explain more of the decision of the conference the following evening. But detective Arnold saw that this Durban mob was determined to hurt me even to the point of death itself. He wisely advised me to leave Durban at once. Arnold was kind enough to take me away from the hall, and pretended that I was to take some breakfast somewhere in a café. We drove towards an Indian café where we did not stop, but passed clear out of Durban, and were seen off by the detective. When the attempt on my life was made in Durban ICU hall, I must put on record here that Arnold alone of those present interfered in order to protect me from the mob.

Immediately on my return to Johannesburg the secession of Natal from the main body was dramatically proclaimed by Champion. Owing to this secession episode, it was now impossible for the sub-committee of the National Council to send down to Durban a commission to investigate the financial affairs of the union, so strongly recommended by the auditors and passed by the conference. This episode would appear to be the turning-point in the history of the ICU, which through its ten years of existence had accomplished as a unit the noble work of unifying the African proletariat with a realization of their contribution to the industrial life of South Africa, and was now to suffer partial dismemberment.[2]

NOTES

1. (p. 164) Perhaps it will interest readers to know that this detective, Arnold, presumably in the course of his duty as a police officer, actually was admitted to membership of the ICU by the Durban branch with Champion's knowledge. He was often seen at the ICU offices in open conversation with

Champion and other officials of the movement, and was known to Durban Zulus as 'Tshaka'.—C.K.

(Champion denied that Arnold was a member; he was known to be a detective, and treated as such.)

2. (p. 165) A. W. G. Champion added his own footnote:
'It should be noted that the report of the auditors did not find that the missing money was in the hands of Champion. They found that there was about £500-£800 which was not accounted for. This amount was accounted for in the case of Sam Dunn, who was sentenced by the Supreme Court to 12 months. Sam Dunn was provincial secretary for Natal. He controlled Natal when Champion acted for Kadalie during 1927-28.

'Sam Dunn was charged by Champion after the books of Durban ICU had been audited. In this autobiography this part of the history is overlooked by Kadalie.'

CHAPTER XI

Fighting the Pass Laws

O N April 22, 1928, I addressed a public meeting in Pretoria
Market Square, Marabastad, under the auspices of the ICU.
I had just returned from Bloemfontein, where I had attended a
conference held by the African National Congress. Of the many
resolutions adopted by the conference, one was in connection
with the pass laws. I had gone to Pretoria to report the decisions
of the conference. The meeting was well advertised. Therefore
a large gathering attended, including police officers. In the course
of the speech I dealt chiefly with the pass laws, which I characterized as relics of the Dark or Stone Age. The Johannesburg *Star*
reported the speech:

'A denunciation of the pass system and a threat that the ICU
might teach the Government a "damn good lesson", were made
by Mr. Clements Kadalie, secretary of the ICU, yesterday afternoon. The ICU and the African National Congress, he said,
were going to approach the Government as diplomats with the
request that passes be suspended for six months. If it was found
that there was a marked growth in native lawlessness, and
hooliganism increased, the Government could tighten up the
regulations. But if, at the expiration of the period, it was proved
that the natives had been law-abiding and crime had decreased,
they were going to appeal to the Government to "play the
game" and abolish the passes. And if the Government refused,
*"we shall teach them a damn good lesson and we'll burn passes
all over the country"*. In regard to the ICU's economic and
political programme, Mr. Kadalie said they were determined to
obtain better wages for the native worker; when a man earned
a poor wage he became a criminal and a nuisance to the public.
Before the Wage Board, the ICU had urged higher wages, and
for the first time in the history of the country natives were to

M

have a legalized wage—"all as a result of the agitation by the ICU."

'Closing an hour's speech, during which he jumped about on the table banging his hands, Mr. Kadalie foreshadowed poor success for the ICU demands. If passes were suspended, everybody in the Native Affairs Department would lose his job, he declared. All over the country the ICU were training men, and when the great day came for burning the passes, he hoped he would be the "Field Marshal". Natives were cowards for the half-hearted resistance offered to the police.'

The Johannesburg and Pretoria newspapers took extraordinary interest in publishing the above speech as well as writing some unsympathetic editorials on it. On April 24, 1928, the *Star* had this full column:

'Mr. Clements Kadalie, national secretary of the ICU, was arrested in Johannesburg this afternoon on a warrant issued from Pretoria under Section I of the Native Administration Act, which reads as follows: "Any person who utters any words or does any other act or thing whatever with intent to promote any feeling of hostility between Natives and Europeans shall be guilty of an offence and liable on conviction to imprisonment for a period not exceeding one year or to a fine of £100 or both."

'At Marshall Square Mr. Kadalie, who now had a legal representative with him, was informed by Sub-Inspector Price that the warrant had been issued in connection with the speech delivered by him on Sunday in the Pretoria Location. Mr. Kadalie was released on bail of £50 to appear before the Pretoria magistrate on May 3. When the two detectives walked into Mr. Kadalie's office, he was just concluding a letter to the editor of the *Star*, referring to the published report of his speech at Pretoria.'

I think the reader will appreciate the fact that whenever I made an important pronouncement during my long public career, I was ever ready at any time to explain afterwards the implications of such utterances. When the two detectives came into my office, I was writing a letter to the press which I am glad to record was published in full by the *Rand Daily Mail*.[1] The following is its text:

'I have read with some concern the leading article entitled "Native Leaders must learn Wisdom". While I do not want to make an apology for the speech I made at Pretoria on last Sunday, I desire, however, to deny the statement attributed to me of having said that the whites are thieves and robbers. As an international trade unionist, I consider it will be wholly unwise for one to attack white people, for it would be contrary to the accepted policy of the ICU. I sincerely realize that the question before us is not white versus black, but capitalism versus the proletariat; therefore, in my speech at Pretoria, I struck the note that under the present system of society our rulers were thieves and robbers when they intend to partition the "land and its fullness thereof which belonged to the Lord". Your article recommends that we should divorce ourselves entirely from politics and lead the Natives strictly along the road of constitutionalism. I would like to point out that the ICU has no intention of copying the stupid and futile and unpolitical attitude of our white contemporaries. As Karl Marx said, every economic question is, in the last analysis, a political question also, and we must recognize that in neglecting to concern ourselves with current politics, in leaving the political machine to the unchallenged control of our class enemies, we are rendering a disservice to those thousands of our members who are groaning under oppressive laws, and who are looking to the ICU for a lead. Our agitation against the pass laws is not a result of our supposed hostility to Europeans, but rather we feel that this measure is characteristic of the days of chattel slavery. It was high time that you should assist us in condemning this slave measure. But I can assure you that whether we get your support or not, we intend to carry on with our propaganda for the total abolition of the pass system—a system which has been responsible for making the Africans criminals and correspondingly painting this Dominion as a "slave State".'

When I arrived at Marshall Square, I asked for bail. This was fixed at £50. In the ICU headquarters we did not keep such a large sum of money in hand. We had only some petty cash which amounted to about £5 at the time. My arrest was made on Wednesday afternoon when the banks had closed their doors. I, however, asked for the use of the Marshall Square telephone to speak to the Standard Bank, where the ICU had accounts. It was arranged that a back door of the bank in Fox Street would be kept open for me to present the ICU cheque to be cashed. After another telephone call to the ICU headquarters, the financial secretary brought a signed cheque for my endorsement, which was cashed at the bank in the presence of an escort detective. I was now on bail; the case was to be heard in Pretoria, by the Chief Magistrate, who was then S. A. McCormick, later the Honourable Judge President of the Natal High Court. It is perhaps worth noting here that immediately I was acquitted, the magistrate was promoted to the Natal Native High Court.

One incident during the hearing of the case, which took some days, may be of some interest to the reader. At this time the ICU provided me with a car, which I took every day to Pretoria during the hearing. One morning the driver, through no fault of his own, came late to fetch me at my house. Consequently we reached Pretoria after 9.15 a.m. When the time came, the court had to wait for my appearance. A big crowd attended the proceedings. On reaching the precincts of the court house, I noticed that everyone appeared to be anxious or worried, including my counsel, Advocate Schreiner, now the Hon. Justice Schreiner, K.C., of the Appellate Division, and Mr. George Findlay, K.C. I had to frame up a big excuse when I entered the dock. I informed the court that my late-coming was due to engine trouble at Halfway House between Johannesburg and Pretoria. All the newspapers echoed this justifiable excuse in reporting to the world that 'Kadalie's engine trouble' brought him late to the court.

I was cross-examined by the Public Prosecutor, who was determined to get a conviction against me. There was a passage in my speech complained of which both learned counsel and the attorney considered would go against me. It was a passage during the oration when I dramatically declared 'I do not care a damn about your Roberts Heights'. The Public Prosecutor insisted that I should submit to the court that I incited to direct action, consequently committing the offence of public violence. To the astonishment of both learned counsel and the attorney, I replied that what I meant to convey to my audience when I spoke about aeroplanes and Roberts Heights (the Union Government military headquarters) was that it was possible that the Government would refuse to suspend the pass laws, and if the natives came out on strike by refusing to carry passes as decided by the Bloemfontein conference, the Government might use force. I was trying to convey that a Government that used force or relied on force could never last, but would go the way the German Empire had gone after the World War of 1914-19.

On May 22, 1928, the magistrate remanded the case and reserved judgment until May 29. Alone with my driver I travelled to Pretoria on May 29. This time I took great care to get there in time. The court house was crowded with spectators. Some of the CID men conversed with me and expressed the opinion that I should lose the case. The newspaper reporters, who also joined in conversation with me, asked in advance what were my plans after the judgment, since my deportation would follow if the case was lost. At 10 a.m. the Chief Magistrate was on the bench, and delivered the judgment to a crowded court. He said:

'The accused is charged with contravening Section 29 (I) of Act 38 of 1927 by uttering words with intent to promote a feeling of hostility between Natives and Europeans. The words are set out in a report of the speech made by the accused at the Marabastad Native Location, Pretoria, to a large gathering of natives on April 22 last. A constable of the South African Police was present at the meeting, and took the speech down in shorthand, making a long transcript of it later. He admits that he did not take down the whole speech as accused spoke too rapidly, and he admits that here and there a word may be wrong, but he asserts that what he took down, and what accused is now charged with saying, is what accused actually said. The accused does not admit the accuracy of the report. He says in many respects it is inaccurate, but I do not gather from his evidence that the report is materially wrong in any respect. From his own evidence I gather that it sets out substantially what he said, although not as fully as he said it. I have compared the report with the one put in by the defence, and one taken by the reporter of *Die Volkstem*, and there is little or no substantial difference in the sentiments expressed, although the words are different. With one or two exceptions, with which I will deal later, I am prepared to accept the report taken by the police constable as being substantially what the accused said at this meeting.

'It deals with three questions, wages for natives, the division of land and the Pass Laws. I do not think any exception can be taken to what accused said on the wages question. He told the meeting that he and another native named 'Mote had been before the Wage Board at Bloemfontein, and as a result of their efforts natives were going to have a fixed rate of wages, and he implies that the rate would be higher than the wages now paid. There is nothing in those remarks to excite any hostile feeling between the natives and Europeans. In dealing with the pass laws the accused used a good deal of wild language, but the general effect of what he said was to constitute an attack on those laws. He told his hearers that they should not be obliged to carry passes. Regarding the *Volkstem* report, in conjunction with the police report, it seems clear that he told his audience that the ICU and the African National Congress at Bloemfontein had passed a resolution that the Government was to be approached with a request to suspend the operation of the pass laws for six months. If during those six months it was found that there was an increase in native crime, then they would ask the Government to put the pass laws in operation again and tighten them up. If the Government refused their request for a temporary suspension of the pass laws, then they were all to meet together and burn their passes and refuse to carry any passes.

'Now I need not stop to consider whether on this language the accused could be charged with inciting to commit an offence. It is an offence for a native to be without a pass, but that is not what the accused is charged with. There is no evidence that advocating the abolition of the pass laws is calculated to promote feelings of hostility between natives and Europeans. It is quite conceivable that numbers of Europeans might welcome the abolition of the pass system, if for no other reason than that it would relieve them of the trouble and responsibility of seeing that their servants are provided with passes and of paying the monthly fee. The accused's talk on the subject of passes was accompanied by an attack on the police in connection with the recent police raids made for the purpose of rounding up passless natives. It is nothing unusual for the police to become unpopular with a section of the community because they carry out their duties and a verbal attack on them for enforcing the pass laws can hardly be said to be calculated to promote hostile feeling between natives and Europeans generally. It is to be remembered that both white and native police took part in the raids. Accused used one phrase, according to the police report, which might bring him within the section with which he is charged, where he says, "I say the whole of this people can go to hell." That might be taken, when read with the context, to mean the European population as a whole. But the *Volkstem* report makes the accused say "Let all the people in the Union Buildings go to hell." Now that supports the version of the defence that accused was not attacking Europeans generally but the Government, and the officials who had to administer the pass laws. The evidence is that the accused frequently pointed to the Union Buildings in the course of his speech. They were visible from the spot where the meeting was held. When the accused spoke of a new Africa arising in which they would be free, and it would not be the South Africa of General Hertzog and Tielman Roos, because they advocated a white South Africa, he was merely using hyperbolical language to express his view that the pass laws would be abolished and that other disabilities under which it is said natives labour, would be removed and even if the Government used force against them, which is what his allusion to aeroplanes, machine-guns and Roberts Heights meant, they would still persevere with their endeavours to have the pass laws abolished and other disabilities removed. And his allusion that the German Empire had gone to hell was meant as an illustration of his argument that the use of force would not benefit the Government. He said in his speech that the money paid by natives went to the Transvaal University College and the poor whites got nothing of it, and when he added "They can all go to hell for my part", he was clearly alluding to the Government and not to the poor whites. And his allusion to being a general or a field-marshal merely meant that he hoped to be at the head of the natives on the day that they destroyed their passes. It had no military significance. Although accused used violent and offensive language, I think that a consideration of this part of his speech shows that it was meant as an attack on the Government for enforcing the pass laws. I do not think an attack on the Government comes within the mischief aimed at by the Section of the Statute under which accused is charged. I do not think such an attack is calculated to promote a feeling of hostility between natives and Europeans generally. The Government of the country is liable at any time to be attacked by some section or other of the community in respect of legislation which it has introduced into Parliament, which has been passed and which it is enforcing. An attack on such legislation would not necessarily promote a feeling of hostility between natives and Europeans. I do not know that I can agree with Mr. Schreiner that the feelings of hostility must be promoted between the natives as a whole and Europeans as a whole, in other words that it must be inter-racial. It is probable that the statute would be contravened if feelings of hostility were prompted between a considerable section of natives and any considerable section of Europeans. But that is a different thing to promoting a feeling of hostility towards the Government of the day.

'Then we come to the other part of the speech, that dealing with the land question. I have left this to the last as it offers the most difficulty. Accused began by saying that the Prime Minister, General Hertzog, had been working on the native question for the last three years, and said he was going to divide it between white and black. Accused said, "We want to know who gave him the right to try and do a thing like that." Then he went on to say that the land did not belong to King George V, Paul Kruger, or Moshesh, or Chaka, or other chiefs, but it belonged to the Lord. Later he said it belonged to the people. His allusion to the native chiefs as well as to King George, Paul Kruger and General Hertzog shows that he was, as he says he was, merely enunciating the well-known socialistic doctrine of the communal tenure of the land. He said the land was robbed by the forefathers, but the *Volkstem* report makes it "General Hertzog's forefathers". It is, of course, an historical fact that with the extension of white civilization northwards in South Africa the natives then living in the country were dispossessed of a good deal of their ground. But the accused's point was not that the natives should take it back again. Had he said that he would clearly have contravened the section, but the context makes it clear what he said. He said, "The ICU likes its workers to know that this land belongs to the people. This land must belong to the poor little natives as well. We have a right to share this country." And the *Volkstem* report makes him say "Black and white have a right to live here. That's our programme." So what he was suggesting was that the natives should have a greater share in the land than they have at present. That suggestion in itself would not necessarily have the effect of promoting hostility between the natives and Europeans. The form of the language used by the accused in this part of his speech was such as to bring it nearer the border-line, but I do think he did not cross it. It goes without saying that the language used by him throughout his speech is very strongly to be deprecated. But the fact he spoke in exaggerated and offensive terms would not of itself create a contravention of the statute. Many natives hold pronounced views on the wages, land and pass laws questions. I think it is not a bad thing, and probably makes for safety in the long run if they are allowed to give free expression to their opinions on these matters, provided they do it in such a way as not to create hostility and antagonism. In so far as the section under which accused is charged limits the rights of free speech, it must be strictly interpreted and the court must be satisfied that the accused intended to create a feeling of hostility between natives and Europeans.

'For reasons I have given I do not think the accused intended to do that. I do think that what he intended to do was to attack the Government in respect of its policy on the land and pass questions. I therefore find him NOT GUILTY and he is discharged.'

Before ending this chapter I must say something about the Onderstepoort strike, which occurred during the first half of 1928. At Pretoria we had a strong branch of the union which was under the control of I. B. Moroe as secretary and A. J. Phoofolo as provincial secretary. At Onderstepoort Government Laboratory the majority of unskilled and semi-skilled labourers were members of the ICU. A decision was made by the Pretoria branch to approach the management for a rise in wages, and a deputation was appointed for this purpose. It was composed of five members of the Union employed at the laboratory, together with Moroe and Phoofolo. The management refused to receive the deputation and dismissed the five workers attached to the deputation. This was a clear case of victimization. It culminated in the other African employees stopping work in sympathy with the men discharged. Immediately news was received that the men were out on strike I proceeded to Pretoria by car from Johannesburg. On arrival at Onderstepoort I was met by a body of police armed with clubs and revolvers. I ventured to ask permission to address the men, but was told that permission could only be granted on condition that I advised the men to resume work unconditionally. I refused to do so and informed the authorities that the union would protect its members involved in the strike. My bold statement caused some commotion, and the police adopted a threatening attitude. I was ordered to leave the premises at once. Finally the Government took drastic action and put all the strikers in prison. The following day seventy-one of the seventy-five who went on strike were fined 10s. each, with the alternative of seven days' imprisonment. Advocate George Findlay defended the men in court. All those who were convicted were subsequently discharged from employment. We intended to appeal to the Supreme Court, but we did not proceed with this course, as we realized that we had little chance of succeeding.

NOTE TO PAGE 168

1. The Johannesburg *Star* published an abridged version.—C.K.

CHAPTER XII

Our European Adviser

WHILE the affairs of the Union were in such turmoil at home as a result of Judge Tatham's strictures and the breakaway of Natal, a refreshing announcement was made from London that an adviser to the ICU had been found at last in the person of Mr. W. G. Ballinger. This news brought some relief to those of us at headquarters. It will be recalled that I had not met Ballinger during my stay in England, but judging from letters received from those I had left with the job of finding an adviser, I was confident that Ballinger's arrival would tremendously help the ICU to save its ship from sinking. It was during the early part of July 1928 when Ballinger reached South Africa. On his arrival at Cape Town I journeyed specially from Johannesburg to Cape Town to meet and welcome him on behalf of the organization of which I was the chief executive officer. When I reached the docks at Cape Town I at once boarded the mail boat. As I was well known there, there was no necessity for me to wait for the usual formalities. The workers who were engaged in unloading the mail boat were all members of the ICU.

As is pointed out in these pages, an African is a shrewd observer of human beings. Thus on seeing our new adviser from overseas at the Cape Town docks that first Monday morning, I felt somewhat disappointed. I think I mentioned this disappointment to a few friends who went down to the docks with me. This disappointment was soon confirmed. On leaving Cape Town station by the mail train for Johannesburg, instead of travelling with me in one compartment which I had previously booked, the new adviser went into a European compartment where he was not booked in advance. I had made special arrangements with the booking authorities for our compartment to adjoin the European section, to enable Ballinger to move freely into the dining-saloon. During the few hours at our disposal in Cape Town before the train left for Johannesburg, Ballinger was taken over by some white people, including a local Scottish clergyman; possibly it was he who persuaded him to make different travelling arrangements.

On our arrival at Park Station we were met by ICU officials and some European well-wishers, including Mrs. Etheldreda Lewis, whose guest Ballinger became during his first days in Johannesburg. To welcome Ballinger to South Africa, the ICU National Council was summoned to meet in Johannesburg. I have to record here with regret that Ballinger's first utterance at the National Council meeting left a very bad impression upon a majority of the members. On that very first day he was attacked by two or three members, who accused him of being a 'dictator', instead of coming out to Africa to be an ICU adviser. I had to intervene in order to protect Ballinger, as the attack developed furiously in the first council meeting. Notwithstanding the fact that peace was temporarily restored, deep-seated antagonism against the adviser was apparently created on his first appearance among the African people.[1]

Before Ballinger came to South Africa, we had European friends who, in one way or the other, afforded us assistance and advice. In the trade union movement we had C. F. Glass, already mentioned; W. H. Andrews and Sidney Bunting also gave unselfish help. It was Bill Andrews who more or less influenced the South African Trade Union Congress to deal sympathetically with our request for co-operation. On some occasions Bill Andrews addressed ICU meetings in the Workers' Hall. During my persecution in connection with pass laws, Andrews supplied the ICU attorneys with a favourable affidavit for use in the Supreme Court. The ICU looked upon Bill Andrews as a great trade unionist who recognized no colour-bar. Sidney Bunting had more to do with the ICU. He helped firstly in his legal capacity, for he took up the work on my behalf when I was refused entry into Natal Province. It was he who obtained free legal opinion from advocate Saul Solomon, K.C. I remember Bunting expressing his strong disgust at the opinion, which he considered was unfair. On many occasions Bunting and Edward Roux used to address

ICU meetings in Johannesburg. Of all European Communists, only these two men were allowed to attend and address our meetings. When a public meeting was organized outside the Workers' Hall to protest against the Bill to amend the Riotous Assemblies Act, both Bunting and Edward Roux participated and spoke. These two men did a lot for individual African leaders, as they conducted a school in Ferreirastown, Johannesburg, where Tantsi, Silwana, Mbeki, Thibedi, etc., were coached educationally. Eddie Roux was also permitted to sell, or sometimes distribute freely, Communist literature at ICU meetings, either in the Workers' Hall or in the open air, in the days before the dangers and implications of Communism were generally understood.

Etheldreda Lewis was a novelist who did much work for the ICU behind the scenes. She, like Margaret Hodgson (afterwards Mrs. Ballinger), introduced many distinguished Europeans to us. Dame Sybil Thorndike, the actress, was one so introduced, and she was impressed by a visit to the Workers' Hall. We have recorded in this book the assistance given to me by Mabel Palmer in Durban, who gave me a number of introductory letters to many people in England when I went overseas in 1927, which included those to the Webbs and A. Creech-Jones.

But, to return to the events following the arrival of W. G. Ballinger with Natal Province out of the picture, we set ourselves to work hard with our newly acquired trade union adviser at headquarters. We had maintained high hopes that, notwithstanding what had happened in Natal, the ship of state which was about to sink would be refloated through the wise aid of our adviser. To our great bewilderment we found that the task our adviser had undertaken seemed to be to put one official at loggerheads with another. Our adviser would one moment fraternize with an official, while in the next breath he would condemn in strong terms that same official.

In this confused atmosphere the work of the union went on into the year 1929. I was privileged during this time of suspicion and confusion to visit some of our branches accompanied by our adviser, notwithstanding the fact that our personal relationships were pointing to a break between us. About this time Ballinger gathered round him unknowingly men who hitherto had taken no active part in the affairs of the union. Early in January 1929 a special meeting of the National Council was held at Bloemfontein at which Ballinger presented his first report after five and a half months in South Africa.

Notwithstanding an apparent undercurrent against me initiated by some Europeans, mostly of the Joint Councils, who had befriended our adviser, the ICU managed, through my personal efforts, to organize African employees at the Johannesburg General Post Office. Representations were made to W. B. Madeley, the Minister of Posts and Telegraphs. I led this deputation to the Minister. The ICU members employed at the General Post Office had their conditions vastly improved, although wage advances were not made. The result of this interview with the Minister brought about a Cabinet crisis. The Prime Minister, General Hertzog, resigned in order to reshuffle his Government, leaving Madeley out of the Cabinet. As the chief actor in this connection, I consider this drama as one of my major achievements on the political stage of South Africa.[2]

In 1929 the ICU had been in existence for ten years. During all this time my name was known both nationally and internationally. Many leading Europeans in South Africa did not like the idea of my domination of the political scene as far as the Africans were concerned. A meeting of the National Council was convened in Johannesburg early in 1929 at which Ballinger suggested the reshuffling of the national officials of the Union. I was asked to assume the duties of organizing secretary, instead of my position as chief executive officer of the organization since its inception. The meeting lasted the whole day because I firmly refused to accept Ballinger's offer. It was about 5 p.m. when I decided to relieve the members of the council, who clearly seemed to see some injustice in Ballinger's suggestion, but could not decide of their own free will. So I tendered my resignation as general secretary.

To me personally this event was serious and important. As soon as the news appeared in the press, I received telegrams and letters from all over South Africa, where branches of the ICU existed, sympathizing with me in my humiliation, while at the same time calling upon me to ignore the decision of the National Council and to carry on. The Johannesburg and Reef branches took a definite lead in expressing strong opposition to the council's attitude. Instead of addressing our usual Sunday afternoon meeting I decided to leave Johannesburg for Lourenço Marques over the week-end to ponder over my future plans. In my absence a huge meeting of the entire membership of Johannesburg and of the Reef branches adopted a unanimous resolution of loyalty towards me, at the same time asking me to form an Independent ICU. I accepted this call, and upon my return from Lourenço Marques opened another office. This decision meant the frustration of those who plotted to antagonize me with the African peoples whom I had led so well and on whose behalf I had sacrificed myself since the 17th day of January, 1919.

By 1929 the ICU had split into three sections: (1) The ICU of Africa which supported Ballinger; (2) The ICU of Natal which followed Champion, and which concentrated itself in Durban; and (3) the Independent ICU which followed me and which secured the largest number of adherents from its former ICU members throughout South Africa. To further the interests of the Independent ICU we established an official organ which was styled *New Africa*. This journal was edited both by me and by my able colleague, H. D. Tyamzashe. Gradually the Ballinger ICU totally disappeared from the scene, and at the time this book is being written the ICU of Natal is also reported to be defunct. I have managed to keep alive the section of the ICU which followed my leadership, with East London, in the Cape Province, as its stronghold as well as its headquarters. Apart from East London we have an active branch at King William's Town, while the Pretoria and Bloemfontein branches, although in existence, show little or no active work so far.

NOTES

1. (p. 178) Yet Kadalie wrote to Winifred Holtby on August 1, 1928, 'Mr. Ballinger is now two weeks with us and he has given us satisfaction already. You could not have made a better choice. In such a short space of time, he has won many friends for the ICU. You sent him at the right moment'. Quoted by Johns, MS. p. 52.
2. (p. 180) The Prime Minister, General Hertzog, had indicated to members of his cabinet that he was unwilling to have them negotiate with the ICU. Madeley had, however, let it be known that he would be willing to have discussions with the ICU

if they met under the auspices of the South African Trade Union Congress. W. H. Andrews, as secretary of the South African Trade Union Congress, acted as an intermediary and the ICU officials accompanied him in meeting Madeley. Roux claims that Hertzog's decision to exclude Madeley from the Cabinet did not stem entirely from his inability to appreciate that Madeley had not met the ICU delegates in their own right. In 1928, with an election imminent, the Labour Party was split between those who thought the Labour Members of Parliament, including the three Cabinet Ministers, should be responsible to the National Council of the Party, and those who accepted that the Parliamentary Party should act independently. Madeley was the only Cabinet Minister to support the National Council's view and Hertzog had to decide which faction to support. The problem was solved for Hertzog by Madeley's meeting the ICU representatives. Roux, *Time Longer than Rope*, p. 182.

CHAPTER XIII

General Strike at East London

WITH the assistance of our official organ, *New Africa*, the Independent ICU was becoming stronger all the time, while Ballinger and his followers on the other hand encountered strong demands from the rank and file of the ICU all over the country asking for an explanation why their leader, Kadalie, had resigned. It was a job that neither Ballinger nor his followers could explain to the satisfaction of the inquisitive and shrewd African audiences. At the close of 1929 the Independent ICU had solidified its activities throughout the country. It was therefore found necessary to bring branches together in a conference which met at East London. In January 1930 delegates came from the Transvaal, Orange Free State and the Cape Province, including the Transkeian Territory. East London is the home of T. B. Lujiza, who had succeeded me as general secretary of the ICU of Africa under Ballinger.

Our conference at East London was a success, and adopted many resolutions, one being to approach the Railways and Harbours Administration for a minimum wage of 6s. 6d. per day for unskilled labourers employed by it at East London. The demand for the increased wage was sent to the Railway Administration while our conference was in session. As was expected, the Railways refused to negotiate with our union. The conference in session therefore had no alternative but to call out its members on strike, firstly in the harbour, and then over the whole railway system at East London.

It was on January 16, 1930, at a public meeting on the location recreation ground that the strike was officially announced. At the same time strike rules were drafted and read out and interpreted at this meeting. One of the strike rules was that all members

N

on strike were not to partake of any intoxicating liquor whatsoever while the strike was in progress. The carrying of sticks or
lethal weapons was also forbidden; the strikers were forbidden
to roam about in the city streets during the strike; and they are
all instructed to gather in the location and take exercises in sports
and various games. These injunctions, I am pleased to record,
the strikers strictly obeyed. For a week the railways and harbours'
strike was a complete success. Ships were lying idle in the harbour, but the authorities did not sit idle either. They brought in
Zulu labourers from Durban who were kept in complete
ignorance when they embarked that they were to scab on their
fellow African workers at East London. When the Zulus found
that the harbour was deserted, they became suspicious and refused
to work. The result was that they were transported back to
Durban.

Meanwhile our members, who were now reinforced by our
African women members (some of them attired in male garb),
began to visit the harbour to pull out local scabs. Strike meetings
were held twice daily in the morning and afternoon in the East
Bank location (now called Duncan Village). It was at these meetings that the strike committee daily announced the progress of
the strike. When it was found that the Railways and Harbours
Administration were adamant in refusing to negotiate, it was
decided by the strike committee to call out members and workers
in other industries and commerce in a sympathetic general strike.
By the second week a general strike was in progress, which
paralysed the whole industrial and commercial system of East
London. The general strike was now complete, as all domestic
workers in hotels and private homes came out. From the city men
and women trekked in orderly manner towards the East Bank
location. I must admit that we were surprised with the complete-
ness of the general strike, which I was called upon to conduct.
The city was now in total confusion, and some people, particularly Coloureds and Indians, thought it was unsafe to stay any
longer in the city. Strike meetings were now being attended by
thousands of people.

As usual the South African police were very active from the
first day of the strike. Aeroplanes flew overhead when strike
meetings were in progress. A European civilian of East London

many years later told me that he was one who piloted some of the machines during the strike, and that he used to see me clearly standing on a lorry addressing the crowd. Police reinforcements were rushed to East London by special trains from all parts of South Africa. At the boundary between the location and the city, military vehicles were parked to transport armed police quickly as required. I remember vividly one Thursday afternoon when I was at the head of a demonstration of the strikers from the location to the sports ground, an ugly situation was narrowly averted by my timely action in diverting the direction of our demonstration as the armed police deliberately marched towards our column.

At night, special civil volunteer police patrolled the location streets. It was then that I decided to disguise myself during the night so that few could identify me. I remember also one evening on my way from the strike committee head-quarters to a certain house where I had arranged to put up for the night, I was accosted by one of the volunteer police who enquired if I knew Kadalie, saying, 'If only I could meet him during the night, I would not hesitate to shoot him, as he is the man responsible for us volunteers staying away from our homes at night.' Needless to say, I walked hurriedly away from this would-be assassin.

Saddest of all, there was a minister of religion among these police volunteers, who shouldered a rifle to shoot at defenceless African men and women strikers whenever the order was given, although in this case it was fortunately not given.

While the strike was in progress, some people, particularly from the African side, led by Dr. W. B. Rubusana and the Reverend Alfred Petros of the Anglican church, tried to contact the railways and harbours authorities to effect mediation, but their worthy efforts did not materialize. As has always been the case, the Government of the Union of South Africa has a large agency of its own, employing non-European labour. In every strike of non-European labour where our Union Government is directly concerned, its attitude had been to employ military force to suppress such strikes. We have many examples to prove this charge. We saw force used in connection with the Port Elizabeth riots in 1920; the Bulhoek tragedy near Queenstown; the Cape

Town dock strike in 1919; at Durban in 1929; and as lately as 1946 in the brutal smashing up of the African mine-workers' strike in Johannesburg.

As is known, I had conducted a previous big strike at Cape Town Docks where I had received my industrial baptism. I was therefore in a position to weigh the present events carefully. Special trains from other parts of the country were pouring into East London, bringing in police reinforcements in large numbers, as if military operations were contemplated. I then suggested to the strike committee to send a telegram to the Minister of Justice, who at the time was Oswald Pirow. But this telegram had no effect at all. Instead of giving consideration to our protest, some high officials from Grahamstown and Pretoria were rushed to East London. We were told (after everything was over) that these high officials had decided on my arrest, but this was ruled out by the then district commandant of police at East London, who thought the general strike would be continued by the other eight members of the strike committee. Eventually it was agreed to rope in the whole strike committee.

When the decision to arrest the entire strike committee was decided upon, we were informed (after the event) that the authorities had another problem to solve. It was this: *would they dare arrest us in the East Bank Location.* At Durban, in Natal, another shooting affair had just taken place towards the close of 1929. Therefore would another massacre follow so soon after at East London? Someone had a brainwave. It was the district commandant of the South African police at East London, who was then Major Lloyd Lister. He suggested that he should write to me a personal letter inviting me to see him at the central police station in the city. He had told his colleagues that Kadalie was a decent and reasonable person, and that he would come along if a courteous letter was sent to him. The letter in question was phrased as follows by Major Lloyd Lister: 'I shall be pleased if you will call on me today before 11 a.m., together with your strike committee. Kindly inform bearer when to expect you.' A European sergeant of police delivered the letter to me in the location while I was on a visit to Dr. Rubusana. When this letter was read to the members of the strike committee, a spirit of optimism prevailed among them, but, as an old warrior, I had my grave doubts about the invitation. I had read about the deportation of European strike leaders in 1913 on the Rand, who were suddenly summoned from their homes and then put on a train at Germiston station secretly and soon found themselves in Durban aboard a liner for England. My colleagues, apparently some of them at least, did not know this story. Instead, they were exceptionally happy, and some even expressed a desire to change into their best clothes.

When the rest of the strike committee went to change their clothes, I went in James Dweni's car. This was one of the first cars driven by an African owner. Dweni was just an ordinary member of the ICU. We passed the General Post Office where we collected our post from the box we rented. Some of the letters contained postal orders and cheques from various parts of the country towards our strike fund. When we reached the central police station, everything on the surface appeared quiet and normal. Nevertheless it was the biggest camouflage one ever experienced. As soon as we reached the police station we were politely ushered into the district commandant's office, where he requested us to sit down. A packet of a hundred cigarettes was passed round, with the remark by the district commandant, 'Let us all smoke the pipe of peace'. When we were all smoking, the district commandant asked me when the other members of the strike committee would turn up. He was informed that they were following presently in another car. I was at the time a vicious smoker, so I continued with my smoking, expecting some good news that the district commandant would convey, since the week just ended was full of various wild rumours.

The district commandant began to speak to us politely at first, presumably so that we should not suspect a sinister action on his part. He then uttered these words: 'You see, Kadalie, a strike is sometimes a bad thing. Someone would injure your child who might attend a strike meeting in curiosity.' Thereupon he pulled out the drawer of his desk, took out a large-sized revolver, levelled it at my forehead and shouted, 'Hands up, you are now my prisoners.' Thereafter his face was transformed into frenzied fury, while the armed police rushed into his office and placed their handcuffs on all of us, most savagely, as if we had attempted to resist arrest. In such a short brutal drama the 'pipe of peace' had been replaced by the most vicious hell in a district commandant's office of boasted civilized South Africa.

After bawling loudly like a perfect savage that we had been keeping him out of sleep for over a fortnight as a result of the strike, while at the same time we did not realize the might of his government, he asked me whether I had anything to say. I replied that I was surprised at this untoward action, since I never expected this brutal and unprovoked treatment. We had conducted a peaceful strike, but the district commandant had used brute force. The court would decide. So I had, therefore, no more to say at this juncture.

This was my darkest hour, but I strove to behave like an African warrior. We were all handcuffed as if we were ordinary criminals. The police, who handcuffed us in the presence of their chief, the district commandant, behaved like savages. On my left hand there is still a mark which reminds me all the time of the brutal act of the South African police. I had not known prison before; this was my first experience at the hands of the South African police. But the drama was not complete! The district commandant asked me again about the next car carrying more strike committee members. This car came in just when the first drama was being completed. As soon as our comrades entered the district commandant's office, I at once warned them to respond to any orders given to them. Whereupon without further ado they were also handcuffed. We were then marched out into the big police yard and from thence outside to a waiting military lorry, wide open and too high for us to get on, since we were singly handcuffed. The inhuman police, who were now swearing at us in Afrikaans, deliberately threw us on to the big lorry, unmindful of whether we were hurt or not. The district commandant came out, witnessed this brutal conduct of his men towards us, and finally drove on a police motor cycle in front of the lorry, while behind us other police cyclists followed. As we were quite ignorant of our destination, we struck up the tune of 'The Red Flag', which we sang as beautifully that Sunday morning as if it were sung in the halls of the Moscow we then imagined. Within a few minutes we found ourselves at the gates of the East London gaol in 'Lock Street'. The gaol gates were already wide open in anticipation of its new important guests.

Inside the gaol the district commandant uttered some more 'peaceful' language stating that we were his 'political prisoners' and that he had made arrangements for our good treatment while awaiting trial. He told us that we could arrange for food to be sent to us from the location. He left us with two packets of C to C cigarettes of 100 each, with some boxes of matches. Thus the South African police deliberately selected a sacred day (Sunday) to demonstrate its brutal force—the force that has kept the African nation in subjection for 300 years![1]

The authorities had decided to keep our arrest a secret affair, but the Africans already knew that we were under arrest on that very Sunday morning. While I was at the police station I pleaded for the release of James Dweni, our driver, as he was not a member of the strike committee. The district commandant acquiesced with the request, but Dweni was kept at the police station while the operation was on to remove us to the local gaol. I also pleaded for the release of my brother, Robert Victor Kadalie, who was not a member of the strike committee, but it was pointed out that Robert had affixed his own name to the list of the strike committee, which was found in our offices, and as such the police held that he accepted responsibility for all the actions of the strike committee.

After we had been securely lodged in prison, the police striking force turned into the location in order to break the general strike. The first action taken by the police on entering the location was to raid the ICU offices. We learned afterwards that a serious situation developed there. Our members did not permit the police to remove our books, etc., so easily, but since the police were fully armed and prepared, they managed to take every document and all books from our offices. My personal papers, including my passport to Europe in 1927, were among the papers removed by the police. I have been unable to recover my passport and a post office savings bank book from the police, in spite of repeated requests for the return of these personal effects.

When the strike was at its peak a local African minister of the Wesleyan church, the Rev. Makaluza, wrote a letter to the *Daily Dispatch*, the East London daily paper, condemning the strike. It was naturally concluded by the strikers that our arrest and the subsequent raid on our offices in the location were due to the

Rev. Makaluza's letter in the press. The strikers decided therefore that a dose of physical punishment on the minister would be an appropriate measure. During the confusion of the police raids at our offices on that memorable Sunday morning a number of young male strikers went to the Wesleyan church for the purpose of visiting the Rev. Makaluza, whom the police had already removed from the location for safety. In his absence some of the young hot-heads of the ICU attempted to set fire to the Wesleyan church, but the fire was quickly put out by the police, while the whole location was in a confused condition.

On the Monday following our arrest we appeared in court before the magistrate, who at the time was D. L. Smit (later chairman of the Native Affairs Commission). No evidence was led against us, and we were remanded in custody. During our preparatory examination the court house was invariably heavily guarded by police armed with a machine-gun. The general strike had apparently transformed the traditional spirit of the English-speaking people of East London, for the legal firms were unwilling to undertake our defence. Under these circumstances we asked the district commandant of the South African police to get into touch, on our behalf, with Advocate Will Stuart, at the time an M.P., at Grahamstown, who hurried to East London during the first week of our ordeal. On reaching East London, Stuart got into touch with the prosecution, who informed him that the Crown was not prepared to grant any bail to the prisoners. This information Stuart conveyed to us at the local gaol on the day of his arrival. He promised us, however, that he would arrange the matter of our bail in the Supreme Court at Grahamstown.

With his departure for Grahamstown on that Saturday afternoon, Stuart left us in a state of hopeless speculation. During that week-end I prepared my notes in gaol as a basis for my application for bail on the following Monday. I did not consult any of my fellow-prisoners about my intention. When Monday came, the court was again crowded to the point of suffocation. The magistrate, as usual, called upon the public prosecutor to lead his evidence, but this official informed the court that the Crown's investigations were not completed, and asked for another remand. As a result of this I caught the eye of the presiding magistrate. 'Accused Number One' (Clements Kadalie) began by saying,

'May it please your worship, I have the honour to apply for bail on behalf of myself and the other eight accused.' I began my address slowly, in a clear voice, and said that I was surprised that in a court of British justice bail is refused to prisoners who have not been arraigned with very serious charges such as murder or high treason. In support of my application I quoted cases in the manner a barrister would do. I first quoted Rex versus H. Selby Msimang at Bloemfontein in 1919, where a disturbance took place resulting in some loss of life, but bail was allowed to Msimang. I then quoted another case in support of my application, viz., Rex versus Samuel Masabalala, who was arrested in 1920 as a result of rioting in Market Square at Port Elizabeth when over twenty people were shot and killed. In this case also bail was granted to Masabalala. As I went on I got 'warmed up' on the course of quoting other legal authorities, to the astonishment of the crowded court. Briefly, I had managed to capture the sympathy of the bench by my unexpected address.

I concluded my speech by stating that there was no evidence of violence whatsoever, or any death, during the strike, and that the court was asked to grant all the prisoners bail. It appeared that this short address had left a profound impression upon the court. Thereupon the presiding magistrate called on the public prosecutor to reply to the application. In reply, this court official said that he had strict instructions to oppose bail being granted. The magistrate then told the prosecutor that since 'Number One Accused' (meaning, of course, myself, as we were all numbered) had quoted legal authorities, he, the magistrate, was prepared to allow all the accused bail which was subsequently fixed as follows: Clements Kadalie and Alexander Maduna £200 each; H. D. Tyamzashe, Philemon Fetsha, Joel Magade, Robert Kadalie, Alfred Mnika, Dorrington Mqayi and Peter Mkwambi £100 each.

While our preliminary examination was in progress on a certain day, to our astonishment as prisoners, we noticed the district commandant of the police hurriedly enter the court-room and with haste whisper something to the presiding magistrate, after which the magistrate, in terrific haste and without any decorum, jumped from his chair and ran towards the exit of the court. Immediately after this our turn came and we were unceremoniously rushed out of court right into the 'Black Maria' outside, and within a few seconds we found ourselves back in gaol, without knowing the reason why. This happened at about 9.30 a.m. The true story of this unorthodox behaviour was first told to us after our release at Grahamstown about three months later. It appears that while our preparatory examination was in progress, the majority of the strikers refused to return to their places of employment as a protest against our arrest. By common consent they camped out on the location recreation ground day and night. The police, on the other hand, were determined to exact their authority, and decided on the prosecution of some of the strikers for location passes (or permits, as these badges of slavery are politely called). About a dozen strikers were arrested for not being in possession of these location permits. When the majority of the strikers heard of what had taken place, they decided by resolution to march in an orderly manner to the court-house to approach the authorities with a request to release those arrested for these permits, failing which the strikers were prepared, as a whole, to join their friends in gaol together with us. The procession from the location to the city was very long and wide.

It was this orderly procession that caused the district commandant of the police to whisper to the presiding magistrate and which resulted in the disruption of the proceedings in court on this memorable day. We learned afterwards that the police were of opinion that the demonstration was an attempt to rescue the strike leaders from custody while at the court-house. The leaders of the demonstration were, however, permitted to interview the chief magistrate, with the result that those men and women who were arrested for failing to possess location permits were released forthwith unconditionally. In the afternoon we were brought back to court, where we were all committed for trial.

The city was still in a state of confusion because all Africans had not yet returned to work. I was permitted by the authorities to address the strikers from an upstairs window of the court-house. I informed the strikers that with our arrest as a strike committee, they no longer had any leader, and with the absence of such leadership mistakes might be made unknowingly which might ultimately involve them in conflict with the police. I strongly advised them to resume work.

In conformity with the statement made to us by the district commandant of police on the day we were locked up, the gaol authorities permitted us to receive our food from the location. Three meals a day were sent to us. Dishes sent to us were numerous and very delicious. We had chicken, legs of mutton, vegetables, fruit galore, puddings of every conceivable make (as we had grand native cooks from hotels and boarding-houses to care for us, who were also on strike). Yes, we were 'political prisoners', our stay in gaol was not so bad. The food that came to us was much too much for the nine of us, so that we gave some of it to the non-European prisoners, who were indeed most grateful to us. From outside our members also delivered to us cigarettes of various brands and baskets of seasonal fruit, including rich cakes. As we were nine prisoners in all, we occupied two cells between us, and in each cell food could be found at any hour of the day or night. Newspapers were also allowed us. It was while we were in gaol that we read of the visit to South Africa of George Bernard Shaw, the famous playwright.

While in East London gaol I became ill. A doctor was summoned one evening to examine me. When I entered the office of the gaol superintendent, I noticed a bottle of whisky and glasses on the table. Somebody evidently had had a good time. I was hurriedly examined and declared to be suffering from diphtheria. The doctor informed me, however, that he would send my swab to a Johannesburg laboratory for certification. That was the end of that alleged diphtheria case! As I was addicted to liquor at the time, I thought to myself that it would have been far better had the doctor offered me a glass of whisky, instead of making a fool of himself!

When our bail was fixed by the court, our members and sympathizers offered to place their houses as sureties for our bail, but the police refused to accept such arrangements, although this procedure was in vogue for many years before the strike. However, when we went back to gaol after our successful application for bail, most of us expected that in a matter of hours we would be set free. The following morning, however, after our bail was fixed by the court, I heard my name being called very loudly. I was ordered to take all my belongings, which consisted of what I daily wore, including my dressing-gown, which was sent to me from the location. While I was proceeding towards the gaol office inside the precincts of the gaol, another order was given for the eight others to come out as well. The main entrance to the gaol was standing wide open. But, alas, here was 'Black Maria' again, into which we were thrown neck and crop.

The van was completely sealed, so we had no idea where we were being despatched now. We learned afterwards that we were motored through Quigney near the beach area. Finally we found ourselves at Summerpride railway siding about five miles from the city. As usual the district commandant of the police escorted us, riding on his motor cycle. At about 11 a.m. the East London-Port Elizabeth passenger train drew up at the above-named siding. We saw a brand-new third-class passenger coach attached to this train, and into this coach we were all bundled. The coach window blinds were drawn so that it was impossible for us to see whither we were going or who were at the various stations *en route*. We were all handcuffed in pairs. We had two European sergeants and numerous European and Native police as our guards. In the compartment we found fresh loaves of bread, one for each of us, and also two new blankets of the army pattern for each of us. The two European sergeants were fairly kind to us, as they were both Englishmen. After their pension they both settled permanently at East London, and are still friendly towards me.

Meanwhile in the train we were heading to an unknown destination. I approached the sergeants to enquire where we were being spirited away, but it was only at 6 o'clock in the evening that I was informed by them that we were being sent to Grahamstown because the authorities at East London did not trust the local Africans, as they might make an attempt to rescue us from gaol by force. The next morning we reached Grahamstown, where we were lodged in the local gaol. We at once arranged with a well-known African family to supply us with food from outside, as was the case at East London.

On the day of our arrival at Grahamstown, Will Stuart came to the gaol and had a long interview with us. He told us that bail would be considerably reduced, but that he had some fear in regard to Alexander Maduna, who was second in command to me, and who had a previous bad police record at Maritzburg, Natal. When Maduna was told of this by Stuart, he broke into tears. We had a big job to pacify him. Stuart was very anxious for our welfare; so without any delay he arranged with the solicitor-general to argue for the reduction of our bail at once before the Judge-President of the Eastern Province Division of the Supreme Court, who at the time was Sir Thomas Graham. Consequently our bail was considerably reduced: Clements Kadalie and Alexander Maduna £50 cash and £50 on their own recognizances; H. D. Tyamzashe, Philemon Fetsha, Joel Magade, Dorrington Mqayi, Robert Kadalie, Peter Mkwambi and Alfred Mnika £25 cash and £25 on their own recognizances. The judge-president, however, made strong criticism of the police (the Crown) for fixing such a high figure in the case of Africans. He also made strong comment on the fact that the gravity of the case did not warrant such high bail. In reducing the bail, the court laid down as conditions that no public meetings were to be addressed by us while awaiting trial, and that those of the accused who did not originally reside at East London should proceed direct to their homes.

I was the first to come out of gaol on the very day the reduction of bail was granted; Mrs. Will Stuart actually paid for my bail. On being liberated I immediately communicated with our people at East London by telephone, and this resulted in Tyamzashe and Mqayi being liberated the following day. We were allowed third-class tickets to proceed to our homes. Both Tyamzashe and I managed to raise funds to transfer our third-class tickets to second-class to Johannesburg. For this aid I may say with gratitude that we were financially assisted by the late Gilbert Tyamzashe, who was then court interpreter at Grahamstown. So we once again breathed the air of freedom after being in gaol for two months.

While in custody some of us made a voluntary vow that we would not cut our hair or shave our beards until we were liberated. The result was that I had grown such a bushy beard that my wife could hardly recognize me when I arrived home in Johannesburg, especially as I entered through the back door. I was indeed ashamed to find myself in such a deplorable and unsociable state for, besides having grown a bushy beard, I had no decent clothes or shoes on, as all my ordinary clothes were left at East London. The reader will remember that during the strike I used to disguise myself at nights. Therefore, when we were arrested I was still wearing the clothes I used for this purpose. Anyway, my wardrobe at home held some other suitable clothes into which I was able to change and become a presentable citizen once more.

Our trial at Grahamstown Supreme Court before Mr. Justice Gutsche lasted a month. The chief Crown witnesses were the district commandant of police (East London), detective-sergeant Mandy and Captain Myers, who was a reporter on the staff of the *Daily Dispatch* at the time. In addition there were African police witnesses for the Crown. When detective Mandy took his stand in the witness-box, I made a suggestion to Advocate Stuart, to put him to a severe cross-examination. I had heard detective Mandy speak the Xhosa language, but he never impressed me as a competent linguist. I suggested, therefore, that his knowledge of the Xhosa language be put to the test now that he was under oath. With this object in view we got one of the accused (Alexander Maduna) who was a good Xhosa speaker, and one of our best Xhosa interpreters during the strike while I was addressing meetings, to write down a Xhosa phrase, which we privately translated for the information of our counsel. At an appropriate moment during the course of his evidence Stuart passed the phrase to Mandy to read out the phrase loud for the benefit of the court, and at the same time he should give its English version. Mandy became helpless, while the learned judge ordered him sternly to comply, but he had to admit now that he was unable to read the phrase or to give its interpretation in English. Thus, owing to this legal strategy, the famous detective's chief evidence collapsed, as far as those speeches which were made in Xhosa were concerned. Both our counsel and attorney complimented me during the usual interview on this smart legal achievement.

When my time came to enter the witness-box, the court was crowded with European spectators. Even the students of Rhodes University, dressed in their gowns, visited the court. The trial was now interesting because there was no interpreting, all my evidence being given in English. I occupied the witness-box for nearly a week. I must say that the solicitor-general was very severe with me. Some of the silly questions he put to me were like this: 'Now, Kadalie, you came down all the way from

Nyasaland: can you tell this court what you have done for the natives of this country?' I promptly informed him about the minimum wages of 8s., 9s., and 12s. 6d. per day at the Cape Town docks which were brought about by my initiative. I also mentioned moneys sent by the ICU in connection with the Port Elizabeth riots in 1920, as well as other moneys sent to Queenstown during Enoch Mgijima's tragedy at Bulhoek. It was through my efforts in the ICU that the Union Government for the first time appointed a Coloured person, Dr. A. Abdurahman, who was an MPC, to the Commission of Inquiry into the Port Elizabeth riots. While I was proceeding to enumerate some of my achievements, the prosecuting solicitor-general disgustedly retorted and asked if I could tell him what I had done for the Nyasaland Africans at my birthplace. Here I scored heavily in my reply, directing the attention of the Court to my activities while overseas in London during 1927.

In the course of my lengthy reply the solicitor-general interrupted me and said that he was not interested in my mentioning matters outside South Africa. The presiding judge, however, ruled that I could continue with my statement, since I was asked to inform the Court about what I had done for both South Africa and Nyasaland. During this period both my counsel and attorney were apparently pleased with my replies, which made the solicitor-general look rather stupid at times, since the learned judge was obviously interested in this evidence.

After all nine accused had given evidence, the solicitor-general addressed the court. We had elected to be tried by a judge without a jury. In his address to the court the solicitor-general argued that all the accused were guilty of the crime of inciting to public violence under the Riotous Assemblies Act, in that we conducted a general strike. The solicitor-general was followed by Will Stuart, who occupied a day and a half in his address in reply. I should have mentioned the fact that Stuart was ably assisted by Mrs. Stuart, who sat next to her husband during the trial. Stuart's job was enormous, as he had to analyse all the evidence of the Crown witnesses, as well as that of our own. He was also quite aware of the fact that the police were very anxious to obtain a major conviction against me personally to afford them the opportunity of deporting me from the Union of South Africa.

In his peroration counsel said emotionally, with tears glistening in his eyes: 'My Lord, you are sitting there as judge and jury. This is a big case which should have been handled by King's Counsel, with myself as junior counsel. I have done my very best, however, in presenting to Your Lordship the case of these nine men in the dock, and where I have omitted anything, I shall rely upon the fair play of our distinguished Court.' When Will Stuart resumed his seat, one could feel that he had made a very important plea on behalf of all the accused, particularly in my own case as leader of the general strike, for the Crown had worked hard to obtain a major conviction. After Stuart's address the learned judge postponed judgment until the following day.

In a lengthy and well-considered judgment, the Hon. Mr. Justice Gutsche analysed the evidence of both the Crown and the defence in detail. The judge had a clear and loud voice, which was heard clearly throughout the big court. He dealt with each indictment, the whole of which consisted of 116 charges, and in each of which I figured as an accessory because of the fact that I was the leader. One by one the learned judge disposed of the various indictments. After a clarifying indictment of each indictment, he would say, 'I find the accused Not Guilty'. This phrase went on as each succeeding indictment was examined and disposed of. This made the solicitor-general, the East London police and their kind, look somewhat shamefully amazed. The process went on for more than an hour; it was only when the last charge was dealt with that the learned judge addressed me in person. He said that on one account I had used the words: 'If the scabs go to work on Monday, we shall give them a damned good lesson by sjambokking them.' The judge said that since Advocate Stuart, my counsel, had led no evidence on this point to explain to the court the meaning underlying the phrase, he found me guilty and sentenced me to three months' hard labour, or a fine of £25.

When this sentence was passed on me, I was not sorry at all, but rather proud, for the leader must suffer for the sake of his followers. Indeed, I felt more than proud when my eight comrades left me in the dock alone. It was better that I bear the penalty instead of one of the lesser ones of my colleagues. The fine was paid there and then, and all nine of us left the court as a victorious team after such a grim and strenuous battle and experience. The East London police contingent that went to Grahamstown, causing the Union Government to shoulder such heavy expenditure, looked somewhat humiliated as a result of our victory. Of the 116 counts arraigned against us, we won on 115. We all came to the conclusion that the learned judge was, in my case, very kind to the Crown when he found me guilty simply because my learned counsel did not explain the metaphor 'sjambok', and not on one of the supposedly serious and inflammatory speeches I was alleged to have made during the strike.

The month-long trial ended in our vindication. Outside the court at Grahamstown was the same driver, James Dweni, and his car, who took us to the East London charge office in Fleet Street on the day of our arrest. There was also a bus that the ICU had hired to convey some of our rank and file to Grahamstown to attend our trial. Before noon after the day of the judgment the two vehicles set out triumphantly for East London with the occupants singing gloriously 'Nkosi sikelela i Afrika' (God Bless Africa), and 'The Red Flag'. All along the route to East London we were celebrating this great victory with all kinds of refreshments. We reached East London at 5 p.m. to find a huge meeting awaiting us. After our five months' absence we found the members and the residents of East London coming to the meeting in their thousands. As I climbed on the wagon platform there was such vociferous cheering as was, perhaps, never heard before at East London. Poor detective-sergeant Mandy happened to attend the meeting, but I was now the great hero of East London among our own people. My oratory on this occasion, after five months' silence, was in jubilant vein in denouncing detective-sergeant Mandy, who, the reader will remember, was the chief Crown witness. I denounced the methods used by Mandy and his chief, the district commandant of the police, on the day we were arrested. The meeting closed amidst scenes of great enthusiasm.

NOTE TO PAGE 189

1. The district commandant invited us to a peaceful conference virtually under a white flag. I have always considered this action on the part of Major Lloyd Lister, district com-

mandant, as unBritish and mean in the extreme. It would have been a more manly act on his part had he gone to the location with his armed police to arrest me and my fellow members of the strike committee on the spot for which I would have respected him more had he done so, instead of acting the part he did.—C.K.

CHAPTER XIV

Right to Reside

AFTER our cordial and most enthusiastic reception at East London, my colleagues, Maduna and Tyamzashe, returned with me to Johannesburg where we were then domiciled. As we were now once more free men, we embarked upon a campaign to acquaint our membership and the public in general on the Rand and Pretoria about our persecution and prosecution at East London. My first public utterance was delivered at Pretoria. This meeting was well advertised by the distribution of handbills which attracted a huge crowd, including both uniformed police and special men of the CID from headquarters in Pretoria. The meeting was quite orderly, but cheered me throughout my speech. I was given a great ovation on rising to address the meeting. Whenever the occasion was big I used to take off my coat in order to enable me to move freely on the platform while pressing important pronouncements home. Indeed, sometimes I used to knock out my interpreters when 'heated' during some of my big orations. When the meeting terminated I motored with friends to the railway station in order to catch a train for Johannesburg.

At the station entrance I was stopped by a well-dressed European gentleman who introduced himself as an inspector of the Criminal Investigation Department. He handed me a document which read as follows:

'I, Oswald Pirow, Minister of Justice, do hereby declare you, Clements Kadalie, prohibited under Section I of Act 27 of 1914 of the Riotous Assemblies Act to attend or address public meetings in the district of the Witwatersrand, viz., from Springs to Randfontein, including the district of Pretoria, for a period of six months from date hereof'.

I argued with the CID officer that I could not accept the document as bearing the name and signature of Mr. Pirow himself as required by the Act, as I was not acquainted with the Minister's handwriting. A witness was obtained then and there, who certified under oath that the signature on the order was Mr. Pirow's handwriting.

With the ban effective I decided not to stay in Johannesburg, but to proceed to another centre where I could employ my public activities. With the approval of my wife I proceeded to East London, to find out on the spot whether we could make our home there. The East London executive committee of the ICU welcomed me wholeheartedly. I found that the branch committee had already purchased a car for my use, which was christened *'Ntshabaziwile'*—meaning literally, 'the enemies have fallen'. After a short stay at East London, in December 1930 I returned to Johannesburg in this car, in order to bring my wife and son down to East London, where we were now destined to make our new and permanent home.

On my arrival in Johannesburg, which was on Dingaan's Day, 1930, my wife told me that the Communist Party, which had organized a public demonstration, came to our house in Doornfontein, after they had destroyed some documents in the ICU office, which was situated near the house. The Communist hooligans (as I am unable to find any other term to describe people who employ such violent methods) threatened my wife with violence when they found that I was absent from the house. The police, however, drove them away before they had time to inflict injury on my wife and son. (Here I may add in parenthesis that the attack by the Communists on my family should be ample proof that I have absolutely no connection with them; yet in almost all official centres I am still looked upon as a rabid Communist.) The Communists were annoyed with me because they believed I had, at Bloemfontein and elsewhere, opposed their pass-burning campaign, which was supposed to culminate on that same Dingaan's Day.

During my stay in Johannesburg I was well established there, for I did not come under pass laws, but the restrictions now imposed on me by the Government under the Riotous Assemblies Act made it imperative for me to seek pastures new. Towards the end of December 1930 I left the Golden City by car with my wife and son for East London, where we have lived to this day, and where this book has been prepared and written. To sum up: The year 1930 witnessed our cruel arrest at East London; our trial in the Supreme Court at Grahamstown; and my prohibition to address or attend any public meeting on the Witwatersrand, including Pretoria; as well as our taking up a new home at East London. The beginning of 1931 found me at Bloemfontein, where I attended the non-European conference under the presidency of Dr. Abdurahman, MPC. In my diary dated January 6, 1931, I wrote thus: 'Non-European conference in full swing. I led the opposition when delegates were discussing non-European Unity. I took up the stand that it was useless for Dr. Abdurahman and his Coloured delegates to talk of non-European unity at Bloemfontein, whereas at Cape Town and Kimberley they never encouraged me and the ICU when we put into practice non-European unity, since our membership consisted of both the African and Coloured workers. I characterized their attitude at Bloemfontein as rank hypocrisy. On the closing of the conference I returned to East London.'

During the time T. B. Lujiza was provincial secretary of the ICU for the Border and Transkei, our Union was sought after by the Africans in the territories. As a matter of fact we had two branches in these territories which clamoured for my personal visit. We tried hard to obtain permission from the authorities during Lujiza's régime, but this was never granted. In 1931, however, it was decided to visit Lady Grey, which is situated outside the Transkei proper. We had a branch of the ICU there, and when we reached the place we were welcomed by Harry Mangcu, who was practising as a law-agent at Lady Frere. We travelled by car via Queenstown. At the time I did not fully realize that our journey and mission were known to the police authorities. I discovered later from the members of the ICU executive committee and its officials that we had some police informers in our ranks who reported every movement of ours.

It rained heavily during our trip through the Transkeian territories, so that all rivers were in spate. We travelled by night from Lady Frere, reaching Tsomo during the early hours of the morning. At Tsomo the river had swept over the bridge leaving a deep layer of mud in which our car got stuck. We had a big job to clear the mud and sand from the road. On both sides of the bridge cars halted and the owners watched our predicament. In the village of Tsomo itself there were two Coloured brothers who happened to know me. They gave us every assistance, as they were both mechanics. With their mechanical help our car was extracted from the bridge, setting us free to move into the heart of the Transkei. We had previously arranged to address a meeting at Kentani where we had a good branch of the ICU. About a mile and a half away from the Tsomo bridge we heard the piercing sound of a motor-hooter, and the car that was hooting was running at over 50 miles an hour. As it approached us, our driver gave way for it to pass, but it suddenly halted and a police sergeant got out, lifted his hand and ordered us to stop. He boastfully told us that he knew who we were and that he was arresting us for entering the Transkei illegally. He ultimately took charge of the wheel of our car and drove us back into Tsomo township.

At the police station I applied for bail, which was refused. I asked, however, to be allowed to interview the magistrate, who also refused to grant us bail, giving his reason that it was a Sunday morning. We were all (five men) therefore committed to gaol together with our motor-car. Our Coloured friends, the Frasers by name, who had assisted us earlier in the morning to extricate our car, supplied us with food at the gaol. On Monday morning we all appeared before the same magistrate. He found myself, Bennett Ncwana, and the driver of the car guilty, and imposed fines of £1 each, or seven days' hard labour, and ordered us to leave the Transkeian territory within a period of six hours. We drove hurriedly to reach the Kei Bridge, the boundary between the Cape Province and the Transkeian territory, before the expiration of the ultimatum. As we had not enough cash in our possession, the Frasers paid our fines, which we refunded immediately on our arrival at East London.

I resided first with my family at the East Bank Location, now known as the Duncan Village, where the City Council refused me a residential permit. I had negotiated to purchase a house in the location, on which I had paid a deposit of £50, but the Council refused to transfer this house into my name, and thus began the legal battle between the Council and myself, which issue was eventually decided in my favour in the Supreme Court at Grahamstown. The newspaper *Imvo*, the oldest African journal in South Africa, wrote editorially on March 14, 1933, on the judgment:

'Location Regulations: Kadalie Succeeds.

'In the Supreme Court, Grahamstown, Justices Gutsche and Pitman, a fortnight ago, granted an application by Clements Kadalie, of ICU fame, to set aside a decision of the East London magistrate which confirmed Kadalie's virtual expulsion from the precincts of the native location. Briefly, the facts are that, acting under location regulations promulgated in 1928 and framed under the Natives (Urban Areas) Act, the location superintendent refused to extend Kadalie's permit for residence, without stating the reasons that led him to do so. The City Council of East London confirmed the action of the Superintendent and the magistrate, instead of deciding the issue in his judicial capacity (when Kadalie appealed to him) confirmed the Council's decision on the strength of a police report from the district commandant. The judges found that an injustice was suffered by Kadalie in that his request for a personal hearing (to support his application for a permit) was refused, and consequently the Supreme Court ordered the Magistrate of East London to reopen the proceedings and deal further with the matter. The costs were ordered to be paid by the City Council, in so far as opposition was made.

'Leaving out all personal considerations, we welcome the decision of the Supreme Court in favour of Kadalie.'

When the case was reopened by the chief magistrate of East London, I had two important witnesses who testified to my character, namely, Dr. W. B. Rubusana, an ex-MPC, and Henry Daniel Tyamzashe, who was then a member of the local location advisory board. Notwithstanding their testimony in my favour, the same magistrate who had dealt with the case before decided against me. On appeal to the Supreme Court at Grahamstown for a second time, my case was dismissed with heavy costs against me, which took me a long time to liquidate at an East London attorney's office. Though banished from the location, I remained in East London, as the following report, which appeared in the local *Weekly Standard*, shows:

'Although Clements Kadalie, the Swahili champion of native rights and leader of the strike in 1930, has been declared to be not fit and proper to reside in the local locations, both by an East London magistrate and a judge of the Eastern Districts Supreme Court, he is residing in East London city itself and remains within the law. This is the curious position which has arisen as a result of the provisions of the Native Urban Areas Act, which entitles Kadalie, as a registered voter of the East London (North) constituency, to live in East London. The matter is exercising the minds of the City Council, and came up for discussion at the last ordinary meeting of the Council, when it was revealed that Kadalie was living at No. 1 Hope Street, East London. Consideration of the question has been delayed, and in the meantime Kadalie is living undisturbed in a house in Hope Street.

'Questioned regarding the position, Mr. Kadalie said that he was merely exercising the rights of a registered voter. He thought he had every right to reside in East London, and could not see how the authorities could remove him if he did not commit a serious breach of the peace or contravention of the Native Administration Act. Asked if he could resist attempts to move him, Mr. Kadalie smiled a little grimly. "I suppose I will," he wheezed, "but I don't think I will be disturbed for a while." '

After taking up my residence in the city itself, the opposition against me by the City Council died away. In order to entrench my position indisputably, I was able in 1936 to buy a property at No. 8 Hope Street, where I now live happily with my family. Our home is well known in East London, and many leading Africans, Coloureds and Indians in the political field, as well as in sport and music, have visited us and admired our home. We have also had the privilege of welcoming to our home some members of the Union Parliament of both Houses. Who could have imagined that I could have survived all the storms which beset me and my family in the early thirties? Besides my home in the city, thank God, I own another house in the very location from which I was supposed to be banned! This property is partly used as branch office by the ICU, while in the city itself

I have my private office in the yard of our house. This office was built during the recent war. And so with the poet I can say:

> Out of the night that covers me,
> Black as the pit from pole to pole,
> I thank whatever Gods may be
> For my unconquerable soul!

CHAPTER XV

The Hertzog Bills and After[1]

B Y the year 1933 I was firmly established at East London, with the ICU functioning smoothly. The country at this time was sitting on a political volcano. The Prime Minister of the day, J. B. M. Hertzog, had announced his Native Policy in an explosive speech at Smithfield, his own constituency in the Orange Free State, the policy which some years later he was able to introduce in Parliament in the form of what was known at the time as the 'Hertzog Native Bills'. In the first draft of these Bills the Prime Minister proposed to abolish the franchise enjoyed by the Africans in the Cape Province since 1853 in the good days of the Victorian era. The Bills were introduced in Parliament at the end of 1935.

[Politically conscious Africans throughout South Africa were roused by these proposals and a conference was called. This proposed conference, the All-African Convention, received widespread support and met in Bloemfontein on December 16, 1935. Kadalie was among those who helped to organize the Convention.]

The Convention decided to send a strong delegation to Cape Town to place the views of the African peoples before the Government and Parliament. Professor D. D. T. Jabavu, B.A., headed the delegation as president of the All-African Convention. Unfortunately for the delegation, when it reached Cape Town it did not strictly adhere to its mandate in regard to the uncompromising attitude of the African people, as expressed at the Convention. The news that came from Cape Town was announced in bold type in the European press, such as 'Major sensation over Compromise Bill', which was passed by 169 votes to 11. With the passing of the Hertzog Native Bills the majority of Europeans

208

in South Africa rejoiced as never before. Toasts and speeches were made both in Parliament and in the country.

[The alleged compromise consisted in withdrawing the clause abolishing the Cape's non-racial franchise and substituting a provision whereby Africans would retain the vote but would be placed on a separate roll and allowed to elect three members of the House of Assembly. These three would have to be Whites. In addition, Africans throughout the Union of South Africa would send four Whites to the Senate by an indirect form of election which would operate through chiefs, headmen, district councils and location advisory boards. Also, a Native Representative Council was to be set up, consisting of a majority of elected Africans and a number of White officials appointed by the Government. The Native Representative Council was given neither administrative nor legislative powers. Ultimately, its members refused to co-operate with the authorities, and it was abolished in 1949 by the Nationalist Government.

It was widely believed that the Convention's delegation accepted the compromise and that in doing so they were prompted by White advisers. This was strenuously denied by Jabavu and other members of the delegation but Kadalie remained unconvinced. The creation of Native Representatives in Parliament, and the Native Representative Council, split those participating in the All-African Convention into two irreconcilable camps. There were those who wished to boycott the new institutions and those who saw them as platforms from which to advocate change. A second meeting of the Convention was held in Bloemfontein in the hope of resolving these differences in July 1936. The ICU in East London sent three delegates who were led by Kadalie.]

I decided before going to Bloemfontein to arm myself fully in regard to the part to be played by me there. With this object in view, I confidentially communicated with various European public men, some of them Members of Parliament with legal status, in order to obtain from them advice on what I thought should be the attitude adopted at the Convention. I therefore addressed letters to four eminent Europeans, the Right Hon. F. S. Malan, who had acted as deputy prime minister in General Smuts' cabinet; C. W. Coulter, ex-M.P. for Cape Town Gardens, a constitutional lawyer; Advocate C. J. Gardner, K.C., now a judge of the Supreme Court, and to Advocate Will Stuart, M.P., who specially represented African interests in Parliament. My letter to all these gentlemen read as follows:

> In view of our forthcoming All-African Convention at Bloemfontein in June, I have taken this liberty of seeking your private opinion on certain suggestions that may be put forth at this Convention in regard to the Native Bills now before Parliament, viz.:
>
> 1. In view of the fact that the Convention, through its Executive, has uncompromisingly rejected the Native Representation Bill, would the Natives be condoning their disfranchisement if they accepted the Native Representative Council, and nominate members to sit on this Council, as well as three Europeans to sit in the House of Assembly?
> 2. Should the Convention, true to the spirit of its resolutions, boycott this Bill when it becomes law, and ignore its entire provisions, what possible effects might such action have; and can such action lay the Natives open to criminal prosecutions for, let us say, obstructing or subverting the machinery of the law?
> 3. Can you suggest any wise course that the Convention should adopt in connection with 'co-operation' or 'non-co-operation' in the matter of this measure?

The reader will observe that I addressed my letter to four gentlemen, all of whom sent me detailed replies.

[Senator F. S. Malan and C. W. Coulter were quoted here by Kadalie, but only Roux's summary of their advice remains. Both men considered that for Africans to participate in the new institutions would not have the effect of condoning their disfranchisement. Africans, they advised, should accept the machinery of the Act to further their cause.]

Notwithstanding the good and sound advice I obtained from some of the outstanding men in public life in South Africa, I nevertheless prepared the following resolutions for submission to the All-African Convention at Bloemfontein:

'Whereas by the passage of the Native Representative Bill, the Parliament and the Government of the Union of South Africa have finally set the seal of the inferior status of the Aboriginal people of South Africa, whereas it has thought fit to deprive the African people of the Cape Province of citizen rights held by them for over three-quarters of a century, and whereas Parliament has thought fit to ignore the plea of the All-African Convention, representing the African people of the Union;

Therefore now this Assembly of the All-African Convention declares itself in favour of a policy of non-co-operation with the Government as far as the working of the Natives Representation Act is concerned.

'Members of this Convention and all organizations here represented pledge themselves as follows:

1. Not to stand as candidates or to support candidates to the Native Representative Council, and to endeavour to persuade others to do likewise.
2. Not to vote or participate in any way in the elections for the Native Representative Council, and to endeavour to organize a complete boycott of such elections and Council.
3. In the Cape Province, to refuse to take part in the election of three Europeans for the Legislative Assembly, and to complete boycott of such elections.
4. To refuse to participate in the election of Europeans to the Senate, and to organize a complete boycott of such elections.
5. Similarly to boycott the Cape Provincial Council elections. In the event of retaliatory measures on the part of the Government, we pledge ourselves to extend the principle of non-co-operation to the non-payment of taxes, in support of the principle of *No Taxation without Direct and Equal Representation*.'

The resolutions were referred to the Standing Committee, but as confusion reigned at the Convention, no consideration was accorded them. Some of the delegates were definitely in favour of my resolutions.

[The majority of members of the Convention decided to participate in elections under the new Act. The lure of possible membership of the NRC seemed to overcome any possible scruples about condoning the new dispensation. Kadalie himself, as we shall see, subsequently tried to become a candidate for this body. This accounts for his description of the remarks by Messrs. Malan and Coulter as 'good and sound advice.']

Having realized the futility of political action which brought about the compromise on the Native Bills of 1936, I decided to tour the country once more in order to champion the economic struggle which I considered as the paramount issue before the African people. With this object in view I addressed a large meeting at Heilbron, Orange Free State, on June 23, 1936. I travelled from East London to Heilbron by rail. On reaching the town at about 6 p.m. I was met at the station by members of the ICU committee, who lived in the location. I was put up at the branch chairman's house. At about 7 p.m. a young European sergeant of the South African Police came to the house. He had his service revolver with him which he conspicuously displayed. He asked me when our meeting would commence on the following day. I directed him to the branch chairman who, being a local man, had the arrangements in hand. When he was told the hour of the meeting he objected, as he evidently thought it would not fit in with his convenience. Here I took a hand in the conversation and told him that I did not leave East London in order to hold meetings that would suit his convenience. My itinerary, I informed him, was arranged in advance to suit *my* convenience, and not that of the *police*. Having swallowed this retort, he changed to another subject by asking me if I had a 'travelling pass'. I told him that I was in no need of a pass as I was not a criminal, while on the other hand, as general secretary of the ICU, my movements were well known to the police authorities. I told him that he came to the location uninvited because he knew beforehand that I had left East London for Heilbron. He then asked whether I carried an 'exemption certificate', but I told him that since such certificate was a camouflaged form of 'pass', I did not carry it either. After some argument he told me that he was going to 'look up' the law, and that he would let me know the true position the next day. When he came the next day he studiously refrained from mentioning the matter, he merely busied himself by taking copious notes of my speech. I doubt, however, whether he had the intelligence to write down that speech.

The following is the speech I delivered at Heilbron, as reported by Reuter:

'Kadalie made his appearance again at Heilbron yesterday. He strongly condemned the Native Bills, and said that a Convention of 600 delegates would be held this week in Bloemfontein when resolutions would be passed which would make the Government tremble, and the least they could do was to postpone enacting these Bills. The Government was afraid of the Natives, regarding them as "a danger", but having no aeroplanes and machine-guns, what else could they do than what they did at East London when he advised all Natives to down their tools and stay at home and hold a holiday in the location. At his word the dock workers, railway employees, municipal labourers and others struck work, and as if by the stroke of a pen commerce, industry and traffic came to a standstill. Ships were held up, trains blocked, and as a result Native wages were increased. In 1924 he helped the Nationalist Party into power. He had never been bought, though. The South African Party members had often tried to persuade him to support them. Dr. Abdurahman had called him a fool, as the Nationalists would enslave them. Now it was done by the United Party. He could swear he had received nothing from General Hertzog, General Smuts or Dr. Malan. He asked whether Natives could be deemed dangerous if farmers left their whole possessions and families in their care? Nothing could check the forward march of the Natives. White people had given them the Bible which taught equality, charity and brotherhood, but ungrateful General Hertzog and his gang did not believe in the Biblical doctrine which they preached to the Natives but did not practise themselves. "The biggest agitation ever experienced would start this week in Bloemfontein," he said. "Give us all the Protectorates outside the Union, but give us sole control, including customs. Drive all the Natives away from the Europeans, and we shall drive all the Europeans away from the Native territories. Then there shall be peace."

'Proceeding he said it was not the Kadalies and the Jabavus who brought about this conflict, and the Riotous Assemblies Act would not stop them. General Hertzog sympathized with the Abyssinian Natives, but their own Natives were downtrodden. For seven years the ICU had been divided, but they were now reorganizing their forces, and would show a united front. It would be of no use praying. He would simply go from dockyard to factory, and with a single word, *"Stop!"* the white people would be held at ransom, the railways would lose over £2,000,000 a day, and while the trouble was on, he (Kadalie) would be looked upon as Prime Minister. They might bring their aeroplanes and police and form big camps everywhere, but he would simply say to the Europeans, "We won't wash your plates, nor clean your boots as long as General Hertzog shows a heart as hard as Pharaoh". An economic struggle was coming, when they would be armed with the knowledge that their children would rise in millions.

'A number of police were present, and the meeting passed off in an orderly manner, concluded the report.'

At East London our Union had another difficulty to overcome, and this was in connection with pensions for their members who had records of long services on the railways. The Railways and Harbours Administration was not prepared to extend the provisions of the Gratuity Acts to our members, for the simple reason that most of them had participated in the general strike called by our Union in 1930. After copious correspondence between our Union and the Railways and Harbours Administration, culminating with the assistance given us by our Parliamentary representative, Mrs. Margaret Ballinger,[2] who worked hard on our behalf, the Administration at last agreed to set aside its earlier decision to debar our members from the provisions of the Gratuity Act of 1928. As a consequence many of our members, as well as other non-Europeans who did not belong to the ICU, received gratuities at East London from the Railways and Harbours Administration. One of our ICU Executive Committee members received £275. With some of this cash he wisely bought himself a big house in the East Bank Location. Other members who received large sums of money as gratuities went back to the reserves, where they apparently spent their shares on buying the cattle. I estimate conservatively that over 200 of our members were paid gratuities by the Railways and Harbours Administration.

The objection by the Railways and Harbours Administration having been removed as a result of the representations made by Mrs. Ballinger, the offices of the Administration were now open to me at any time, and any representations I made thereafter were, as a rule, favourably adjusted. I remember during the war of 1939-45 that the Buffalo Harbour was sealed off from the public, but I was allowed to enter there whenever I had representations to make to the authorities. In passing I should mention here that it is in the Harbour that the ICU has its strongest support at East London.

The reader is, or may be, aware that one of the disabilities against which the African is clamouring is the poll-tax. Nearly every day many of our people go to gaol on account of this obnoxious poll-tax. I am not ashamed to mention here that I was subjected to this poll-tax iniquity at East London, and was placed under arrest and locked up in the local gaol, in May 1932. This was at the time when the police were hot after my blood, as was publicly admitted by a detective-sergeant at the Circuit Court at East London when I was falsely charged (criminally) on one occasion and was acquitted by a judge. The ICU Committee brought cash to the local gaol for my poll-tax during the evening, but the gaol authorities refused to release me at night. Next morning my comrades went to the Native Affairs Department where they paid my poll-tax, which amounted to £4 for four years. I was then released from prison.

In 1943 when I was a member of the Location Advisory Board of East London, I set out to contest a seat on the Native Representative Council. I issued two manifestos. When the campaign opened, I toured various towns to get into personal touch with members of the various Advisory Boards of the Cape Province, for it is the members of these Boards who nominate and finally vote for members of the Native Representative Council. Promises for support reached me from many Advisory Boards, and consequently I felt quite confident of winning the election in the Cape urban areas. My opponents, as well as the Government, must have been aware of this. One day I happened to interview a certain European official in the course of my work when this official raised the question of the election. He looked up Act 12 of 1936, which regulates these elections, and drew my attention to the birth clause which states that a candidate must be born within the Union of South Africa. As I was born in Nyasaland, outside the Union, the official in question advised me to apply for permission to contest the election from the Governor-General,

P

which I did at once, but that merely resulted in the refusal of my application.

In November 1943 I addressed a lengthy memorandum to the Secretary for Native Affairs, Dr. D. L. Smit. His reply engendered some hope for me. It read as follows:

'Dear Mr. Kadalie,

Replying to your letter of November 19 asking to be declared a Union National, I have looked into the law on the subject, and it would appear that, in terms of paragraph (b) of section one of the Act No. 40 of 1927, read with paragraph (a) of sub-section (I) of Section One of Act No. 18 of 1926, you are in fact a Union National already. This fact alone is, however, insufficient in itself to entitle you to seek election as a member of the Native Representative Council, having regard to the fact that you were not born in the Union of South Africa. Your petition last year in this connection was refused by the Governor-General, and I feel that no good purpose would be served by asking for reconsideration of the matter at this stage, as the next general election will not take place until 1947. It would be more appropriate for you to raise the matter again then, should you so desire.'

On July 15, 1946, I renewed my application in the above respect, but it was again rejected. Having exhausted all avenues, I decided on February 25, 1947, to direct my appeal to 'Caesar'— the Right Honourable Field-Marshal J. G. Smuts, C.H., K.C., O.M., M.P.

[In a lengthy letter to the Prime Minister, Kadalie pointed out that he had lived 29 years in the Union of South Africa, that he had entered the country legally, that he had travelled to Europe with a passport describing him as a 'Union national', and that poll-tax was exacted from him every year.]

The reply to the above letter came from the Minister of Native Affairs, instead of from the Prime Minister, and once more rejected my appeal. As to the reasons which prompted the Union Government to refuse to grant me the necessary 'licence' to contest the election of the Native Representative Council under Act 12 of 1936, I for one have come to the conclusion that the Government, being aware of my debating powers, as well as the influence I still possess among my fellow Africans, does not desire me to become a member of the NRC. Added to this, the Minister of Native Affairs will not so easily forgive me for my audacity at the first National Anti-Pass Conference held in Johannesburg in 1944, when I moved a motion of 'no confidence' in him as our Minister. On top of this I added another deadly bombshell when I sent a cable to the Secretary-General of the United Nations in New York on October 23, 1946, which read:

'THE INDUSTRIAL AND COMMERCIAL WORKERS' UNION OF AFRICA, PARENT BODY OF AFRICAN TRADE UNIONISM, STRONGLY OBJECTS TO THE INCORPORATION OF SOUTH-WEST AFRICA INTO THE UNION OF SOUTH AFRICA BECAUSE OUR GOVERNMENT, HEADED BY FIELD-MARSHAL SMUTS, IS THE ARCHITECT OF COLOUR BAR DISCRIMINATION. WE FAVOUR A UNITED NATIONS MANDATE OVER SOUTH-WEST AFRICA.'

While the ICU ceased to function in other parts of the Union of South Africa years ago, I am able to record that at East London this once powerful trade union of the African workers has existed with a growing membership running into four figures. For three years the ICU held all the six seats on the Location Advisory Board for the East Bank Location, now Duncan Village, while I topped the poll at each election. We revolutionized the proceedings of the Board, inasmuch as we made it possible for the residents of the locations to attend its meetings. ICU members as a rule crowded the Peacock Hall where joint Advisory Board meetings are held monthly. During our time of service on the board we made some history. When the City Council decided in 1946 to demolish houses in the East Bank Location—actually a few houses were pulled down by owners themselves who were not members of the ICU, and were scared by officials of the City Council—on my initiative a public meeting was held where a petition was read out by me and unanimously adopted for transmission by telegraph to the Ministers of Native Affairs and Public Health at Cape Town, drawing their attention to the injustices being imposed on the owners of houses at the East London location. A memorandum prepared by me was subsequently forwarded to the ministers concerned, who in turn sent a commission of inquiry to East London to investigate the matter on the spot. They met the members of the Advisory Boards in the Peacock Hall. Both Mr. R. H. Godlo and I read out memoranda to the Commission. I was complimented afterwards by Major Collings for my memorandum, which he described as excellent and very interesting. In March 1946 the demolition of the location houses was suspended by the City Council. As was expected, late in the year, the City Council served summonses on some owners of houses for refusing to demolish or remove from such houses. The matter came up before the magistrates' court at East London, when both the ICU and the Vigilance Association jointly engaged the services of two firms of local attorneys for the defence. The court decided in our favour. Thus a long battle came to an end as a result of my initiative, through the agency of the ICU representatives, who were then in a majority on the Advisory Board.

The ICU was honoured by the Natives Law Commission of Inquiry which invited it to submit evidence when the Commission held its sittings at East London in October 1946. My old colleague Henry Daniel Tyamzashe and I gave evidence which was duly published by the press. We had, of course, prepared replies to twenty-nine questions which covered all aspects of Native life in South Africa. In its heyday the ICU advocated the abolition of the Pass Laws, and this point was strongly emphasized in our replies to the questionnaire on the subject. We submitted that all forms of passes, including the application of poll-tax collection, should be abolished. We also advocated the registration of all citizens, irrespective of colour, for identification purposes in the case of accident or death. This system was invoked on the European continent before the first World War. Our evidence went on further to say that

'. . . while recognizing that the commission was investigating a very important aspect affecting two-thirds of the Union's population, and that it will take a considerable time before its findings and recommendations may be known to the public, our union would humbly request the commission to consider the methods usually employed by the South African police, who round up Africans in our locations in the early hours daily. In East London one finds that a state of martial law exists; for raids are carried out by the police early in the mornings for passes and poll-tax receipts. Our union has made representations to the City Council on the matter, but without receiving any redress. The African population of East London will respect-fully appreciate it if the honourable commissioners would give immediate attention to our humble request in regard to these frequent police raids.'

The reader will appreciate from the numerous activities recorded in this chapter, that the ICU at East London and King William's Town has continued actively to the day this book is being prepared to support the various demands of the African people and to protest against disabilities and grievances. Only recently another comprehensive memorandum was presented to a Government commission which is inquiring into the affairs of the East London locations. Notwithstanding the fact that the ICU is not functioning in many parts of Africa, I record here with pleasure that at East London the work of the Union goes on smoothly every day, rendering yeoman service to its members.

NOTES

1. (p. 208) Roux made substantial rearrangements to this chapter and inserted explanatory passages into the text. Since no earlier version of this chapter appears to exist, Roux's notes, in an amended form, have been retained and appear in brackets.
2. (p. 214) Margaret Ballinger was returned by the Cape Eastern Division in 1937 as a Native Representative. She retained her seat until 1959 when the last vestiges of African Parliamentary representation were abolished.

CHAPTER XVI

What of the ICU?

A s the reader has gathered from the beginning of this book, the ICU was inaugurated early in January 1919, as the aftermath of the first Great War. Africans, as well as other non-Europeans, had just returned from the war more disillusioned than ever. The war was supposed to have been fought to make the world safe for heroes. Unemployment was raising its ugly head. The rising cost of living was making the necessities of life unobtainable. While leaving insufficient at home, these commodities were exported overseas. Amidst this uncertainty we witnessed the formation of the first trade union of the non-Europeans of South Africa.

In Cape Town there was a considerable number of West Indian Negroes at that time. Some of these men were highly cultured, and most of them were employed at the docks as stevedores in various occupations such as shipwrights, foremen, etc. The second chairman of the ICU, James King, was a Negro, and a good tradesman, while J. G. Gumbs, another Negro, and third chairman, who afterwards occupied the ICU presidency from 1924 until his death in 1929, was a qualified chemist, as well as a rigger at the Cape Town docks. On the executive committee of the union we often had three or four of these Negroes. When the Marcus Garvey movement was at its height, these Negroes in South Africa tried their best to use the ICU as an auxiliary of the Universal Negro Improvement Association, but, just as was the case with the Communist Party of South Africa, I became the stumbling block against their machinations, since I abhor serving two masters at the same time in my political make-up. I did not believe in the slogan of 'Africa for the Africans' which was popular during the post-war period among the oppressed peoples of African descent throughout the world. I believed, as I believe now, that the salvation of the Africans in this country will be brought about through their own sweat and labour.

The ICU could never have flourished easily in the country if economic hardships of the non-Europeans had been satisfactorily redressed by the powers that be. Notwithstanding the high cost of living, there was no corresponding adjustment of the wages of the African workers. The feeling of frustration was soon evident. In the northern provinces passes were forcibly loaded on the African people. Nowhere was there a silver lining to show the masses the way to human freedom. In this hopeless frustration the advent of the ICU was like a beacon of light on the horizon. There was a great desire to find the way towards human emancipation, and the advent of the ICU promised the only way. It was in this atmosphere of discontent that the ICU spread from Cape Town like a veld fire over South Africa, with Port Elizabeth and East London, seaport towns first, then to the country districts of the central and eastern provinces, then to Natal province, the Orange Free State and finally to Johannesburg and the Transvaal. But the ICU did not confine its activities to the Union of South Africa only; we had branches at Lüderitz-bucht and Keetmanshoop in South-West Africa, whence came James A. La Guma.

Our destination was the 'ICU of Africa'. In pursuance of this designation we had two branches in Southern Rhodesia, at Bulawayo and Salisbury. At the end of 1927 the ICU had spread its wings throughout the sub-continent of Africa. Is it not a wonder that the exploiters of African labour saw the writing on the wall when they witnessed this new evolution of once down-trodden people on the march! The reader has read in these pages of the efforts by the ICU to approach the South African Trades Union Congress with the object of presenting a united front against 'the arbitrary and unlimited powers of capitalism'. A few joint meetings were held between us and the Trades Union Congress, but the split in the union, coupled with the advent of Ballinger, brought about the suspension of this worthy consultation. There is no gainsaying that if this consultation had continued, a revolutionary change for good could have taken place in the industrial world of South Africa.

We have chronicled in these pages the Natal episode involving the financial aspect of the ICU, while at the same time giving reasons why young teachers flocked to take up appointments as secretaries in the organization. Some of these secretaries in Natal were grossly incompetent, and they disobeyed orders in regard to handling monies belonging to the Union, with the result that the organization was thrown into confusion and distrust grew among our supporters and members.

With the rapid rise of the ICU which attracted people of various upbringings, the question of rivalries between leaders was bound to come. For a time the president and I were able to keep together the various elements that were antagonistic to each other, but as time went on, I was in turn marked out for attack, owing to my being born outside the Union of South Africa. When Champion broke away, the fact of my birth was used by him to rally the Zulu workers around his leadership. Following my resignation, the ICU leaders were more or less aligned tribally. It is a fact worth recording that the majority of the ICU membership lacked political knowledge. The rank and file mentality, being African, was to follow the 'chief', whether right or wrong.

Many causes can be cited for the disintegration of the ICU. First of all we have to realize that the union was organized on the same lines as the Grand National Consolidated Trades Union in Great Britain in the early stages of the trade union movement there. Most of our secretaries were drawn from the teaching profession. These men had never in their lives studied the trade union movement or even politics in general. They were attracted to the ICU, which offered them higher pay than they could earn as teachers. The ICU offered them wages ranging from £8 to £15 per month in the case of provincial secretaries. The morals of some of these young men were definitely not suited for public appointment. Some of them indulged in intoxicants freely. The membership of the union was drawn from all classes of our people, and the great mass of the Africans are religiously minded. It is obvious that many of our members did not approve of the behaviour of the secretaries.

The bad financial management of the affairs of the union in Natal hastened its doom. Mr. Justice Tatham's judgment has already been mentioned. The withdrawal thereafter of the Natal Province following the lead of Champion, brought about the decline of the union from its former glory. The Natal situation could have been retrieved, because the breakaway movement was at first strictly confined to Durban. The northern portion of Natal solidly adhered to the mother body. With the advent of W. G. Ballinger as our new adviser, the rift between the rest of the union and Durban widened. At this particular time our adviser, we think, had not gained enough experience to understand the African mind. By his methods, Ballinger put many of us at loggerheads one against another, thus making it very difficult for us to compromise for the good of the movement we all loved and some of us suffered for. With a wiser and more experienced adviser I am sure that the ICU could have been saved from shipwreck.

In spite of its shortcomings and failures, the ICU demonstrated to the world the powers of the African workers once they were properly organized. Throughout the twenties and thirties the ICU dominated the African industrial and political scenes. Who could have doubted that had it not been for the disintegrating forces caused by rivalries amongst its higher officials, which to a great extent were unscrupulously engineered by the European elements, backed of course by the powers that be, the industrial as well as the political emancipation of the African people just around the corner would have dawned upon the toiling masses of this sub-continent!

I have taken great care to bring into this book a worthy story of the ICU organization in which I played a very important part—one may call it 'drama'. I must confess, however, that if there are some errors in it, the reader will appreciate that I have entirely depended upon my own memory, as most of the early ICU documents were left with W. G. Ballinger at ICU headquarters in Johannesburg at the time of the split in 1929. The story of the ICU, which is closely interwoven with my own struggles and triumphs, now told to the public at large, may perhaps unfold the difficulties with which the pioneers of African trade unionism had to contend with in its infancy. The many trade unions of the African workers which have now sprung up in all big cities of the Union of South Africa owe their existence to the pioneering work of the 'mother ICU' which blazed the trail in the industrial field. For my part, I should like to borrow a phrase from the late Booker T. Washington, and say:

'To me the history of African Trade Unionism seems like the story of a great adventure, in which for my own part I am glad to have had a share. So far from being a misfortune, it seems to me that it is a rare privilege to have taken part in the early struggles, the plans and the ambitions of over eight million people who are making their way from industrial serfdom into a place in the social and political system of our South African nationhood.'

INDEX

A

Abdurahman, A., 47, 51, 197, 203
Acts and Bills:
  Colour Bar, 133, 155
  Emergency Powers, 77
  "Hertzog Native Bills", 208
  Immigrants Regulation, 46
  Industrial Conciliation, 73, 76
  Master and Servants, 13
  Miners Phthisis Acts Consolidation Bill, 77
  Minimum Wage, 75
  Native Administration, 21, 22, 126-9, 144-6, 155, 156, 168, 206
  Native Labour Regulation, 76
  Native Representation, 210 ff.
  Native Urban Areas, 206
  Riotous Assemblies, 13, 146, 179, 197, 201, 202
  Wage, 69
Adelaide, 163
African National Congress (ANC), 17, 18, 25, 28, 58, 59, 60, 61, 67, 79, 88 f.n., 167, 172
African Voice, 55, 56
Afrikaner Bond, 17
Aisler, Lady, 106
Alice, 56
All-Indian Trades Union Congress, 144
American Methodist Episcopal Church (AME), 50, 70, 85
Andrews, W. H., 74, 143, 146, 151, 152 f.n., 178, 182 f.n.
Argyle, W. J., 9
Arnold, Detective, 92, 164, 165
Austrian Trade Union Congress, 133

B

Ballinger, Margaret, 57 f.n., 85, 179, 214, 219 f.n.
Ballinger, W. G., 23-4, 25, 177-81, 183, 221, 223

Bandawe Mission Station, 31, 32, 33
Barlow, Arthur, 16, 17, 60
Basutoland, 145
Batty, A. F., 12, 37, 40, 128
Bedford, 163
Benoni, 42, 48 f.n., 152 f.n.
Berea, 92, 97
Berlin, 122, 133, 134-5, 136
Bethlehem, 69, 96
Binda, Rev. Edwin, 52
Birmingham, 119
Bloemfontein, 14, 15, 16, 17, 51, 58-61, 69, 70, 71, 72, 74, 102, 161, 162, 164, 167, 172, 180, 181, 202, 209
Bondfield, Margaret, 137
Boydell, Thomas, 55, 142
Bradford, 118
Brailsford, H. N., 114, 140
Brakpan, 42
Brande, E., 46
British Labour Party, 116, 125, 126
British Trade Union Congress, 136, 137, 148, 149
British Trade Union Movements, 21, 63, 115, 125, 222
Brockway, A. Fenner, 106, 108, 113, 114, 115, 127, 128, 137, 139, 140
Brown, A. Barratt, 138, 140
Buffalo Harbour, 53, 215
Bulawayo, 35, 36, 145
Bulhoek, 16, 58, 62, 149, 185, 197
Bunting, Sidney, 91, 101 f.n., 178, 179
Butler, A., 155
Buxton, C. R., 139

C

Cape Argus, 39, 42
Cape Federation of Labour Unions, 21, 41, 42, 60, 101 f.n. 3, 103, 112, 149

225